I0313272

Theology in Language, Rhetoric, and Beyond

Theology in Language, Rhetoric, and Beyond

Essays in Old and New Testament

Jack R. Lundbom

CASCADE *Books* • Eugene, Oregon

THEOLOGY IN LANGUAGE, RHETORIC, AND BEYOND
Essays in Old and New Testament

Copyright © 2014 Jack R. Lundbom. All rights reserved. Except for brief quotations in critical publications or reviews, no part of this book may be reproduced in any manner without prior written permission from the publisher. Write: Permissions, Wipf and Stock Publishers, 199 W. 8th Ave., Suite 3, Eugene, OR 97401.

Cascade Books
An Imprint of Wipf and Stock Publishers
199 W. 8th Ave., Suite 3
Eugene, OR 97401

www.wipfandstock.com

ISBN 13: 978-1-62564-480-0

Cataloguing-in-Publication data:

Lundbom, Jack R.

Theology in language, rhetoric, and beyond : essays in Old and New Testament / Jack R. Lundbom.

xii + 204 pp. ; 23 cm. Includes bibliographical references and indexes.

ISBN 13: 978-1-62564-480-0

1. Bible. Old Testament—Criticism, interpretation, etc. 2. Bible. Jeremiah—Criticism, interpretation, etc. 3. Bible. Old Testament—Theology. 4. Bible—New Testament—Relation to the Old Testament. I.Title.

BS1171.2 L85 2014

Manufactured in the U.S.A.

Unless otherwise noted, all Bible translations are the author's own.

Biblical references marked (NRSV) are from the New Revised Standard Version Bible, copyright 1989, Division of Christian Education of the National Council of the Churches of Christ in the United States of America. Used by permission. All rights reserved.
Biblical references marked (RSV) are from the Revised Standard Version of the Bible, copyright 1952 [2nd edition, 1971] by the Division of Christian Education of the National Council of the Churches of Christ in the United States of America. Used by permission. All rights reserved.

To

Richard and Herbert Anderson

Contents

Permissions ix

Preface xi

Abbreviations xiii

1 Grace and Favor in the Old Testament: Hebrew *ḥnn* 1

2 Burning Anger in the Old Testament: Hebrew *ḥrh*, *yṣt*, and *yqd* 21

3 God in Your Grace Transform the World 37

4 Biblical and Theological Themes 43

Translation into Lingala—Rev. Richard Anderson

5 Deuteronomy 58

6 Yahweh Comes to Be King on Earth (Deut 33:2–5) 72

7 And the Word of the Lord Came to Huldah 76

8 Jeremiah and the Created Order 80

9 The Confessions of Jeremiah 99

10 Psalm 23: Song of Passage 132

11 Mary Magdalene and Song of Songs 3:1–4 145

12 All Great Works of God Begin in Secret 150

13 Theology in Language, Rhetoric, and Beyond 164

Index of Scriptural References 183

Index of Authors and Names 187

Permissions

The author and publisher are grateful to the following journals and publishers for permissions to publish the following essays:

"*ḥnn*" (coauthored with David Noel Freedman). In *Theological Dictionary of the Old Testament* 5 (Grand Rapids: Eerdmans, 1986), 22–36.

"*ḥrh*" (coauthored with David Noel Freedman). In *Theological Dictionary of the Old Testament* 5 (Grand Rapids: Eerdmans, 1986), 171–76.

"*yṣt*" (coauthored with David Noel Freedman). In *Theological Dictionary of the Old Testament* 6 (Grand Rapids: Eerdmans, 1990) 266–69.

"*yqd*" (coauthored with David Noel Freedman). In *Theological Dictionary of the Old Testament* 6 (Grand Rapids: Eerdmans, 1990) 271–74.

"God in Your Grace Transform the World." *Currents in Theology and Mission* 34 (2007) 278–81.

"Deuteronomy" in *The Oxford Encyclopedia for Bible and Ethics* (New York: Oxford University Press, 2014).

"And the Word of the Lord Came to Huldah." *The Covenant Companion* 73/6 (June, 1984) 26–27.

"Jeremiah and the Created Order." In Jack R. Lundbom, *Jeremiah Closer Up* (Sheffield: Sheffield Phoenix Press, 2010), 42–57.

"The Confessions of Jeremiah." In Jack R. Lundbom, *Jeremiah Closer Up* (Sheffield: Sheffield Phoenix Press, 2010), 75–103.

"Psalm 23: Song of Passage." *Interpretation* 40 (1986) 5–16.

"Mary Magdalene and Song of Songs 3:1–4." *Interpretation* 49 (1995) 172–75.

"All Great Works of God Begin in Secret." In *Exploring Bible, Church and Life: Essays in Celebration of the 100th Anniversary of Lutheran Theological Seminary, Hong Kong*, ed. Simon Chow, Dieter Mitternacht, and Nicholas Tai (*Theology and Life* 36; Hong Kong: Lutheran Theological Seminary, 2013), 289–99.

"Theology in Language, Rhetoric, and Beyond." *Theology & Life* 34 (2011) 253–76.

Preface

THEOLOGY IN THE JUDEO-CHRISTIAN tradition, which is discourse about God and the things of God, has benefited enormously from philosophic inquiry at various times in its history, most prominently in the Hellenistic period, the High Middle Ages, and the Modern Era, where Greek thought, for the most part, has been pressed into service to give systematic expression to revelations in the Bible, salvation history, and the experience of faith. The yield has been significant, and what is here presented should not be taken as a dismissal of this enterprise, which is a legitimate one, except as it has become the only means to do theology, or for one reason or another has gone awry.

The present collection of essays draws upon other resources for theological insight. The essay on Psalm 23 makes use of anthropology and human-development theory; the essay on Deuteronomy incorporates wisdom themes; the essay "Jeremiah and the Created Order" looks not only at ideas about God and creation but about the seldom considered idea of God and a return to chaos; and the essay "The Confessions of Jeremiah" examines, not words this extraordinary prophet was given by God to convey, but what he himself felt and experienced in the office to which he was called. Other essays argue that theology is rooted in biblical words—in and of themselves, and in context—and in rhetoric, where the latter must also include composition. And it goes without saying that careful exegesis of the biblical text continues to be as necessary as it has always been in developing proper theological understanding, in spite of more recent trends to read back into the Bible ideas emanating from here, there, and everywhere in our modern world.

I am dedicating this book to Richard and Herbert Anderson, two pastors in my family who, over the years, have had an important influence in my life. Rev. Herbert Anderson spoke to me when I was yet a young boy about entering the Christian ministry, and over the years has followed me with prayers and pastoral concern. During an unusually long life he has been, among other things, a Baptist pastor, teacher, mission executive, and college president. His elder brother, the late Rev. Richard Anderson, was for many years a missionary with the Evangelical Free Church in Congo (Kinshasa), and served as a consultant in translating the Bible into Lingala, giving the people of that country a Bible in their own tongue. The essay "Biblical and Theological Themes," given originally in 1981 as lectures to CEUM pastors in Congo (then Zaire), was translated by him into Lingala for pastors attending the seminar, and is here included following the lectures.

Jack R. Lundbom
November 2013

Abbreviations

AB	The Anchor Bible
ABD	*The Anchor Bible Dictionary*, edited by David Noel Freedman, 6 vols., New York, 1992
AfO	*Archiv für Orientforschung* (Graz)
AHw	Wolfram von Soden, *Akkadisches Handwörterbuch*, 3 vols., Weisbaden, 1959–81
AnBib	Analecta Biblica
ANE	Ancient Near East
ANET^3	*Ancient Near Eastern Texts Relating to the Old Testament*, 3rd ed. with Supplement, edited by James B. Pritchard; Princeton, 1969
AOAT	Alter Orient und Altes Testament (Neukirchen)
AOS	American Oriental Series (New Haven)
ArOr	*Archiv Orientâlní* (Prague)
AS	Assyriological Studies (Chicago)
ASOR	American Schools of Oriental Research
ATD	Das Alte Testament Deutsch
BA	*Biblical Archaeologist*
BDB	*A Hebrew and English Lexicon of the Old Testament*, ed. F. Brown, S. R. Driver, and C. A. Briggs, Oxford, 1962
BibOr	Biblica et orientalia (Rome)
BLe	H. Bauer, P. Leander, *Historische Grammatik der hebräischen Sprache des Alten Testamentes*, Halle, 1918–22; repr. Hildesheim, 1962
BZAW	Beihefte zur Zeitschrift für die altestamentliche Wissenschaft
CAD	*Chicago Assyrian Dictionary*, ed. Ignace J. Gelb et al., Chicago, 1956–
CBQ	*Catholic Biblical Quarterly*
CBSC	The Cambridge Bible for Schools and Colleges (OT ed. A. F. Kirkpatrick)
CEUM	Communauté Evangélique de l'Ubangi-Mongala (Evangelical Covenant Church of the Ubangi)
CIM	China Inland Mission

CIS	Corpus inscriptionum semiticarum
CWA	Covenant Woman's Auxiliary
DJD	Discoveries in the Judaean Desert
DLZ	*Deutsche Literturzeitung*
EA	El-Amarna tablets. According to the edition of J. A. Knudtson, *Die el-Amarna-Tafeln*, Leipzig, 1908–15; repr. Aalen, 1964; Continued in A. F. Rainey, *El-Amarna Tablets*, 359–79, 2nd rev. ed. Kevelaer, 1978
Heb	Hebrew
HBM	Hebrew Bible Monographs
HSM	Harvard Semitic Monographs
HTR	*Harvard Theological Review*
IB	*The Interpreter's Bible*, ed. G. A. Buttrick. 12 vols. New York, 1951–1957
ICC	International Critical Commentary
Int	*Interpretation*
JAOS	*Journal of the American Oriental Society*
JB	The Jerusalem Bible (Garden City, NY, 1966)
JBC	*Jerome Biblical Commentary*, ed. R. E. Brown et al; Englewood Cliffs, NJ, 1968
JBL	*Journal of Biblical Literature*
JJS	*Journal of Jewish Studies*
JQR	*Jewish Quarterly Review*
JSOTSup	Journal for the Study of the Old Testament, Supplementary Series
JSS	*Journal of Semitic Studies*
JTS	*Journal of Theological Studies*
KAI	*Kanaanäische und aramäische Inschriften*, 2nd ed., 3 vols, ed. Herbert Donner and Wolfgang Röllig; Weisbaden, 1962–71
KAT	Kommentar zum Alten Testament, ed. E. Sellin and J. Herrmann, Leipzig
KBL^3	Ludwig Köhler and Walter Baumgartner, *Hebräisches und Aramäisches Lexikon zum Alten Testament*, 3rd ed., Leiden, 1967–1990
KMT	Kuomintang (Chinese Nationalist Party)
KTU	*Die Keilalphabetischen Texte aus Ugarit*, ed. Manfred Dietrich, Oswald Loretz, and Joaquin Sammartin, AOAT 24, Neukirchen, 1976
KJV	The Authorized King James Version (1611)
Lat.	Latin

LTS	Lutheran Theological Seminary, Hong Kong
LUN	Laws of Ur-Nammu
LXX	Septuagint, according to *Septuaginta* II, 8th ed.; ed. Alfred Rahlfs, Stuttgart, 1965
MDP	Mémoires de la délégation en Perse
MT	Masoretic Text, according to *BHK*[3] or *BHS*
NAB	The New American Bible (New York, 1970)
NEB	New English Bible (Oxford and Cambridge, 1970)
NJV	The New Jewish Publication Society of America Translation of the Holy Scriptures: The Prophets (Philadelphia, 1978)
NRSV	The New Revised Standard Version (New York, 1989)
NT	New Testament
OT	Old Testament
OTL	Old Testament Library
OTM	Old Testament Message
RevQ	*Revue de Qumrân*
RGG[1]	*Die Religion in Geschichte und Gegenwart*, 1st ed., Tübingen, 1909–1913
RGG[2]	*Die Religion in Geschichte und Gegenwart*, 2nd ed., Tübingen, 1927–1931
RSV	Revised Standard Version (New York, 1953)
SBLDS	Society of Biblical Literature Dissertation Series
SBLMS	Society of Biblical Literature Monograph Series
SEÅ	*Svensk Exegetisk Årsbok*
TCL	*Textes cunéiform du Musée du Louvre* (3 vols; Paris, 1910–67)
TDOT	*Theological Dictionary of the Old Testament* (17 vols; ed. G. Johannes Botterweck, Helmer Ringgren, and Heinz-Josef Fabry; Grand Rapids, 1974–
TDNT	*Theological Dictionary of the New Testament*, 10 vols, ed. Gerhard Kittel and Gerhard Friedrich, Grand Rapids, 1964–76
THAT	*Theologisches Handwörterbuch zum Alten Testament*, 2 vols; ed. E. Jenni and C. Westermann, Munich, 1971–76
UF	*Ugarit-Forschungen*
UT	*Ugaritic Textbook*, C. H. Gordon, AnOr 38, Rome, 1965.
VAB	Vorderasiatische Bibliothek (Leipzig, 1907–16)
VT	*Vetus Testamentum*
WCC	World Council of Churches
ZA	*Zeitschrift für Assyriologie* (Leipzig, Berlin)
ZAW	*Zeitschrift für die alttestamentliche Wissenschaft*

1

Grace and Favor in the Old Testament

Hebrew *ḥnn*[1]

ḤĀNAN ("TO BE GRACEFUL, to be gracious, to show favor"); *ḥēn* ("grace, favor"); *ḥannûn* ("gracious"); *ḥănînâ* ("favor"); *tĕḥinnâ* ("favor; supplication for favor"); *taḥănûn* ("supplication for favor").[2]

Linguistic Background

Etymology and Occurrences

The basic meaning of the root *ḥnn* is "grace," which is one of two primary translations for its cognate noun *ḥēn*. The noun is first a term of beauty. It denotes an aesthetically pleasing presentation or aspect of someone or something, and is properly the quality someone or something possesses. The response to this projection of beauty is also *ḥēn*, "favor." The derived

1. Coauthored with David Noel Freedman; "*ḥnn*," in *TDOT* 5 (1986) 22–36.

2. D. R. Ap-Thomas, "Some Aspects of the Root ḤNN in the OT," *JSS* 2 (1957) 128–48; Hans Conzelmann and Walther Zimmerli, "χαρίς," in *TDNT* 9:372–402; Mitchell J. Dahood, "Hebrew-Ugaritic Lexicography II," *Biblica* 45 (1964), 409; David Noel Freedman, "God Compassionate and Gracious," *Western Watch* 6 (1955) 6–24; W. F. Lofthouse, "*Ḥēn* and *Ḥesed* in the OT," *ZAW* 51 (1933) 29–35; Karl Wilhelm Neubauer, "Der Stamm ChNN im Sprachgebrauch des AT" (doctoral diss., University of Berlin, 1964); J. L. Palache, *Semantic Notes on the Hebrew Lexicon* (Leiden: Brill, 1959), 32; William L. Reed, "Some Implications of ḤĒN for OT Religion," *JBL* 73 (1954) 36–41; Hans-Joachim Stoebe, "חנן *ḥnn* gnädig sein," in *THAT* 1:587–97; Ina Willi-Plein, "חן Ein Übersetzungsproblem: Gedanken zu Sach. XII 10," *VT* 23 (1973) 90–99.

sense is used in Hebrew primarily for the pleasing impression made upon one individual by another. It is possible to show *ḥēn* to the beloved ruins of Jerusalem (Ps 102:14–15[Eng 13–14]), but this usage is rare. The verb *ḥānan* means "be gracious," used almost exclusively in the derived sense, "show favor," but it evidently could also be used in the aesthetic sense, "possess grace" (Prov 26:25). The same dual meaning is found in Gk *cháris*, the word most often used to translate *ḥēn* in the LXX. Both meanings of *cháris* can be seen relatively close together in Sir 40:17, 22.

Akkadian *enēnu* A is invocatory, like the Hebrew hithpael of *ḥānan* "ask for mercy," "pray."[3] It is almost always used of someone supplicating either a god or a king. The verb *enēnu* C[4] corresponds to the Hebrew qal, "grant a privilege," "do a favor." The ruler of Elam, for example, graciously returns to his servant fields that he had earlier bought from him at full price.[5] The West Semitic loanword *enēnu* D[6] appears frequently in the Amarna Letters.[7] In EA 137, Rib-addi, prince of Byblos, says to Pharaoh: "If the king, my lord, be gracious to me and return me to the city."[8] The term likewise occurs in royal correspondence. Cognate nouns *ennanātu* and *ennu* [9] are also known with the meaning "grace," "favor," or "mercy," although *eninnu* and *ennanātu* are "favors" (as in "do a favor" or "ask a favor" of someone),[10] which is not one of the meanings of *ḥēn*.

Ugaritic *ḥnn* is similar to Hebrew, meaning "be gracious," "show favor."[11] Exchanges here also involve gods and kings: "Be gracious, O El,"[12] and "Secure me favor with the king."[13]

Two basic meanings are distinguished in Arabic *ḥanna*: 1) "yearn or long for," and 2) "feel tenderness or compassion," "express sympathy." The latter is more closely connected with the Hebrew root, most noticeably in

3. *CAD* 4 (1958) 162–64; *AHw* 1:217.

4. *CAD* 4:164; cf. *AHw* 1:217, *enēnu* 1.

5. MDP 23, 282, 5; cf. *CAD* 4:164.

6. *CAD* 4:164–65; *AHw* 1:217 *enēnu* 1.

7. EA 137, 81; 253, 24.

8. *ANET*³, 484.

9. *CAD* 4:168–70.

10. Cf. the Old Assyrian name *Ennana-la-Aššur* in W. Mayer and G. Wilhelm, "Altassyrische Texte aus Privatsammlungen," *UF* 7 (1975 [1976]) 319; reading of W. von Soden.

11. *KTU*, 1.10 I, 12; 1, 65, 6; 4.75 IV, 5; 2.15, 3; 1, 17 I, 16.

12. *KTU*, 1.65, 6.

13. *KTU*, 2.15, 3.

the adjective *ḥannûn*. The verb *ḥanna* is used when one yearns for home, a former wife, or one's children. Common to both Arabic and Hebrew is the use of the respective verbs in situations that presuppose a prior alienation. For example, one may show favor to someone who has spurned one. In Later Phoenician inscriptions from the Persian and Greek periods we find both *ḥnn* and *ḥēn.*[14] In CIS 1:3, 12 a rare niphal occurs (*nḥn*); the only other known occurrence is in Jer 22:23.[15] The use of *ḥēn* in the idiom "give favor in the eyes of" parallels common OT usage. In the Yeḥawmilk inscription,[16] the king asks his patron deity to give him "favor in the eyes of the gods and in the eyes of the people" (cf. the Pa'ala—'ashtart inscription: "and give them favor and life in the eyes of the gods and the sons of mankind"[17]). The 1st person singular suffix form *ḥny* occurs in the Larnax tes Lapethou inscription in the construct chain *mnḥt ḥny.*[18] In this phrase, "offering of my grace," "grace" has the meaning of "thanks" (as in "say grace"; Lat. *gratia*). The offering made in the sanctuary is in gratitude to Melqart for life and offspring given to the king. The verb is also found in Aramaic (Dan 4:24[27]; 6:12[11]). In all cognate languages, as in Hebrew, the root was commonly employed in compounding proper names.

Meaning

a. In the OT, the verb *ḥānan* occurs primarily in the qal and hithpael. The qal has the meaning "be gracious," "show favor." The hithpael means "seek favor," mainly the favor of God, but also of humankind (Gen 42:21). Isolated uses of the niphal, piel, and polel appear in the OT. The hiphil does not occur; the causative is expressed by *nāṯan ḥēn*, as in Gen 39:21 (cf. the Yeḥawmilk and Pa'ala—'ashtart inscriptions). But only Yahweh is ever said to be able to give favor. In the absence of a hiphil, a hophal is unlikely; *yuḥan* in Isa 26:10 and Prov 21:10 should be read as a qal passive.

In two OT texts, *ḥnn* carries an aesthetic meaning. Prov 26:25 contains a lone denominative piel in the phrase *kî-yĕḥannēn qôlô*, "when he

14. See Zellig S. Harris, *A Grammar of the Phoenician Language*, AOS 8 (1936), 102.

15. G. A. Cooke, *A Text-Book of North-Semitic Inscriptions* (Oxford: Clarendon, 1903), 30–31, 36.

16. *KAI*, 10.9–10; cf. Cooke, *A Text-Book of North-Semitic Inscriptions*, 18–19; *ANET*³, 656.

17. *KAI*, 48.4; Cooke, *A Text-Book of North-Semitic Inscriptions*, 91.

18. *KAI*, 43.13; Cooke, *A Text-Book of North-Semitic Inscriptions*, 83.

speaks graciously"; Prov 22:11, another mention of gracious speech, uses an anomalous stative participle in *ḥēn śĕpāṭāyw*, one "who is gracious of speech."[19]

In all other cases, *ḥnn* is used of favor shown in personal relationships; it can refer to ordinary acceptance or kindness, or else favor of a special nature, such as pity, mercy, or generosity. In the latter case, the usual limits established by law or custom are transcended. In Hebrew, *ḥnn* does not imply preferential treatment, a favoring of A over B (like רצה *rāṣâ* in Deut 33:24 and חפץ *ḥāpēṣ* in 2 Sam 20:11). Compared with *rāṣâ*, *ḥānan* is more active. The former refers to what satisfies the desire: delight, enjoyment, and the like, and basically denotes a passive disposition. It refers more specifically to the kind of acceptance Yahweh displays when a sacrifice with its pleasing odor reaches him (e.g., Lev 22:27; Ezek 20:41). By contrast, *ḥānan* is active acceptance and active favor. To be gracious means to aid the poor, feed the hungry, deliver those in distress from defeat and death.[20] In all cases *ḥnn* is a positive term. It is inconceivable that one can be angry and at the same time show favor. Nor can one receive favor from someone who is at the same time angry. Favor cannot coexist with judgment. It is given or withdrawn according to whether one is positively disposed toward another. To show someone favor is perhaps a more superficial expression of oneself than to show love (אהב [*ʾāhab*] [*ʾāhabh*]). Love can coexist with judgment (Prov 3:12) and exists at a deeper level of the inner consciousness, where conflicting emotions are allowed to coexist.

b. The noun *ḥēn* occurs 67 times in the OT, only once with the article (Prov 31:30) and once with a suffix (Gen 39:21); it never appears in the plural. It has two basic meanings: "grace" and "favor." The latter is the more important in the OT, referring to the positive disposition one person has toward another. It can also mean "respect" (Prov 28:23; Lam 4:16). It appears most often in the familiar idiom *māsāʾ ḥēn bĕʿênê*, "find favor in someone's eyes." This was a favorite expression of the Yahwist. In much later usage, *nāśāʾ ḥēn* replaces *māṣāʾ ḥēn* (Esth 2:15, 17; 5:2). Only in the conditional request form *ʾim-māṣā ʾṭî ḥēn bĕʿēneykā* (Esth 7:3; cf. 5:8; 8:5) is the verb *māṣāʾ* retained. This idiom is more than a mere figure of speech; it describes very concretely what in fact was taken for granted in ancient Israel, as in the rest of the ANE: "favor" is פנים *pānîm*, "face" (Ps 119:58; Zech 7:2; Mal 1:9;

19. Dahood, "Hebrew-Ugaritic Lexicography II," *Biblica* 45 (1964) 409.

20. Cf. d. *ḥannûn*, below.

Dan 9:13). Yahweh is frequently asked to "turn" (פנה *pānâ*) and show favor (Ps 25:16; 86:16; 119:132; cf. 2 Kgs 13:23), i.e., turn and show his face (in mercy or kindness). To show one's face then means to be favorably disposed toward a person. In anger one's face is hidden (e.g., Ps 13:2[1]; 27:9; 30:8[7]). Moreover, if Yahweh's face is hidden, he might not hear one's "cry for favor" (Ps 31:23[22]; 55:2[1]). If the favor should be more than a simple expression of common courtesy, the face becomes bright. "Light of face" is a common metaphor for beneficence in the Amarna Letters and the Ugaritic correspondence.[21] Ancient people tended to measure *ḥēn* more precisely by the look in someone's eyes. Modern people look instead to the smile. In reality, both go together. *ḥēn* can be like *kābôd*. Psalm 84:12[11] says: "For Yahweh is a sun and shield, he bestows favor (*ḥēn*) and honor (כבוד *kābôd*)." The brightness of a face giving *ḥēn* can also be reflected on the face that receives *ḥēn*. After Hannah finds *ḥēn* in the eyes of Eli, she departs with a *pānîm* no longer sad (1 Sam 1:18; cf. Exod 34:29–35, where Moses's face shines after his private meeting with Yahweh).

The concept of *ḥēn* is not as profound as *ḥesed*. The terms rarely occur together (Gen 19:19; Esth 2:17) and in fact are found in quite different environments, despite the fact that both can be translated "kindness" or "mercy." The word חסד *ḥesed* is a covenant term most often meaning "covenant love." It presupposes rights and obligations, and demands a favorable attitude from both parties to a relationship. A relationship built on *ḥesed* is meant to be long-term. *Ḥesed* should be kept. In this sense it is more like *'ĕmet* (אמן *'āman*). But *ḥēn* is not mutually practiced by both parties. It is given by one to the other, and sustains the relationship only so long as the giver so desires. It can be given for a specific situation only. If it is given and sustained over a longer period of time, there is always the possibility that it may be withdrawn unilaterally. Unlike *ḥesed*, *ḥēn* can be withdrawn without consequence, since it is given freely.

c. The word *ḥănînâ* is found only once (Jer 16:13); it is another noun meaning "favor." A similar form appears in 3Q5 2:1.

d. The adjective *ḥannûn* means "gracious," and with one possible exception (Ps 112:4) is always used of Yahweh.

The subject for *ḥannûn wĕraḥûm wĕṣaddîq* in Ps 112:4 has been problematic since ancient times. Although the triple chain is unique in the OT,

21. Mitchell J. Dahood, *Psalms 1–50*, AB 16A (Garden City, NY: Doubleday, 1965), 26.

ḥannûn wĕraḥûm is otherwise a standard cliché applied only to Yahweh (as in Ps 111:4). Psalm 112, however, is not a psalm about Yahweh; it is in its entirety about humankind—the righteous person (vv. 1–9) and the wicked one (v. 10). One manuscript (Alexandrinus) adds *kýrios ho Theós* (cf. RSV). But there is otherwise nothing to preclude *yĕšārîm* from being the subject in 112:4. Note also that the cliché *(wĕ)ṣidqāṯô ʿōmedeṯ lāʿad* refers to Yahweh in Ps 111:3 and to the upright person in 112:3, 9.

In most cases, *ḥannûn* occurs with *raḥûm*, "merciful"; older usage prefers *raḥûm wĕḥannûn* (Exod 34:6; Ps 86:15; 103:8), while later usage prefers *ḥannûn wĕraḥûm* (Joel 2:13; Jon 4:2; Ps 111:4; 112:4; 145:8; 2 Chr 30:9; Neh 9:17, 31). The mercy that a mother shows to the issue of her *reḥem* is *raḥûm* and so also *ḥannûn* appears to carry the idea of motherly (or fatherly) compassion (cf. "Etymology and Occurrences," above, for meaning of the Arabic). Yahweh is *ḥannûn* in his capacity as father (Exod 22:26[27]). The overall goodness of Yahweh's favor can be seen from Ps 145:8–9, where *ḥannûn wĕraḥûm* is broken up for reiteration in the following cola, with the poet substituting *ṭôb* for *ḥannûn* (cf. also Ps 86:16–17: *pĕnēh ʾēlay wĕḥonnēnî . . . ʿśēh-ʿimmî ʾôṯ lĕṭôbâ*).

e. The noun *tĕḥinnâ* can mean "favor" or "mercy" (Josh 11:20; Ezra 9:8; the LXX translates both with *éleos*; cf. 1 Esd 8:75), or more commonly "cry for favor," "supplication." It is often used in parallel with *tĕpillâ*, but can also designate supplications made to other human beings (Jer 37:20; 38:26). The chiastic ordering of terms in 1 Kgs 8:28, *tĕpillaṯ / tĕḥinnāṯô—hārinnâ / hattĕpillâ*, argues for linking *rinnâ*, "ringing cry," with *tĕḥinnâ*, "cry of supplication."

f. The noun *taḥănûn* occurs only in the pl. abstract *taḥănûnîm*, "cries for favor" or "supplications."

Concrete Usages in the OT

Grace as a Possession

In its aesthetic sense, *ḥēn* denotes a quality that a person, animal, or inanimate object possesses. This usage is exclusively nontheological, although the sages judge the use to which possessed grace is put as either good or bad. The OT speaks on numerous occasions about gracious speech. It is the mark of refinement to be able to speak graciously. Such is to be desired of kings (Ps 45:3[2]), and it is an absolute prerequisite for one who aspires to the ruling elite (Prov 22:11; Eccl 10:12). But gracious words can be intolerable if they mask deception. Prov 26:25 warns of one concealing hatred: *kî-yĕḥannēn qôlô 'al-ta 'ămen-bô*, "when he speaks graciously, believe him not."

In describing women, *ḥēn* can refer to the total impression a woman makes (*'ēšeṯ-ḥēn*, Prov 11:16), although the focus no doubt is chiefly on her carriage and speech. A youthful wife is praised by comparison to a graceful animal (Prov 5:19). Another proverb says that a gracious woman receives honor (Prov 11:16). But in some women *ḥēn* is also a mark of deception (Prov 31:30), and it is commonly associated with the behavior of prostitutes (Nah 3:4). In these latter cases, *ḥēn* certainly includes among the woman's enticing qualities her use of gracious or seductive words. Wreaths worn on the head or *gargĕrôṯ* (neck?) can be *ḥēn*, and the wisdom teachers liken their teaching to such (Prov 1:9; 3:22; 4:9). Prov 17:8 compares a bribe to an *'eben-ḥēn* (beautiful or precious stone), which again does not negate the beauty implied in *ḥēn*, but makes clear the unfortunate ends to which *ḥēn* can be used.

Grace or Favor in Human Relationships

More beautiful than gracious words or graceful forms, delicate wreaths, or precious stones are human relationships built upon *ḥēn*. In the derived sense, *ḥēn* is a human disposition. It is present in the heart of one who is positively disposed toward another.

Favor as a Gift

When used of human relationships, the verb clearly includes the idea of giving. In some passages the notion of giving is implied so strongly as to require explicit translation, e.g., Judg 21:22: *ḥonnûnû 'ôṯām*, "Grant them graciously to us" (cf. also Gen 33:5, 11 in "Divine Favor to Individuals," below). In the case of Yahweh, *ḥēn* is commonly coupled with the verb נתן *nāṯan*, "give." It follows that *ḥēn* is in the nature of a gift. This explains in part why people must request it. It is freely given and cannot be grasped or seized by force. The giver has every right to withhold his *ḥēn*, and unless he is a person of rank, this may be done even at some risk. For the one receiving *ḥēn*, this gift is unlike most in that it never really becomes his possession. One quite literally finds favor in the eyes of another, and that is where the favor remains. It is comparable to one's reputation, which is likewise not its owner's possession. The two are nicely juxtaposed in Prov 22:1: "A good name (שׁם *šēm*) is to be chosen rather than great riches, and favor (*ḥēn*) is better than silver or gold."

Favor Sought

Favor is sought and found, and because it can be withheld, it demands a peculiar stance from the seeker, namely, subordination. The ancient Near Eastern world was a world of kings and lords, and consequently it was deemed proper to use language of deference. Typical is the expression *māṣā'tî ḥēn bĕʿêneykā*, not uncommonly accompanied by bowing and prostration (Gen 33:3ff.; 2 Sam 14:22; 16:4; Ruth 2:10; Ps 31:10[9]). Deferential language was necessary when a person of low station spoke to someone of high station. Prov 18:23 says that while the rich may speak roughly, the poor must use entreaties (*taḥănûnîm*). It is thus ironic when Job says he must ask his servant for favor (Job 19:16). But persons of means commonly employ deferential language when speaking to each other, in order not to be thought presumptuous. It is found most often in the OT when lords and kings are present (i.e., in patriarchal and royal narratives). It is even possible for a person of higher rank to speak with deference to another of lower rank. This is done when one prefers to ask for something rather than command it. Jacob, for example, speaks with deference to his son Joseph (Gen 47:29); it cannot be assumed here that Joseph's rise to power in Egypt necessitates such language from his father. David also speaks with deference when relaying a message to Nabal (1 Sam 25:8). In the case of Laban speaking to his nephew Jacob (Gen 30:27), we have nothing more than flattery: Laban is pretending to be obligated to Jacob.

Favor can be sought on two levels. The first is the level of formality. In a specific context, *ḥēn* is sought as a preamble to a request. The expression *'im-māṣā'tî ḥēn bĕʿêneykâ* is an elaborate way of saying "please." The suppliant is not out to find favor per se; his main concern is having his request granted. A more profound type of favor is that which is granted for a longer period of time. On this level, *ḥēn* is a general disposition toward someone, signifying a relationship of some importance. In ordinary usage, however, requests for *ḥēn* are usually made on the first level. Laban asks Jacob's favor only that he may be allowed to speak (Gen 30:27). Shechem requests the favor of Jacob and his sons in hope of marrying Dinah (Gen 34:11). Jacob entreats Joseph to take an oath regarding Jacob's burial (Gen 47:29). Joseph seeks favor from his brothers only to avert his sale (Gen 42:21), and later he seeks the favor of Pharaoh's household when he wants to go and bury his father (Gen 50:4). The sons of Reuben and Gad want land in Transjordan (Num 32:5); David wants Jonathan's permission to take leave (1 Sam 20:29), provisions for his troops (1 Sam 25:8), and later sanctuary from Achish (1 Sam 27:5). Jeremiah presents his *tĕḥinnâ* to Zedekiah that he may not be sent back to the house of Jonathan to die (Jer 37:20; 38:26), Esther seeks the favor of the king that she and the Jewish people may be spared (Esth 4:8; 5:8; 7:3; 8:3, 5).

Favor Found

Found favor can also be received on two levels. For specific acts of kindness, one can employ the same sort of deferential language used to seek favor. The imperfect in *'emṣā'-ḥēn bĕ'êneykā 'ădōnî* (2 Sam 16:4; Ruth 2:13) is to be translated as a present perfect: "I have surely found favor in your eyes, my lord." This is an embellished "thank you." It acknowledges favor already shown. The equally difficult form *nimṣā'-ḥēn bĕ'ênê 'ădōnî* in Gen 47:25 appears also to be equivalent to "thank you, my lord." But favor of the more profound and lasting kind is more commonly reckoned as found. When the Yahwist says that Joseph found favor in the eyes of Potiphar (Gen 39:4), he does not mean that Joseph did a single thing that pleased Potiphar, but rather that Joseph had overall good standing with his superior. The same is true of David with respect to Saul (1 Sam 16:22) and Jonathan (1 Sam 20:3). He had established a deep relationship with both, so much so that *ḥēn* implies deep affection. The favor Ruth found in the eyes of Boaz (Ruth 2:2, 10, 13) as well as the favor Esther found in the eyes of King Ahasuerus (Esth 2:17; 5:2)—not to mention others who saw her (Esth 2:15)—likewise included lasting affection. Whether Joab attains lasting favor with David (2 Sam 14:22) or merely exults because the king has granted his request is not clear. Neither is it clear whether Hadad had lasting favor with the pharaoh of Egypt (1 Kgs 11:19). For the most part, however, found favor transcends a single event and signifies a relationship of some depth. Found favor, being also a gift, can also be given in response to merit. Good sense wins *ḥēn* (Prov 13:15), and it was apparently also given to people of skill, as we can surmise from Eccl 9:11, although the Preacher himself is making a very different point.

Favor Lost

Even if *hēn* has created a relationship of some depth, it can still be lost. Deut 24:1 presupposes the right of a husband to give his wife a bill of divorce if she no longer finds favor in his eyes. Likewise a curse upon a guilty man consigns both him and his children to subsequent disfavor (Ps 109:12). In this latter case, disfavor is a result of judgment, whereas in the former case judgment comes after loss of favor. The sequence is not important; what matters is that favor and judgment cannot coexist.

Favor Anticipated

Prov 28:23, too, assumes that judgment and favor are incompatible: *môkîaḥ 'adām 'aḥăray ḥēn yimṣā' mimmaḥălîq lāšôn*, "He who rebukes a man will afterward find more favor than he who flatters with his tongue." If someone rebukes another he will no doubt lose that person's *ḥēn*. But the proverb does more than praise the rebuker over the flatterer; it says that *ḥēn* will come to the rebuker later on, but he must be willing to wait for it.

Royal Favor

In Dan 4:24[27], Daniel warns the king to repent of his sins and begin showing favor to the oppressed. Only so can he hope to escape a coming judgment.

Favor toward a City

Psalm 102:15[14] records a single instance of human favor that is not directed toward another individual or group. Here people show favor to—or more likely have pity on—the ruins of Jerusalem, which have too long lain neglected.

Theological Usages

Human Benevolence

Benevolence is an act of grace shown by the rich toward the poor, or at least by an individual with means toward one who has little or no means. It is what can be expected of a person toward his *rēaʿ*, "friend," "neighbor." Benevolence is extolled in Wisdom literature as a prime virtue. Therefore the generous person is *ṣaddîq*, "righteous" (Ps 37:21, 26; 112:4–5). The רשׁע *rāšāʿ*, on the contrary, is not benevolent (Prov 21:10). Job appeals to his friends' better nature: "Be gracious to me, be gracious to me, O you my friends" (Job 19:21). If they are now exalted over Job as they maintain (v. 5), that is all the more reason to be gracious to one who stands in need. Generally speaking, someone who is gracious to the *ʿānî* will be happy (Prov 14:21). But more important is the knowledge that showing grace to the needy honors Yahweh (Prov 14:31). A loan to the דל *dal* is a loan to Yahweh, and Yahweh will repay the gracious one for his deed (Prov 19:17). According to Prov 28:8, retribution will be meted out to the rich person who augments his wealth by extortion. In the end he gathers it only for another, namely the one who is gracious to the *dallîm*.

Brotherly Favor: Jacob and Esau

The account of Jacob and Esau in Genesis 32–33 takes us to the pinnacle of OT teaching on *ḥēn*, although the divine presence is at best peripheral. This is the dramatic episode in which the two brothers become reconciled. The Yahwist has incorporated the story into his history, but without editorializing. We might have expected him to tell us explicitly of Jacob's finding favor with Esau (cf. Gen 6:8; 39:4), but he prefers to let the story speak for itself.

The story contains four quotations from Jacob in which he seeks *ḥēn* from Esau (Gen 32:6[5]; 33:8, 10, 15). It is apparent throughout the narrative that this is not the usual request for favor.[22] Jacob does not seek Esau's *ḥēn* as preamble to something else. This *ḥēn* is the goal of his activity (32:6, 8[5, 7]), namely, a permanent change of disposition or attitude on Esau's part.[23] Even Jacob's use of the polite *ʾim-nāʾ māṣāʾṯî ḥēn bĕʿêneykā* shows that he has no ulterior motive. He has no request to make; instead he comes

22. See earlier section in this chapter, "Favor Sought."

23. See earlier section in this chapter, "Favor Found."

with gifts to give, and he compliments Esau with this phrase by urging him to accept them (33:10). Jacob knows that if Esau accepts the gifts it will demonstrate that Esau has accepted him as well, i.e., that Jacob has indeed found favor in his brother's eyes. The phrase is also used later when Esau's offer of men is turned down (33:15). Jacob's quest is successful, as 33:4–11 makes clear.

This event became quite important in later biblical tradition. It was remembered by Hosea (Hos 12:5[4]): *bākâ wayyitḥannen-lô*, "he wept and sought his favor."[24] It also appears quite likely that this story served as a prototype for Jesus's parable of the lost (prodigal) son in Luke 15:11–32. In the Jacob-and-Esau story, favor is restored almost entirely on the human level. We get only one hint of what its significance might be in the divine economy. After Jacob and Esau have come together, Jacob says to Esau: "Truly to see your face is like seeing the face of God" (Gen 33:10). The acceptance Jacob experiences from his brother is no less than what he might expect from a gracious God. (Jacob also saw the face of God in the face of the *'îš* at the Jabbok [Gen 32:31(30)]; Hos 12:5[4] therefore changes *'îš* to מלאך *mal'āk*.)

Divine Favor

Yahweh Himself Is Gracious

Graciousness is a divine attribute. The adjective *ḥannûn* is used almost exclusively of Yahweh in the OT, and almost always it is joined by other adjectives in liturgical concert. Yahweh is gracious and merciful, slow to anger, and abounding in steadfast love and faithfulness (Exod 34:6; Joel 2:13; Jonah 4:2; Pss 86:15; 103:8; 111:4; 116:5; 145:8; Neh 9:17, 31; 2 Chr 30:9). After the apostasy of the golden calf, and in response to Moses's specific request, Yahweh reveals his essential qualities and character: he is first of all *raḥûm wĕḥannûn* (Exod 34:6). The sequence is crucial. Grace comes after confession of sin, even as it came before the giving of the law. Law is delicately balanced against grace, and in fact the entire conversation between Moses and Yahweh in Exodus 32–34 focuses on this subject. In the single text where *ḥannûn* is used alone (Exod 22:26[27]), Yahweh warns

24. Cf. William L. Holladay, "Chiasmus, the Key to Hosea XII 3–6," *VT* 16 (1966) 55, who credits me with this interpretation.

that he will come as a protecting father to aid one of his children should strict justice interfere with humanitarian concerns.

The *idem per idem* constructions in Exod 33:19 use *ḥānan* and *riḥam*: "I will be gracious to whom I will be gracious, and I will show mercy on whom I will show mercy." *Idem per idem* constructions are used when one does not wish to be more specific.[25] Here in Exod 33:19 the form has normally been taken to express Yahweh's supreme authority in dispensing grace and mercy, when, where, how, and as he pleases.[26] Its rhetorical function (likewise in Exod 3:14) is to terminate the debate with Moses.[27] An alternate suggestion is that the form emphasizes Yahweh's nature to be merciful and gracious (cf. Exod 34:6–7). According to this view, Yahweh is saying to Moses, "I will surely be gracious; I will surely be merciful," or, "I am the gracious one; I am the compassionate one" (cf. Exod 3:14).[28] The form expresses the force of *ḥannûn* and *raḥûm* as attributes of God. It is assumed also that Yahweh ranks higher than humankind when he shows favor: "As the eyes of servants look to the hand of their master, as the eyes of a maid to the hand of her mistress, so our eyes look to Yahweh our God, till he have mercy upon us (*'ad šeyyĕḥonnēnû*)" (Ps 123:2).

Divine Favor to Individuals

Whereas *ḥēn* is always a gift from one person to another, only God is ever explicitly said to "give favor" (*nāṭan ḥēn*). He can give his own favor to someone or else negotiate favor between individuals, as in Gen 39:21. Yahweh never seeks the favor of humans. Only in Job is there even the hint of such a thing, and then the question is raised indirectly. Speaking of the mighty Leviathan, Yahweh answers Job rhetorically: "Will he make many supplications (*taḥănûnîm*) to you?" (Job 40:27[41:3]). The argument here is part of a much larger *qal waḥōmer*: if Leviathan would not ask for Job's favor, how much more will Yahweh not have to ask for it (41:2b–3[10b–11)! Apparently Yahweh thought this is what Job was waiting for.

25. S. R. Driver, *The Book of Exodus*, CBSC (Cambridge: Cambridge University Press, 1911 [repr. 1953]), 362–63.

26. See earlier section of this chapter, "Favor as a Gift."

27. Jack R. Lundbom, "God's Use of the *Idem per Idem* to Terminate Debate," *HTR* 71 (1978) 193–201.

28. David Noel Freedman, "The Name of the God of Moses," *JBL* 79 (1960) 154.

Divine favor is given to the righteous and humble (*'ānî*), i.e., the poor and oppressed. According to Ps 84:12[11], "Yahweh bestows favor and honor (*ḥēn wĕkābôd yittēn*)" on "those who walk uprightly." Prov 3:4 teaches that keeping the commandments and practicing other virtues will give one *ḥēn* in the eyes of God and human beings. The wicked person, says Isa 26:10, should not be shown favor, for it will not help him to learn righteousness. Others who can expect Yahweh's favor are the *'ăniyyîm* (Exod 22:24–26[25–27]; Prov 3:34).

Specific individuals also seek and find divine favor. The most affirmative statements are made by the Yahwist in Genesis. Gen 6:8, "But Noah found favor in the eyes of Yahweh," is the only statement of its kind in the entire OT. We hear of no supplications, and the assumption is that Yahweh's favor was a general disposition lasting over a long period of time. The Priestly writer gives us the further insight that Noah was a "righteous man" (*'îš ṣaddîq*), in contrast to the rest of the populace (Gen 6:9). This shows again that the OT has no aversion to merited favor. Later the Yahwist tells us that Yahweh gave Joseph favor in the eyes of the prison warden (*wayyittēn ḥinnô bĕ'ênê śar bêṭ-hassōhar*, Gen 39:21). In the Jacob cycle, *ḥānan* is used twice to mean "graciously given" (Gen 33:5, 11). God has graciously given Jacob children and other possessions. Thus when ancient history is looked at from a distance, and looked at also in legends that are markedly compressed, Yahweh's favor to particular individuals is stated briefly and unequivocally. If these individuals ever sought divine favor or experienced crises where divine favor was in doubt, such was forgotten by the time these stories reached generations of the tenth century BC.

When we leave Genesis, a different situation obtains. Individuals seek divine favor more than they claim to have found it. Despite Yahweh's assurances that he is gracious, even the greatest figures of the OT cannot rest secure in the knowledge that they have Yahweh's continuing favor. Moses has the favor of Yahweh, but when Yahweh says he will not accompany him on the journey, Moses begins to question it (Exod 33:12–13, 16–17; 34:9). The same thing occurs later when he sees the burden he is being asked to carry as Israel's leader (Num 11:11). But it must also be recognized that, although Moses may have Yahweh's overall favor, this is not to say that Yahweh will grant his every request for favors. Yahweh does accede to the request that he accompany Moses on the journey, but he does not honor the oxymoronic request that Yahweh kill him (Num 11:15),[29] nor does he

29. Walther Zimmerli in Hans Conzelmann and Walther Zimmerli, "χαρίς," in *TDNT*

honor Moses's request to cross the Jordan: *'el-YHWH bā'ēṯ hahî' lē'mōr . . .* (Deut 3:23). David twice sought Yahweh's favor. Once, when his child was sick, he fasted and wept, saying: "Who knows whether Yahweh will be gracious to me, that the child may live" (2 Sam 12:22); but the child died. And when Absalom drove him from Jerusalem, David wondered whether Yahweh in his favor would allow him to return (2 Sam 15:25).[30] In this instance Yahweh was gracious. For David, then, favor is seen mainly in deliverance from trouble and death.

According to the Chronicler, Manasseh also prayed for Yahweh's favor when in straits very similar to those of David. He left Jerusalem (only by hooks and chain), but like David was eventually restored to his kingdom; God heard his *tĕḥinnâ* (2 Chr 33:13). When Job is in distress, Bildad advises him to seek Yahweh's favor (Job 8:5). According to Bildad, Yahweh rewards the righteous and punishes sinners; therefore if Job is righteous, Yahweh will receive his cry with favor. Job, however, answers that he has sought Yahweh's favor but received no answer (Job 9:15, NEB). Daniel dutifully seeks Yahweh's favor despite the royal decree (Dan 6:12[11], Aramaic). This appears to refer to an act of piety performed customarily by the Jews in exile.

The Psalms are of course filled with pleas for Yahweh's favor. Although expressions of corporate worship, they nevertheless come from the heart of the individual. Very personal trials are articulated—sickness, personal enmity, loneliness, fear of death, and so forth. The impv. *ḥonnēnî*, "be gracious to me," is found only in the Psalms (although Job 19:21 contains the pl. *ḥonnunî*), where it occurs seventeen times (Pss 4:2[1]; 6:3[2]; 25:16; 26:11; 27:7; 30:11[10]; 31:10[9]; 41:5, 11[4, 10]; 51:3[1]; 56:2[1]; 57:2[1]; 86:3, 16; 119:29, 58, 132). The hapax legomenon *ḥānĕnēnî* (*ḥonĕnēnî*) in 9:14[13] adds an eighteenth instance. The terms for "supplication(s)," *tĕḥinnâ* (6:10[9]; 55:2[1]; 119:170 and *taḥănûn* (28:2, 6; 31:23[22]; 116:1; 130:2; 140:7[6]; 143:1; [86:6, *taḥănûnôṯāy*], indicate further the extent to which Yahweh's favor is sought in the Psalms. Almost all these psalms are individual laments; the main exceptions are Psalms 4, 30, and 116, which are psalms of confidence or thanksgiving, and 119, a psalm on the law. It may also be noteworthy that all (except for 116, 119, and 130) are ascribed by tradition to David. The psalmist usually begins his song with *ḥonnēnî*. His need may be accompanied by a consciousness of sin (25:16, 18; 41:5[4]; 51:3ff.[1ff.]; 130:2ff.), or he may come as a righteous person who is being

9:380.

30. Cf. Rib-addi, EA 137, 81.

oppressed by the wicked (26; 140). In the latter situation, the psalmist is concerned to affirm his innocence, since adversity implies Yahweh's judgment to outside observers. Thus favor can be sought on either the ground of righteousness or on the ground of unrighteousness coupled with repentance for sin. In Ps 59:6[5], the poet asks Yahweh not to be gracious to the wicked. In many cases a psalm that begins with a supplication for Yahweh's favor will later incorporate the answer received, e.g., 6:3, 10[2, 9]; 28:2, 6; 31:10, 23[9, 22]. Such psalms, whether compilations or not, tend to compress human experience. Psalm 77:10[9] (of Asaph) preserves for us the frustration of one who must wait for divine favor: "Has God forgotten to be gracious (*hăšākaḥ ḥannôṯ*), or in anger shut up his compassion?" Psalm 30 speaks of earlier favor that the psalmist sought—and evidently found—and then later adds a further plea for Yahweh's favor (vv. 9, 11[8, 10]).

Divine favor can also be sought indirectly through people chosen by Yahweh. In early times the divine emissary par excellence was Yahweh's *mal'ak*; to seek out his favor was to seek out the favor of Yahweh. Abraham wants *ḥēn* from the *mal'ak* in order to have him stop for a visit (Gen 18:3), but, more important, he anticipates a possible word from Yahweh about the promised son. In the Yahwist's later reworking of this passage, it is Yahweh himself who appears to Abraham on this occasion (18:1). This messenger together with two others show *ḥēn* to Lot by rescuing him from Sodom, and Lot's words to them, "Your servant has found favor in your sight," are words of thanks (Gen 19:19). Lot knows that they are favorably disposed toward him, and he is naturally grateful. When the *mal'ak YHWH* appears to Gideon, the latter requests a specific favor in the form of a sign to assure him that it is indeed Yahweh who is speaking with him (Judg 6:17). For Hannah, whose name is also derived from *ḥānan*, the divine emissary is Eli the priest. She wants a child, and when Eli grants her supplication (in the name of the *'ĕlōhe yiśrā'ēl*), she responds with a joyful "thank you": "Your maidservant has surely found favor in your eyes" (1 Sam 1:18). And Hannah's own face brightens as well.[31] At a later time in Israel the *nābî'* became the principal messenger of God. Fifty men plead for a favorable response from the prophet Elijah that their lives may be spared (2 Kgs 1:13); after receiving it, they become part of the prophet's entourage.[32] The remnant left in Judah after 586 BC presents a *tĕḥinnâ* to the prophet Jeremiah, which he in turn refers to Yahweh (Jer 42:2). Yahweh answers this

31. See "Linguistic Background: Meaning, b," above.

32. Jack R. Lundbom, "Elijah's Chariot Ride," *JJS* 24 (1973) 46–49.

supplication, but tells the people to remain in the land (42:9–10). Job looks for another kind of divine mediator, who might be gracious enough to save humankind from going down into the Pit (Job 33:24).

Divine Favor to Israel

At Sinai, Yahweh introduced himself to Israel first and foremost as a God of grace. He said it was his nature to be *rāḥûm wĕḥannûn* (Exod 34:6). Thus he granted Israel *ḥēn* in the eyes of the Egyptians, so the latter would bestow gifts on them when they left Egypt (Exod 3:21; 11:3; 12:36). But the Sinai revelation also made clear that Yahweh was a demanding God, who would not clear the guilty but would visit the iniquity of the fathers upon their children to the fourth generation (Exod 34:7). This dual nature of Yahweh as God of grace and God of judgment finds expression throughout the OT, where grace or favor to Israel is always seen vis-à-vis judgment. During the long period of growth into nationhood, when Yahweh surely persisted in showing Israel particular favor, the OT remains strangely silent on the subject, except perhaps in some of its divine blessings.[33]

But when judgment came upon the nation, the awareness of Yahweh's favor (past and future) became acute. The prophets especially foresaw military defeats at the hand of enemies, destruction of Israelite cities and death for their inhabitants, and finally exile. All signified a loss of Yahweh's *ḥēn*. In the dedication prayer of 1 Kgs 8 (cf. 2 Chr 6), recorded by the Deuteronomistic historian, Solomon correctly anticipates what is to come. The prayer speaks frequently of supplication (*tĕḥinnâ* and hithpael of *ḥnn*) necessitated by sin and its consequences: both the present supplication Solomon is making and future supplications that the people may find it necessary to make (1 Kgs 8:28, 30, 33, 38, 45, 47, 49, 52, 54, 59; 9:3 [cf. 2 Chr 6:19, 21, 24, 29, 35, 37, 39]). These future supplications are to be made either in the temple or, if the people are outside the city, facing in the direction of the temple. With the exception of the plea for victory in battle (1 Kgs 8:44–45 [cf. 2 Chr 6:34–35]), all are pleas for favor when the people are in some sort of distress, e.g., when they are defeated in battle (1 Kgs 8:33 [cf. 2 Chr 6:24]), when they are weak from lack of food, whether through famine or siege (1 Kgs 8:37–38 [cf. 2 Chr 6:28–29]), or when they have been taken into captivity (1 Kgs 8:46–49 [cf. 2 Chr 6:36–39]). In every case there is also to be a plea for forgiveness (סלח *sālaḥ*) of sins. Some time after Solomon concludes

33. See below the section of this chapter called "Favor in Blessings."

his prayer, Yahweh acknowledges his *tĕḥinnâ* (1 Kgs 9:3) and blesses the temple. Nothing is said about Yahweh's response to future supplications. Yahweh merely ends with a warning of judgment if apostasy ensues (9:7–9). This is the substance of Deuteronomistic theology: sin leads to loss of divine favor and issues in judgment. Implicit also in Deuteronomistic theology is the idea that Yahweh's disfavor finds expression in the hostility shown to Israel by the enemy. Favor will be shown neither to the young (Deut 28:50) nor to the old (Lam 4:16). The sin that precipitates Yahweh's disfavor and judgment is apostasy.

Isa 27:11 (which presupposes the destruction of Jerusalem in 586 BC) states that Yahweh cannot show favor to his people because they are without discernment (בין *bîn*). For Jeremiah and Deuteronomy, the ultimate sin is "forsaking Yahweh and going after *'ĕlōhîm 'ăḥērîm*." Jeremiah says that after Yahweh withdraws his favor, the people can serve these *'ĕlōhîm 'ăḥērîm* "day and night" (Jer 16:13). Jeremiah is more bitterly ironic when addressing the inhabitants of Jerusalem's royal complex: "How you will be favored (*mah-nnēḥant*) when pangs come upon you!" (Jer 22:23). In Deuteronomistic-Jeremianic theology we also find the idea that Yahweh's favor could avert judgment. The Deuteronomistic historian says that Yahweh was gracious to Israel during the reign of Jehoahaz and had compassion on the Israelites because of his covenant with the patriarchs (2 Kgs 13:23). This averted destruction at the hands of Hazael, the Aramean king. Jeremiah holds out hope that Yahweh will avert judgment when he sends Baruch to the temple to read his scroll. Jeremiah says: "It may be that their supplication will come before Yahweh . . ." (Jer 36:7). The weeping and supplication described in Jer 3:21 may express a similar hope on the part of the people.

It is Amos who introduces the idea that Yahweh's favor would be seen in his leaving a remnant of Israel, although his tone of uncertainty gives the word an original sting: "It may be that Yahweh, the God of hosts, will be gracious to the remnant of Joseph" (Amos 5:15). Jeremiah declares that "the people who survived the sword found grace (*māṣā' ḥēn*) in the wilderness" (Jer 31:2). Thus despite his message of judgment, the prophet saw a measure of divine favor reserved for Israel that Yahweh did not originally grant to the inhabitants of Canaan (Deut 7:2; Josh 11:20).[34]

In the postexilic period, Ezra acknowledges Yahweh's favor in the survival of a remnant: "But now for a brief moment favor (*tĕḥinnâ*) has been shown by Yahweh our God, to leave us a remnant . . ." (Ezra 9:8). In another

34. See below the section of this chapter called "Divine Favor to Other Nations."

prayer he expands the ritualized statement of Yahweh's attributes, adding that Yahweh did not forsake (עזב *'āzab*) the people or make an end (כלה *kālâ*) of them, i.e., he left a remnant (Neh 9:17, 31).

Another theme reiterated by the prophets was that Yahweh would be gracious to Israel if she repented. To the people of Jerusalem the prophet Isaiah says: "You shall weep no more. He will surely be gracious to you at the sound of your cry" (Isa 30:19). Jeremiah anticipates the return of the northern exiles: "with weeping they shall come, and with supplications (*ûbĕṭaḥănûnîm*) I will lead them back" (Jer 31:9). Joel says to rend hearts and not garments, and return (*šûb*) to Yahweh, for he is *ḥannûn wĕraḥûm* (Joel 2:13). The Chronicler records that Hezekiah addressed the remnant in the north to the effect that if they would return to Yahweh (i.e., repent: *šûb*) and come to Jerusalem to celebrate the Passover, then the exiles taken away by the Assyrians would be able to return (*šûb*) home. This would come about because Yahweh is *ḥannûn wĕraḥûm* (2 Chr 30:9).

As individuals must, so Israel, too, must sometimes wait for Yahweh's favor. Ps 123:3 expresses the impatience people feel after long periods of abuse: *ḥonnēnû YHWH ḥonnēnû kî-rab śāba 'nû bûz*, "Be gracious to us Yahweh, be gracious to us, for we have had more than enough of contempt." Ps 102:14[13] expresses a similar sentiment with regard to the city of Zion: "It is time to favor her (*lĕḥenĕnâ*); the appointed time (*mô'ēd*) has come." The need for patience was perhaps best understood by Isaiah: "Therefore Yahweh waits to be gracious to you . . . Blessed are all those who wait for him" (Isa 30:18). In Isa 33:2, the confession of the people articulates the same theme: "Yahweh, be gracious to us; we wait for you." Later, the prayer of Daniel predicates its request for Yahweh's favor on the fact that the seventy years predicted by Jeremiah are now up and it is time for Yahweh to be gracious (Dan 9:2ff.). With its rhetoric of accumulation, this prayer is reminiscent of Solomon's prayer in 1 Kgs 8. In fact it actualizes, perhaps intentionally, what was only anticipated earlier. Now Yahweh's favor must be sought, and Daniel rather than Solomon is the intercessor for the people. He does not prostrate himself before the altar, but he does accompany his supplication with fasting, sackcloth, and ashes (Dan 9:3). He, too, is concerned about the temple, now lying in ruins (v. 17), and he stands before Yahweh not in righteousness (v. 18) but in repentance for the sin of himself and his people (v. 20). Daniel realizes that Yahweh's favor is his to give or withhold; it cannot be assumed as a right or compelled

(v. 18; cf. Exod 33:19). Yahweh subsequently hears Daniel's supplications and sends word to him by the angel Gabriel (Dan 9:20–27).

Zechariah and Malachi have different concerns that call for Yahweh's favor. In Deutero-Zechariah, the prophet speaks of "a spirit of compassion and supplication" (*rûaḥ ḥēn wĕṭaḥănûnîm*) that Yahweh will pour out upon the people of Jerusalem following the murder of their prophet (Zech 12:10). This is in contrast to the spirit of judgment that had prevailed earlier. Malachi is concerned to upgrade the quality of sacrifice. The people are told to seek the face of God with first-rate offerings, that he may be gracious to them (Mal 1:9).

Divine Favor to Other Nations

At the time of the conquest, Yahweh commands Moses explicitly not to be favorably disposed to the inhabitants of Canaan (Deut 7:2; Josh 11:20). Here *ḥānan* refers to special favor, i.e., mercy. Later, however, the book of Jonah argues that the favor available to Israel is also available to Assyria, providing of course that they repent (Jonah 4:2).

Favor in Blessings

Yahweh's favor is conveyed in the giving of blessings. On seeing his brother Benjamin after years of separation from his family, Joseph blesses him with the words: "God be gracious to you (*yoḥnĕkā*), my son" (Gen 43:29). In the Aaronic benediction, the bestowal of Yahweh's favor is artfully reiterated at the center:

> Yahweh make his *face* to shine upon you
> and be *gracious* to you (*wîḥunnekkā*)
> Yahweh lift up his *face* on you. (Num 6:25–26)

A similar blessing is echoed in Ps 67:2[1]: "May God be gracious to us and bless us, and make his face shine upon us."

In an obscure passage in Zechariah, Zerubbabel, the builder of the second temple, is described as bringing forth the cornerstone or keystone accompanied by shouts of "Grace, grace to it!" (*ḥēn ḥēn lâ*, Zech 4:7).[35]

35. Others translate *ḥēn* as "salvation," "beauty," or the like.

2

Burning Anger in the Old Testament

Hebrew *ḥrh*, *yṣt*, and *yqd*[1]

Hebrew *ḥrh*

ḥārâ ("to burn"); *ḥārôn* ("burning anger"); *ḥărî* ("burning").

Linguistic Background

Etymology

The verbs *ḥārâ* and *ḥrr* have the basic meaning "burn."[2] Both most probably derive from a biliteral *ḥr* in Old Hebrew. Ugaritic *ḥrr* means "burn," "scorch," or "roast."[3] Akkadian *erēru* and Arabic *ḥarra* also mean "burn" (although Rabin[4] takes *waḥara* to be the real Arabic cognate). The Aramaic *ḥrr* of the Targumim (Pss 2:12; 102:4[3]; Ezek 15:4–5) has the meaning

1. Coauthored with David Noel Freedman; "*ḥrh*," in *TDOT* 5:171–76; "*yṣt*," in *TDOT* 6:266–69; and "*yqd*," in *TDOT* 6:271–74.

2. G. Sauer, "חרה, *ḥrh* entbrennen," in *THAT* 1:633–35; W. H. Simpson, "Divine Wrath in the Eighth Century Prophets" (PhD diss., Boston University, 1968).

3. *KTU* 1.5, 2:5; 1:23, 41, 44, 48; cf. 1:12, 2:38, 41; *UT*, no. 902.

4. Chaim Rabin, "Etymological Miscellanea," in *Studies in the Bible*, Scripta Hierosolymitana 8 (Jerusalem: Magnes, 1961), 390–91.

"burn" or "be blackened, charred." At Boghazköy, *re-e-ú* is attested as a Canaanite loanword = **ḥrē*, "angry."[5]

Meaning

The verb *ḥārâ* occurs mainly in the qal with *'ap* as the expressed or implied subject: *ḥārâ 'ap* "(someone's) nose / anger burned hot." Apparently *ḥārâ* is more intense than קצף *qṣp*, although *qāṣap* substitutes for *ḥārâ* in P and the Holiness Code.[6] Anger directed toward another person is expressed by *ḥārâ 'ap bĕ* (except in Num 24:10, where *'el* is used instead). Without *'ap*, *ḥārâ* + *lĕ* means simply "(he) was angry": *wayyiḥar lĕya'ăqob*, "and Jacob was angry" (Gen 31:36). The niphal appears with *bĕ* in Cant 1:6; Isa 41:11 and 45:24 and means "be angry (with)." The piel does not appear in biblical Hebrew, although it may have existed later. The form *ḥryty* in 11QPs[a]; Sir 51:19 (*ḥryty npšy*), "I kindled my desire"),[7] is either piel[8] or qal.

Two hiphil readings are problematic. In Neh 3:20, *heḥĕrâ* is left untranslated by most modern versions, but it could mean "burned with zeal,"[9] which would reflect a meaning similar to the tiphel forms (Jer 12:5; 22:15; see below). Job 19:11 contains a hiphil *wayyaḥar*, but this should probably be repointed as a qal.[10] Causitive meaning in the sense of "provoke to anger" is expressed by the hiphil of כעס *kā'as* (frequent in Deuteronomy, Jeremiah, and the Deuteronomistic history). The hithpael of *ḥrh* has intensive meaning: "fly into a passion" (Ps 37:1, 7–8 [4QpPs 37:8 has *tiḥar*[11]]; Prov 24:19). Jeremiah contains two rare t-formations: *tĕṯaḥăreh* (Jer 12:5) and *mĕṯaḥăreh* (22:15), which are most likely piel forms derived from a quadriliteral root *tḥrh*.[12] But the meaning in both cases is clear: "be in a

5. *AHw*, 2:976.

6. BDB, 354.

7. James A. Sanders, ed. *The Psalms Scroll of Qumrân Cave 11 (11QPs[a])*, DJD 4 (Oxford: Clarendon, 1965), 80, 82.

8. KBL[3], 337, under hiphil.

9. BDB, 354.

10. See for example, Georg Fohrer, *Das Buch Hiob*, KAT 16 (Guttersloh: Mohn,1963), 308.

11. Hartmut Stegemann, "Der Pešer Psalm 37 aus Höhle 4 von Qumran (4 Qp Ps 37," *RevQ* 4 (1963) 247.

12. For a different view, see Joshua Blau, "Über die t-Form des Hif'il im Bibelhebräisch," *VT* 7 (1957) 385–88, especially 387–88; according to Blau, we are dealing here with a t-causitive, a hitafel formed from a triliteral root.

heat (of a race)" or "compete." Jastrow[13] lists a *taḥărûṯ* in Talmudic Hebrew meaning "heat, rivalry, contention." A cognate noun *ḥārôn* means "anger" or "burning anger."

Concrete Usage in the OT

In the OT, anger is frequently expressed when someone has heard something—either firsthand or through a report—that makes him very displeased. It can also erupt quickly in conversation. It is a spontaneous response to a threat of some sort directed at the individual or a group to which the individual belongs. But threats to one's sense of justice, truth, or right behavior can also evoke anger. Jacob becomes angry with Rachel because she has blamed him for her barrenness (Gen 30:2). An accusation by Ish-bosheth against Abner makes Abner angry (2 Sam 3:8). Balak's anger is kindled against Balaam for disregarding explicit instructions and invoking a blessing on Israel rather than a curse (Num 24:10).

Anger is also expressed when someone has been insulted or degraded. Potiphar becomes angry after hearing a report that Joseph has insulted (*ṣḥq*) his wife (Gen 39:17–19; cf. v. 14, where she claims an insult to the entire household: "See, he has brought among us a Hebrew to insult us"). Balaam became angry at his ass when the ass refused to move (Num 22:27). Saul, too, was angry when the women sang that David's exploits surpassed his own (1 Sam 18:8). The Israelite troops were angry with Judah when Amaziah refused to let them join in the fight against the Edomites (2 Chr 25:10).

In some instances, anger is expressed together with jealousy or in the heat of competition. Saul's jealousy of David led to anger towards David and Jonathan (1 Sam 20:7, 30). Jealousy also was behind Israel's anger at Judah when Judah took the lead in escorting King David back to Jerusalem (2 Sam 19:43[42]). Sanballat and his comrades were angry when they heard that Nehemiah was rebuilding the walls of Jerusalem (Neh 3:33[4:1]; 4:1[7]). Perhaps, too, it was sibling rivalry (*bĕnê 'immî niḥărû-bî*) that made the "sons of my mother" force the bride to be a keeper of vineyards (Cant 1:6).

News of treachery or suspicion of deceit could also arouse anger. Jacob became angry at Laban for his persistent searching for the household gods, not knowing that the real deceit lay with Rachel (Gen 31:36; cf. v. 32). Zebul

13. Marcus Jastrow, *Dictionary of the Targumim, the Talmud Babli and Yerushalmi, and the Midrashic Literature with an Index of Scriptural Quotations* (1903; reprinted, Brooklyn: Traditional Press, 1975), 2:1662.

the Shechemite became angry when he heard of the plot against Abimelech (Judg 9:30). Eliab's anger towards David (1 Sam 17:28) was prompted by his suspicion that David had ulterior motives in coming to the battle front. Elihu was angry at Job because Job justified himself instead of God; he also was angry at Job's three friends because despite their condemnation of Job they were unable to refute him (Job 32:2–3).[14] The anger of David in 2 Sam 12:5 is over an injustice, although David is no doubt surprised to find out that the greedy man in Nathan's parable is none other than himself. Nehemiah is likewise angry over the injustice of the nobles in Israel forcing fellow Jews into slavery by exacting high interest (Neh 5:6).

In the elevated speech of the patriarchs we find polite circumlocutions intended to avert another's anger. A request is prefaced with the polite formula *'al-yiḥar bĕ'ênê 'ădōnî*," let not (anger) burn in the eyes of my lord" (Gen 31:35), or *wĕ'al-yiḥar 'appĕkā bĕ'abdekā*, "let not your anger burn against your servant" (Gen 44:18). A vestige of this remains in Exod 32:22, where Aaron says to Moses: *'al-yiḥar 'ap 'ădōnî*, "let not the anger of my lord burn hot."[15] When Joseph has revealed himself, he says to his brothers: *wĕ'al-yiḥar bĕ'ênêkem*, "and do not be angry in your own eyes," i.e., at yourselves (Gen 45:5); but in this instance we find words of genuine consolation.

Usage in Theological Contexts

Divine Anger

The verb *ḥārâ* occurs most commonly in the OT with Yahweh as subject (cf. *ḥārôn*, which is used only in reference to God). Yahweh becomes angry primarily because people's behavior displeases him; when his anger is kindled, it is always directed at people, whether individuals, the people of Israel, or, less commonly, the foreign nations. In Deut 29:26[27] the phrase "against that land" means in the rhetorical language of Deuteronomy "against the people of that land." Abraham and Gideon seek to avert Yahweh's anger: *'al-nā' yiḥar l'ădōnāy* (Gen 18:30, 32); *'al-yiḥar 'appĕkā bî* (Judg 6:39). This is more than mere politeness; both are making humble but extraordinary requests of God.

14. For a different interpretation, see Fohrer, *Das Buch Hiob*, 446; cf. III.1.

15. חנן *ḥānan* "Favor Sought": *māṣā'tî hēn bĕ'ēneykā*.

Yahweh is not recorded as becoming angry in Genesis, despite his many judgments in the primeval history. In the wilderness, however, a different situation obtains. Here we often are told of Yahweh's anger, despite the idyllic picture later prophets paint of the wilderness period (Jer 2:2–3; Hos 2:16–17[14–15]). Yahweh is angry at Moses because he resists being Yahweh's mouthpiece (Exod 4:14); this may also explain why Abraham and Gideon are cautious in presenting their arguments.

Many of the same things that make humans angry make Yahweh angry. Jealousy heads the list. Yahweh's anger with his people in the wilderness stems from their apostasy: they build a golden calf (Exod 32:10–11; cf. v. 19; Hos 8:5; see below). In response, Yahweh threatens to consume the people with anger. This anger is represented as a consuming fire. He will instead make a great nation of Moses. Moses wisely rejects this idea, and his intercession prevents disaster.

The consuming power of Yahweh's anger is also shown in the Covenant Code where justice is at issue. The people are told they will be judged proportionately if they wrong strangers or harm widows and orphans (Exod 22:23[24]). The complaints of the people in the wilderness can also be answered by God's anger. The people complain in Yahweh's hearing that they lack food (Num 11:1, 10, 33). Here anger takes the form of a fire that consumes parts of the camp (v. 1) and a plague that takes the lives of numerous people (v. 33). Yahweh's anger also burns against Aaron and Miriam when they challenge Moses's right to be the sole spokesman for God (Num 12:9; cf. Exod 4). Yahweh also becomes angry at Balaam for going to meet Balak (Num 22:22), but in light of v. 20 the reason for his anger is not at all clear. At Shittim, Israel bows down before Baʿal of Peor, and Yahweh responds in anger with a plague that kills some twenty-four thousand (Num 25:3, 9).

Yahweh becomes angry when his commands are not carried out. The timidity of some in pursuing Yahweh's holy war evokes Yahweh's anger (Num 32:10, 13; cf. Num 14). The punishment on this occasion is the extension of the period of wandering to forty years, so that the wicked generation would perish entirely before being able to enter the promised land. In Deuteronomy, Yahweh becomes angry when Israel goes after other gods (*'ĕlōhîm 'ăḥērîm*, Deut 6:14–15; 7:4; 11:16–17; 29:25–26[26–27]: *'ĕlōhê nēkar-hā'āreṣ*, Deut 31:16–17). Anger here results in famine (11:17) and ultimately death.

The Deuteronomistic history reflects earlier sources. Yahweh becomes angry with Israel when the Israelites seek other gods or in any way transgress the covenant (*ʿābar ʾeṯ-bĕrîṯ* Josh 7:1, 11; 23:16; Judg 2:13–14, 20; cf. 3:7–8; 10:6–7). This leads inevitably to defeat in battle (cf. the defeat at Ai due to Achan's sin; Josh 7) or total subjection to the surrounding enemy (Judg 2:14; 3:8; 10:7). Failure to drive out all the Canaanites from the land is likewise traced to Israel's transgression of the covenant (Judg 2:20–23); Yahweh's lack of support is regarded as being another manifestation of Yahweh's anger. During the monarchy, idolatry continues to be the most detestable offense against Yahweh. Now, however, the kings receive the blame (2 Kgs 13:3; 23:26; 2 Chr 25:15). Even the great reform of Josiah could not prevent the anger of Yahweh from destroying the nation (2 Kgs 23:26).

A similar perspective appears in the historical summary of Psalm 106 (v. 40). Uzzah apparently violates a command of Yahweh not to touch the ark, and in so doing is the victim of Yahweh's anger (2 Sam 6:7; cf. 1 Chr 13:10), which in turn arouses the anger of David (2 Sam 6:8; cf. 1 Chr 13:11). Yahweh also becomes angry when David takes a census (2 Sam 24:1), and so sends a plague. The background is unclear: 2 Sam 24:1 states that Yahweh himself incited David against Israel, whereas 1 Chr 21:1 says that David was incited by Satan.

The prophets use *ḥārâ* sparingly, despite their message of judgment. But their usage is consistent with that of the rest of the OT. Isaiah says that Yahweh's anger will burn against Israel for rejecting *tôrâ* (Isa 5:24–25); the entire created order will suffer the consequences. Hosea sharply reminds Israel of Yahweh's anger over the bull cult sponsored by the government in Samaria: *zānaḥ ʿeglēk šōmĕrôn ḥārâ ʾappî bām* (Hos 8:5;[16] cf. also Exod 32:10–11). Zechariah declares Yahweh's anger at unworthy kings and their officials (Zech 10:3).

Only twice in the OT is *ḥārâ* used to refer to Yahweh's anger towards other nations. Here his jealousy manifests itself *in behalf of* Israel. Habakkuk asks rhetorically if Yahweh's anger was against the rivers and the sea when he trampled the nations (Hab 3:8). This mythological language probably echoes Yahweh's primordial struggle against the sea monster. In the royal psalm attributed to David (Psalm 18 = 2 Samuel 22), the poet recounts the cosmic manifestations of Yahweh's anger against the enemy (v. 8[7]). Finally, Job thinks Yahweh's anger is directed at him because of his lamentable plight (Job 19:11), while the epilogue speaks of anger towards Job's three friends for speaking falsely concerning Yahweh (Job 42:7; cf. "Concrete Usage in the OT," above).

16. Jack R. Lundbom, "Double-duty Subject in Hosea VIII 5," *VT* 25 (1975) 228–30.

Human Anger

In the early period, the *rûaḥ* of God could descend upon an individual, making him angry. Samson, whose pride was injured when the answer to his riddle was discovered, went down to Ashkelon under the power of the spirit and killed thirty men, taking their garments to gather payment for his opponents (Judg 14:19). Saul, too, becomes angry under the influence of the *rûaḥ*, and responds to an injustice about to be done to the men of Jabesh-gilead (1 Sam 11:6). As was the case with Samson's anger, Saul's anger too leads to war.

People could reflect divine anger when the Torah was broken. Moses's anger burns hot at the sight of the golden calf (Exod 32:19). Twice the rape of one of Israel's daughters occasioned bitter anger. David became very angry (*wayyiḥar lô mĕʾōd*) when he heard of Ammon's rape of Tamar (2 Sam 13:21). Shechem's rape of Dinah (Gen 34:7) is recalled as a similar event (cf. Gen 38); here and elsewhere the Yahwist finds in the patriarchal history certain prototypes illuminating the history of David. But on the earlier occasion it was the sons of Jacob rather than Jacob himself who became very angry (*wayyiḥar lāhem mĕʾōd*). In both cases the fathers withhold judgment while the sons mete it out to the offenders (e.g., Absalom avenges Tamar). Anger regularly leads to destructive actions, and such actions are usually carried out by the one who is angry, though occasionally by another. David thus shows unusual restraint in refraining from vengeance.

Certain wisdom texts counsel against becoming angry, even against the wicked (Ps 37:1, 7–8; Prov 24:19). But the exclusive use of the intensive form (hithpael) indicates that the warning is against passionate anger: *ʾal-tiṯḥar*. Passionate anger can only lead to evil (Ps 37:8); besides, the wicked have no future anyway (Prov 24:19–20).

Israel occasionally incurs the anger of their enemies, but Deutero-Isaiah asserts that Yahweh will frustrate the enemies' plans, and their anger will be of no avail. On the day of salvation they will all be shamed (*yēbōšû*, Isa 41:11; 45:24). Ps 124 also asserts that, had Yahweh not been on the side of Israel, their angry enemies would surely have consumed them (vv. 2–3).

Humans Angry before God

While the OT never speaks of anyone becoming overtly angry towards God, frequently someone expresses anger in God's presence or in conversation with him. Occasionally one gets the impression that God is the real object of the anger; but if this is so, it remains hidden from view. On three occasions such anger is associated with sacrifices. Cain is angry because Yahweh accepts Abel's offering but rejects his own (Gen 4:5–6). Moses angrily tells Yahweh not to accept the offering of Korah and his rebellious priests (Num 16:15). And when Saul violates the requirements of the ban (חרם *ḥāram*), Yahweh refuses his subsequent offering and rejects Saul himself from being king (cf. Achan, "Divine Anger" above). Saul's behavior arouses Samuel's anger and he cries to Yahweh all night (1 Sam 15:11).

Anger before Yahweh can also involve Yahweh's judgment—inflicted, postponed, or omitted. When Uzzah is punished for touching the ark, David verges on anger toward Yahweh (2 Sam 6:7–8; cf. 1 Chr 13:10–11); but he holds his peace, out of respect or fear. Jonah becomes angry during his conversation with Yahweh because Yahweh withheld punishment from Nineveh (Jon 4:1, 4); but he was also angry about the plant that perished (Jonah 4:9); and according to the biblical author the latter anger should have cancelled the former, since Jonah would understand Yahweh's mercy toward Nineveh and share his attitude.

Hebrew *yṣt*

yāṣat ("to kindle, to burn")

Meaning, Occurrences

Hebrew *yṣt* is another, less common root used in the OT to mean "kindle" or "burn" (cf. *dlq*, *ḥrh*, *ḥrr*, *yqd*, *lhṭ*, *qdh*). The more common roots are בער *bʿr* and שׂרף *śrp*.

The root has no cognates in the other Semitic languages, including Aramaic. In the OT, it appears primarily in Deuteronomic material and in prophetic writings (including Lamentations) from the eighth to the sixth centuries BC. About half of its thirty occurrences are in Jeremiah, both in the poetry and in the prose. The verb appears later in Neh 1:3; 2:17, and continues in use into the postbiblical period.[17] In the OT, *yṣt* is used with reference to the burning of land and property, and by metaphorical extension to include the populace (Jer 11:16), which, especially during war,

17. Jastrow, *Dictionary of the Targumim*, 590–91.

is tied closely to property and land (Judg 9:49). Moreover, when Yahweh pours out his wrath, he does not discriminate between people and land (2 Kgs 22:13, 17). The common word in P for the burning of sacrifices is *śārap* (Leviticus). Our root is nevertheless interchangeable with *bʿr* and *śrp*, both of which are used for burning of all kinds.

There are four occurrences of the qal. With *bĕ*, it means "kindle" (Isa 9:17[18]; with *bāʾēš*, it means "be kindled with fire" (Isa 33:12; Jer 49:2; 51:58). The niphal means "be kindled, burned"; it is found only in the 3rd person. The common form *niṣṣĕṯâ* (3rd-person sg. fem.) appears in 2 Kgs 22:13, 17; Jer 9:11[12]; 46:19, although the two occurrences in Jeremiah may be derived from the root *nṣh*, "be ruined, laid waste" (cf. Jer 4:7). The kethib of Jer 2:15, *nṣth*, is an old 3rd-person pl. fem., as in Aramaic,[18] although it could also come from *nṣh*.[19] The 3rd-person pl. *nṣtw* appears in Jer 2:15 (Q); 9:9[10]; Neh 1:3; 2:17. In the hiphil with *bāʾēš* the meaning is "set on fire" (Josh 8:8, 19); with *ʾēš* alone, it is "set fire to" (Amos 1:14; Jer 17:27). In Jer 51:30, *hiṣṣîṯû miškĕnōṯeyhā* means "they set her houses on fire."

Concrete Usage in the OT

Land and property—fields of grain, pastures, uncultivated groves of trees, and especially cities—are burned by enemies as an act of war. To finish the destruction of the city of Shechem, Abimelech sets fire to the fortified tower with bundles of brushwood he and his people have gathered (Judg 9:49). Absalom, too, as an act of war has his servants set fire to the barley fields of Joab (2 Sam 14:30–31).

Usages in Theological Contexts

In a holy war, Yahweh expressly commands the burning of cities. Ai (or Bethel?) was thus set on fire after it had been taken by Joshua (Josh 8:8, 19). By the time of Amos, however, Yahweh's judgment is conceived in more universal terms. In his great sermon in Amos 1:2—3:8, Amos prophesies destruction by fire against seven nations, including Judah. Against six of them—Damascus, Gaza, Tyre, Edom, Moab, and Judah—Yahweh says

18. BLe, §55ć; cf. §42ó.

19. Graf, Duhm, Driver, Peake, and Rudolph.

wĕšillaḥtî ʾēš, "and I will send fire" (Amos 1:4, 7, 10, 12, 2:2, 5), whereas against the Ammonites he says *wĕhiṣṣattî ʾēš bĕḥômaṯ rabbâ*, "and I will kindle a fire in the wall of Rabbah" (Amos 1:14).

Isaiah speaks of thorns and briars (*šāmîr wāšayiṯ*) as symbolizing wicked people who are set afire. One hears echoes of Jotham's parable and the subsequent debacle suggested by Abimelech in his discourse (Judg 9). In Isa 9:17[18], Isaiah speaks of the civil wars that characterized the closing years of the northern kingdom: each is like a fire that consumes briars and thorns and devours the thickets of the forest (*wattiṣṣaṯ bĕsibĕkê hayyaʿar*; cf. Hos 7:7; 2 Kgs 15:8–30; cf. Judg 9:15–20). Yet through it all, the wrath of Yahweh is manifested (Isa 9:18[19]; cf. Judg 9:56–57). In Isa 33:10–12 we find the same idea: when Yahweh exalts himself on the day of judgment, the chaff that the nation has conceived and borne will be consumed; people will treat one another "like thorns cut down, that are burned in the fire (*qôṣîm kĕsûḥîm bāʾēš yiṣṣattû*; v. 12). Later, however, when Yahweh sings his new Song of the Vineyard (Isa 27:2–6; cf. 5:1–7), wrath is gone because the wicked are no more. To emphasize the point, Yahweh says that if only he had some thorns and briars he would trample them and burn them up (Isa 27:4), but none are left.

Before this can take place, however, judgment must come upon Jerusalem. In 622 BC, a lawbook was found in the temple and subsequently read to King Josiah. After hearing its contents, he rent his clothes, saying, *kî-gĕdôlâ ḥĕmaṯ YHWH ʾăšer-hîʾ niṣṣĕṯâ bānû*, "for great is the wrath of Yahweh that is kindled against us" (2 Kgs 22:13). A divine oracle confirmed his assessment of the situation. The scroll may have included the Song of Moses found in Deut 32 (vv. 15–22 are echoed in the oracle uttered against Judah by the prophetess Huldah).[20] In Deut 32:22a, Yahweh says, *kî-ʾēš qādĕḥâ bĕʾappî wattîqad ʿad-šĕʾôl taḥtîṯ* "for a fire is kindled in my anger, and it burns to the depths of Sheol"; in Huldah's oracle, he says, *wĕniṣṣĕṯâ ḥămāṯî bammaqôm hazzeh wĕlōʾ tikbeh* "therefore my wrath will be kindled against this place, and it will not be quenched" (2 Kgs 22:17b).

Jeremiah was chosen to bring this message to both king and people after the time of Josiah. He grieves over the damage already inflicted, while predicting worse in the days ahead. The enemies arising against Judah did not come from within, as in the case of the northern kingdom, but from without. They came and burned the countryside, the cities, and the inhabitants of the land. They came in a steady stream: first the Assyrians, then the

20. Jack R. Lundbom, "The Lawbook of the Josianic Reform," *CBQ* 38 (1976) 293–302.

Egyptians, followed by various mixed hordes (Jer 18:22; 2 Kgs 24:2), possibly including Scythian tribes,[21] and finally the mighty Babylonian army. The lions that burned up the cities of Judah are not named (Jer 2:15) but are probably the Babylonian kings who oppressed Judah for many years. The enemy burning the pastures in Jer 9:9[10] is also not named, but it too leaves the land without inhabitants. Even the animals and birds are gone. Jeremiah weeps over this destruction (following MT *ʾeśśāʾ* in 9:9[10]), but in the following verse Yahweh answers that Jerusalem and what remains of Judah's cities will suffer a similar fate. In Jer 32:29, Yahweh says explicitly that he is sending the Babylonians to set fire to Jerusalem. Behind every particular enemy stands the ominous figure of Yahweh, who has declared holy war on his people.

But after the burning of Jerusalem, fires will be set in other nations: Yahweh says he will kindle a fire in the temples of the gods of Egypt (Jer 43:12); Memphis will be burned and left without inhabitants (46:19). The villages of the Ammonites will be burned with fire (Jer 49:2). Yahweh will again kindle fire in the wall of Damascus (v. 27; cf. Amos 1:4). When Babylon's time comes, her cities and the surrounding area will be consumed by Yahweh's fire (Jer 50:32; 51:30, 58). Ezekiel speaks on one occasion of Yahweh's kindling a fire among the trees of the Negeb (Ezek 21:3[20:47]). Whenever Yahweh kindles fire in a foreign land, no reason is given. This stands in stark contrast to the judgment oracles against Israel, in which Yahweh states reasons in almost every case. The message proclaimed by Jeremiah is essentially the same as that of Deut 32:15–22 and Huldah's oracle: the people have forsaken Yahweh and his law and have provoked his anger by worshiping other gods; therefore Yahweh's wrath will burn against them and their land like an unquenchable fire. The burned cities in Jer 2:15 are the consequence of forsaking Yahweh (v. 17). In the sapiental comment in Jer 9:11–13[12–14], the reason given for the burning of the land is that the people have forsaken Yahweh's law and gone after the baʿals. In the sermonic prose of Jer 11:16–17, the prophet says that Israel was once a green olive tree that bore much fruit, but now Yahweh will set fire to her because she has burned incense to Baʿal. In Jer 17:19–27, he declares that if the people do not keep the Sabbath and desist from bringing burdens through the gates of Jerusalem on the Sabbath, Yahweh will burn those gates along with the palaces of the city (v. 27). The destruction of Jerusalem announced in Jer 32:29 results from the worship of baʿals and other gods: this is a clear echo of Huldah's oracle

21. Herodotus, *Hist.* i.105.

in 2 Kgs 22:17. When Zedekiah of Judah sins by not practicing justice and by not turning from self-righteous arrogance about Jerusalem's security, Yahweh declares that Israel's forest will be burned (Jer 21:14). Here, as in Jer 22, reference is to the cedar-lined buildings of Jerusalem's royal complex.[22] What finally took place in Jerusalem is summed up in Lam 4:11: "Yahweh gave full vent to his wrath, he poured out his hot anger; he kindled a fire in Zion, which consumed its foundations (*wayyaṣṣeṯ-'ēš bĕṣiyyôn wattō'kal yĕsôdōṯeyhā*).

The city was still in the same condition many years later, when Nehemiah inquired about Jerusalem from visitors who had come to Babylon (Neh 1:3). The news he received made him weep, but he responded by confessing Israel's sin to Yahweh. Shortly afterwards, he went to Jerusalem himself to initiate and supervise the great task of rebuilding the city wall upon the burned ruins (Neh 2:17).

Hebrew *yqd*

yāqad ("to be kindled; to burn"); *yĕqōd* ("burning"); *môqēd* ("burning mass")

Linguistic Background

Etymology, Meaning

Hebrew *yqd* is a less common root used in the OT to mean "be kindled" or "burn" (cf. *bā'ar, ḥārâ, yāṣaṯ, śārap*). Akkadian *qādu* is attested in Middle and Late Babylonian; while it normally means "light, kindle," it can also mean "burn."[23] Besides *qādu*, Akkadian also has *qalû* and *qamû* (both transitive), which mean "burn," in addition to the more common *šarāpu* (cf. Heb *śārap*). We know that *qādu* and *šarāpu* are synonyms.[24] The former appears frequently in cultic texts, where it denotes the lighting of a torch,

22. Jack R. Lundbom, *Jeremiah: A Study in Ancient Hebrew Rhetoric*, SBLDS 18 (1975), 48 (2nd ed.: Eisenbrauns, 1997, 67); Lundbom, *Jeremiah 21–36*, AB 21B (New York: Doubleday, 2004), 124; cf. Géza Vermès, "The Symbolic Interpretation of *Lebanon* in the Targums: The Origin and Development of an Exegetical Tradition," *JTS* n.s. 9 (1958) 1–12.

23. *AHw* 2:892.

24. Bruno Meissner, *Beiträge zum Assyrischen Wörterbuch*, AS 1 (Chicago: University of Chicago Press, 1931), 1:71, 14.

lamp, or cultic fire.[25] In "A Nightly Ceremony in the Temple of Anu,"[26] *qādu* alternates with *napāḫ*, which also means "kindle," but more in the sense of "blow into a flame." During this ritual, the high priest "lights" a great torch (*gizillû rabû*) from a fire containing aromatic spices, makes a recitation to Anu, and then carries the torch out into the street; there the other priests "light" their lamps and bring the fire to the outlying temples.[27] In an incantation text from ca. 1000 BC,[28] the ritual calls for "lighting" a torch in spices and then using it to ignite a brazier where clay images are to be baked. Torches are also kindled for lighting funeral pyres.[29] Assyrian kings burn cities, temples,[30] and cedars.[31] Tukulti-Ninurta I (1243–1197 BC) possesses might and energy that "burns the unsubmissive left and right."[32]

In Ugaritic, the root *srp* is attested but not *yqd*, although Dahood reads *mqdm* as "braziers."[33] Arabic *wqd* means "burn," and Old South Arabic *mqdn* means "altar hearth." In Aramaic, *yqd* is attested in all periods, which could mean that it comes into Hebrew as a loanword.[34] In the Sefire inscriptions,[35] Barga'ya pronounces a curse on Matî'el should he break their treaty: *'yk zy tqd šĕwt' z' b'š kn tqd 'rpd w*[*bnth r*]*bt*, "just as this wax is burned by fire, so may Arpad be burned and [her gr]eat [daughter cities]." Again, in II. 37–38 we find: *'ykh zy tdq sĕwt' z' b'š kn yqd m*[*tĕ'l*] "just as this wax is burned by fire, so may Matî['el] be burned by fi]re."[36] In the Bible,

25. Erich Ebeling, *Tod und Leben nach den Vorstellungen der Babylonier* (Berlin: de Gruyter, 1931), 17, 23: *išāta aqâd*, "I kindle the fire"; 93, 16: *gizillâ iqâda*, "[the priest] lights a cultic torch."

26. F. Thureau-Dangin, *Rituels Accadiens* (Paris: Leroux, 1921), 1:118ff.; *ANET*³, 338–39.

27. Ibid., 119, 30; 120, 15; cf. *CAD* 4 (1956), 114.

28. *AfO* 18 (1957–58), 297, 8–9.

29. Maximilian Streck, *Assurbanipal und die letzten assyrischen Könige bis zum Untergange Ninevehs*, VAB 7 (1916), 266, 10; Erich Ebeling, "Beschwörungen gegen den Fiend und den Bösen Blick aus dem Zweistromlande," *ArOr* 17 (1949) 187, 17.

30. Sargon II; F. Thureau-Dangin, *Une Relation de la huitième campagne de Sargon* TCL 3 (Paris, 1912); Zusätze *ZA* (34) 113–22; E. F. Weidner, "Neue Bruchstücke des Berichtes über Sargons achten Feldzug," *AfO* 12 (1937–39) 144–48; cf. *AHw*, 2:892.

31. Ebeling, *Tod und Leben*, 36, 24.

32. W. G. Lambert, "Three Unpublished Fragments of the Tukulti-Ninurta Epic," *AfO* 18 (1957–58), 48A, 11.

33. *KTU*, 4.158, 19; cf. Dahood, *Psalms 101–150* (AB 17A, 1970), 11.

34. KBL³, 410.

35. *KAI* 222A, 35–36.

36. Joseph A. Fitzmyer, *The Aramaic Inscriptions of Sefire*, BibOr 19, Rome: Pontificial

Shadrach, Meshach, and Abednego survive the furnace of *nûrā' yāqidtā'*, "burning fire," which Nebuchadnezzar has prepared for anyone who refuses to bow down to his image (Dan 3:6, 11, 15, 17, 20–21, 23, 26). In Dan 7:11, the beast is destroyed and consigned to *lîqēdaṯ 'eššā'*, "the burning fire," which is undoubtedly an unceremonious funeral pyre.

Occurrences

There are at least three occurrences of *yqd* in the qal (Deut 32:22; Isa 10:16; 65:5) and five in the hophal (Jeremiah and Leviticus). BDB takes *yāqûd* in Isa 30:14 to be the qal passive participle ("that which is kindled"; NEB: "glowing embers"), but KBL³ considers it a noun meaning "hearth."[37] Sherds, as we know, were used to take fire from the hearth. In Isa 10:16, the prophet plays on *yēqad* and *yĕqôd*, which may derive ultimately from the infinitive absolute but are used here as nouns: *wĕṯaḥaṯ kĕbōdô yēqad yēqōd kîqôd 'ēš*, "and under his glory a burning [fever?] will be kindled, like the burning of fire." The noun *môqēd* may mean "burning embers" (Ps 102:4[3]; Isa 33:14), or, as in Rabbinic and Modern Hebrew, simply "hearth" or "fireplace." The *môqĕdâ* is a "hearth" (Lev 6:2[9]).

Theological Usage

Theological usage of *yqd* in the OT is quite similar to usage in extrabiblical sources. Fires lit by priests in the temple are part of divine worship. Fires also burn when Yahweh the king comes in judgment.

The Perpetual Altar Fire

The law (Exod 29:38–42; Lev 6:2–6[9–13]; Num 28:2–8) prescribes both a morning and evening whole burnt offering (*'ōlâ*); the fire from the evening offering is to be kept burning (*tûqad*) on the hearth (*môqĕdâ*) all night. This allows for a perpetual altar fire. It has been argued, however, that having an *'ōlâ* both morning and evening is a postexilic ritual, and that during the monarchy only a morning *'ōlâ* was prescribed.[38] Ahaz, for example, directs

Biblical Institute 1967), 14–15.

37. Also RSV, JB, NAB.

38. W. O. E. Oesterley, *Sacrifices in Ancient Israel* (London: Hodder & Stoughton,

his priest to perform a morning *ʿōlâ* and an evening *minḥâ* (cereal offering) but no evening *ʿōlâ* (2 Kg 16:15). Ezekiel, too, mentions only a morning *ʿōlâ* (Ezek 46:13–15). On the other hand, Elijah offers an *ʿōlâ* on Mount Carmel late in the day (1 Kgs 18:38; cf. v. 29). A schematic view seems to be precluded since different traditions no doubt existed in preexilic times. The three passages formally prescribing both a morning and an evening *ʿōlâ* are legislative and seek standardization. Furthermore, Ahaz is hardly a model for the preexiic period, since he modified worship in other respects to conform to Assyrian practice.

Yahweh's Burning Wrath

Yahweh's anger burns when his people go after other gods (cf. *ʾelōhîm ʾaḥērîm*). The classic expression of this is found in the Song of Moses, where in response to Israel's apostasy Yahweh declares: *kî-ʾēš qādĕḥâ bĕʿappî wat-tîqad ʿad-šĕʾôl taḥtît*, "For a fire is kindled in my anger, and it burns to the depths of Sheol" (Deut 32:22). Isaiah and Jeremiah both show familiarity with this song, which goes on to say that after judgment Yahweh will turn to punish the enemy—which has served as an agent of destruction—lest the enemy's own arrogance become too great (Deut 32:26–27). This latter part of the song is appropriated in Isa 10:16 and its context: Assyria, Yahweh's agent of destruction, will now be punished. Assyrian warriors will be smitten with disease, while under the king's glory (splendid attire?) "a burning will be kindled, like the burning of fire" (Isa 10:16; cf. 37:36–38). Isaiah has in mind the boastfulness of the Assyrian kings, who, as we have seen, were wont to speak of their own glory as "burning the unsubmissive left and right."[39] Isaiah also anticipates later apocalyptic thought in the idea that Yahweh's punishment serves to separate the righteous among his people from the wicked. In Isa 33:14, the sinners in Zion say: "Who among us can dwell with the devouring fire? Who among us can dwell with everlasting burnings (*môqĕdē ʿôlâm*)?" The answer is immediate: Those who walk righteously and speak uprightly . . . (Isa 33:15ff.). They will survive and will see the good times that lie ahead. Their eyes will see Judah's kings arrayed in splendor (v. 17) and Jerusalem a quiet habitation (v. 20).

1937), 221; Roland de Vaux, *Studies in Old Testament Sacrifice* (Cardiff: University of Wales Press, 1964), 36; R. J. Faley, "Leviticus," *JBC*, 71.

39. Cf. W. G. Lambert, "Three Unpublished Fragments of the Tukulti-Ninurta Epic," *AfO* 18 (1957–58), 48A, 11.

The influence of Deut 32 on Jeremiah appears not only in Jeremiah's poetic diction[40] but also in phrases occurring in the sermonic prose. In Jer 15:14; 17:4, the prophet quotes Deut 32:22 more closely even than Huldah, who draws upon this verse (and that immediately preceding) for her oracle against Judah (2 Kgs 22:17.[41] The first colon *kî-ʿēš qādĕḥâ bĕʾappî* is quoted verbatim in Jer 15:14 and almost verbatim in 17:4 (with *qĕdaḥtem* instead of *qādĕḥâ*). The second colon is abbreviated to *ʿad-ʿôlām tûqād* in 17:4 and also in some manuscripts of 15:14 where the MT has *ʿălēkem tûqād*. For Jeremiah Yahweh's wrath comes as a perpetual fire causing exile in a foreign land. It looks as though Jeremiah is using *tûqād* to play deliberately on the usage found in Lev 6:2, 5, 6[9, 12, 13], especially since there are no other occurrences of the hophal. In Jer 17:1–4, too, the sin is clearly illicit worship, engraved "on the horns of their altars" and on "their altars . . . in the open country."

Deutero-Isaiah likewise associates Israel's sin with the cult, Isa 65:5 quotes the Zadokite priests as saying that they alone may approach Yahweh's altar. As Hanson has shown,[42] these words echo almost precisely those found in the pro-Zadokite statement of Ezek 44:13, 15, 19. But Yahweh is not pleased, at least so far as this prophet is concerned. The smoke they send up, which he might normally enjoy (Gen 8:21, e.g.) is now converted by his anger into *ʾēš yōqedeṭ kol-hayyôm*, "a fire that burns all the day" (Isa 65:5). Therefore, the perpetual altar fire evokes a perpetual fire of Yahweh's anger,

Finally, in Ps 102:4[3] the psalmist speaks of his bones burning "like a furnace" (*kĕmôqēd*). His sickness and the transitory quality of his life he takes as a divine judgment, showing that Yahweh is angry with him (v. 11[10]). He nevertheless finds enough strength to praise Yahweh, who is enthroned forever (v. 13[12]).

40. William L. Holladay, "Jeremiah and Moses: Further Observations," *JBL* 85 (1966) 18–21.

41. Lundbom, "The Lawbook of the Josianic Reform."

42. Paul D. Hanson, *The Dawn of Apocalyptic*, 2nd ed. (Philadelphia: Fortress, 1979), 147–49.

3

God in Your Grace Transform the World[1]

The theme for the ninth Assembly of the World Council of Churches (WCC) at Porto Alegre, Brazil, "God in Your Grace Transform the World," consisted of a prayer by the church that God in his infinite grace transform his world and ours.

The New Testament witness that God graciously sent Jesus Christ into the world has to be the preeminent transforming act overshadowing every other transformation, past or future. The gospel writer John says: "And the Word became flesh and dwelt among us, full of grace and truth" (John 1:14). Paul too tells the church at Rome that "all have sinned and fall short of the glory of God, they are justified by his grace as a gift, through the redemption which is in Christ Jesus" (Rom 3:23–24).

We may say then at the outset that God has already transformed the world, continues to transform the world, and will in the future transform the world through the living Christ, making our first word on the WCC theme of 2006 also our last.

But I should like to give our theme a bit more specificity, and to do this I think it useful to have a look at some foundational teachings in the Old Testament on "grace," also "favor," which translate the same Hebrew word, *ḥēn*. It is the Old Testament that gives us the basic meanings of grace and favor, providing us also with contexts in which these concepts are seen to

1. Lecture given at Thomas Mar Athanasius Memorial Orientation Centre Seminar, Kottayam, Kerala, India, August 12, 2005; published in *Currents in Theology and Mission* 34 (2007) 278–81.

be operative. There we see grace at work in human relationships, gracious activity within Israelite society, and grace both sought and found in a covenant relationship with Yahweh, God of heaven and earth.

Grace, at base, is a term of beauty. It denotes a pleasing aspect or presentation of someone or something and is the quality that this someone or something possesses. The Old Testament speaks of a graceful doe bounding through the field, also a graceful woman, or woman who is gracious (Prov 5:18–19; 11:16). It speaks about gracious words befitting kings (Ps 45:2), or words that please kings along with other people (Prov 22:11; Eccl 10:12).

Even more important than possessed grace is grace finding its way into the eyes of the beholder. Here grace becomes favor. The common Old Testament expression is "to find favor in the eyes of" someone. In our modern world we look for a smile on the face, having now even a stylized face with upturned mouth to display when we are favorably disposed to this or that.

But in the ancient world people looked into the eyes to find favor or a lack of favor. The other Hebrew word most often translated "favor" in the Old Testament is *panim*, meaning "face." One conveys favor by showing the face; one hides the face to withhold favor. The psalmist knows well that divine anger is conveyed in a "hidden face" (Pss 13:1; 27:9; 30:7).

Grace is a totally positive response in personal relationships. It is so with human beings; it is so with God. Grace cannot coexist with anger or judgment (Prov 28:23), being unlike "love" (Heb *'hb*) in this respect, which can coexist with anger and judgment. Prov 3:12 says: "The Lord reproves him whom he loves." How the multifarious dispositions of God are harmonized remains a grand mystery, but in humans it appears that love resides at a deeper level of the inner being where conflicting emotions are allowed a coexistence. Grace lies closer to the surface.

Grace is freely given and is thus in the nature of a gift (Gen 33:5–11; Judg 21:22; cf. Rom 3:24; Eph 3:7). Grace can also be freely withdrawn. One is under no obligation to show favor or to continue showing favor. Here it is unlike steadfast love or covenant love (Heb *ḥesed*), which is a bonding virtue that presupposes rights and obligations. Steadfast love must be kept, demanding as it does positive attitudes and positive actions from both parties to a relationship.

Grace may also and usually does find mutual expression in relationships, but in a different way. It is given freely by one to another, and a relationship in grace is sustained only so long as the giver desires. Grace and favor can be lost (Deut 24:1).

Finally, grace is *active* acceptance, both with human beings and with God. In the Psalms God's grace is paralleled to his "mighty works" (Pss 111:4; 145:4–9). To be gracious means to aid the poor, feed the hungry, deliver those in distress from defeat and death. It also means not oppressing the same and executing justice on their behalf (Exod 22:22–27). If Israel fails to so act, distressed souls in their helplessness will cry to God, and he will hear them, for God says, "I am gracious" (v. 27). Prov 14:31 says that (human) grace to the needy honors God.

Elsa Tamez, a Mexican theologian and biblical scholar, wrote recently on the WCC theme calling for "God's grace and human dignity."[2] She said, "Grace is not only experienced in a passive way. Grace is a gift that invites us to radiate it from our spirit, mind and body, to manifest it through our attitudes and practices and not just through what we say."

Grace in the Bible is active grace. In the book of Deuteronomy it translates into benevolence to the sojourner, orphan, and widow, also the Levite in town who is out of a job (Deut 14:29; 16:11, 14; 24:17, 19–21; 26:12–13). Israel is to care for these because they are objects of Yahweh's special care (Deut 10:18–19; cf. Jas 1:27).

Yahweh reveals himself first and foremost in the Old Testament as a God of grace. In fact, graciousness is nothing less than a divine attribute (Exod 34:6; Joel 2:13; Jonah 4:2; Ps 86:15). But because of this and other grand testimonies regarding God in both Old Testament and New—and I am thinking here of

a. God's initiative in electing Israel, and later the church as the "new Israel";

b. God's saving of Israel in the Exodus, and his saving of the world in the life, death, and resurrection of Jesus Christ;

c. God's profound love for the world in general, and sinners in particular; and

d. God's unconditional covenants to Noah, Abraham, David, and the Church—we are likely to overestimate the scope of God's grace and favor.

A danger of misunderstanding occurs at the following points. First, because God's grace is entirely positive in nature, it cannot coexist with divine anger or divine judgment (Exod 34:6–7; Ps 77:9). Solomon anticipated

2. Elsa Tamez, "God's Grace and Human Dignity," *Ecumenical Review* 57 (2005) 276–77.

this in his prayer of dedication for the temple, telling God in the people's hearing that when the people sin and are judged, they will have to make supplication to God (1 Kgs 8:28–53). Supplications are pleas for divine favor. In the theology of Deuteronomy, sin leads to a loss of divine favor and issues in judgment upon young and old (Deut 28:50; Lam 4:16). Israel understood the loss of nationhood as a loss of divine favor.

Second, because God's grace is freely given and freely taken away, we may come to think that human actions are irrelevant, or at least marginal, in importance. Nothing could be further from the truth. Not only does meritorious behavior figure into God's dispensation of grace; it is also true that because of sin, divine grace must be sought from the human end. Grace is therefore sought and found, which gets to the heart of our WCC prayer. We are seeking divine grace when we pray "God in your grace, transform the world."

Favor can be sought and found by the righteous. While it is certainly true that God loves us and is gracious to us even when we are undeserving, it is similarly true that God gives grace to the righteous and the humble (Ps 84:11; Prov 3:34). Noah, we are told by the Priestly writer, received favor in the eyes of the Lord because he was righteous (Gen 6:8–9). The psalmist, too, knows that he can seek God's favor not only because he is poor and needy, but because he is godly and trusting (Ps 86). Prov 3:1–4 says that those who keep God's commandments will find favor with God and with other people.

Favor can be sought and found by the sinner. David seeks divine favor to blot out his transgression (Ps 51:1–2). More often, the psalmist seeks divine favor when he is sick, when he is threatened by enemies, and when he fears death (Ps 116). Here he may be conscious of having sinned, or he may claim to be righteous. The psalms are filled with the supplication, "Be gracious to me" (Pss 6:2; 9:13; 31:9), which appears only there. They are also filled with the plea "Turn and be gracious to me" (Pss 25:16; 86:16; 119:132; cf. 2 Kgs 13:23), where the psalmist imagines that God has turned his face away in anger or in judgment.

In Exod 34:1–9, the great revelation of Yahweh as "a God merciful and gracious" comes immediately after Israel's preeminent sin in the wilderness: the crafting of a golden calf. Moses in response to this divine self-disclosure pleads for God to pardon the people's iniquity and continue the journey with them (Exod 34:9).

After people have sinned, God will again be gracious and merciful if they return to him (Isa 30:19; Jer 31:9; Joel 2:13; 2 Chr 30:9). Sometimes individuals and Israel as a whole have to wait for God's favor (Pss 26; 102:13; 123:3; 140). The prophet Isaiah says:

> Therefore the LORD waits to be gracious to you;
> therefore he exalts himself to show mercy to you.
> For the LORD is a God of justice;
> blessed are all those who wait for him. (Isa 30:18)

We need then to know that favor can be sought and found, on the ground of righteousness or on the ground of unrighteousness—the latter if it is accompanied by a confession of sin.

In light of what has been said thus far, what more can we say about our prayer that God in his grace transform the world?

1. We can say, first, that God can indeed transform the world by his grace, no matter what we or anyone else does. Our God is a God of grace, and we can always pray for transforming grace, expecting that it will be given as God chooses, despite all worldly forces working against the divine will.

2. We cannot expect that divine grace will coexist with divine anger or divine judgment. Even with the transforming gift of Christ to the world, there is still the divine wrath to contend with, which Paul says is kindled against all manner of wickedness. In the chilling passage of Rom 1:18–32, Paul says that "the wrath of God is revealed from heaven against all ungodliness and wickedness of those who by their wickedness suppress the truth." The modern church, particularly in the West, would do well to heed to this sobering word if it hopes to be an agent of God's grace in today's world.

From Paul we learn also that, in spite of salvation by grace alone (Rom 3:24), there is a judgment of God meant to lead people to repentance, also another judgment to be revealed on the final day of the Lord's coming, where every person will be rendered according to his works (Rom 2:1–11). Luther appears to have read right past the important verses 6–8 in Romans chapter 2: "For [God] will repay according to each one's deeds: to those who by patiently doing good seek for glory and honor and immortality, he will give eternal life; while for those who are self-seeking and who obey not the truth but wickedness, there will be wrath and fury" (NRSV). So if God does not transform the world by his grace, he will transform it by his wrath, and once again, the modern church will ignore this correlative truth only to its great sorrow.

3. We can say that divine grace is promised and can be expected to come to individuals and to a church that leads a life of obedience to God's commands, that seeks the higher righteousness Jesus talks about in his Sermon on the Mount. God desires righteous living, and our world will experience great transformation if both individuals and the corporate body of Christ live up to their calling to be God's holy people. The bar of Christian living needs to be raised considerably higher than many have it at the present time.

4. We can say that divine grace will surely abound when individuals and the church repent of their sin. Enormous transformation can come about in our world if those who bear the name of Christ will simply humble themselves and repent rather than seeking to justify, as they so often do, evil and evildoers.

5. Finally, divine grace will surely abound when the church emulates God and carries out active grace to the poor, the needy, and those in distress. Here we become channels of the divine grace, allowing ourselves to be used by a God who cares deeply for all who suffer in our world.

4

Biblical and Theological Themes[1]

The Biblical Idea of Grace

Grace in the Old Testament is, first of all, a beauty or perceived beauty that is possessed. Genuine beauty is seen in the gracious woman (Prov 11:16), but charm can be deceitful (Prov 31:30), as, for example, in harlots (Nah 3:4). A doe bounding through the forest is graceful (Prov 5:19). Even a stone can possess graceful beauty, but one must be on guard against bribes that are likened to it (Prov 17:8). The one having gracious speech will have the king as his friend (Prov 22:11), but gracious speech can also be a cover for deceit in the heart (Prov 26:25).

Grace in the Old Testament is also the response given by a person to what is beautiful. Here the Hebrew terms means "favor." Favor (or grace) is seen on the face of one pleased with what he or she sees. In modern culture we look for a smile on the face, but for the ancient Hebrews favor was seen in the eyes. The biblical expression was to "find favor in the eyes" of someone. This is the more important meaning of the Hebrew verb and related nouns in the Bible.

One can ask for grace or favor in a limited way or for a limited period of time, which is simply another way of saying "please" (Gen 47:29; 50:4). One can also say a gracious "thank you" for some act of kindness (Gen 47:25; 1 Sam 1:18). But grace or favor can extend for a longer period of time, in which case it denotes a special relationship between two persons

1. Lectures at a Pastors' Seminar of the Communauté Evangélique de l'Ubangi-Mongala in Gemena, Zaire (Congo), August 4–8, 1981.

or a person and God. Joseph, before he was wrongly accused by the wife of Potiphar in Egypt, had Potiphar's favor (Gen 39:4). Moses had overall favor with the Lord (Exod 33:17). And David, early on, had favor with King Saul (1 Sam 16:22).

In the Bible the Lord is a God of grace, giving grace to individuals and also to the people Israel. It is in God's very nature to be gracious (Exod 33:19; 34:6).

The grace of God is always a *positive* disposition. Grace cannot coexist with anger or with judgment, making it different in this respect from love, which can coexist with both (Prov 3:12).

The grace of God is always *active*. Grace is not just a thought in the mind of God, although it is surely that; it is shown in concrete acts, such as aiding the poor, feeding the hungry, delivering people from distress, and the like.

The grace of God—like grace extended also by people—is *freely given* and can be *freely taken away*. There is no obligation to give or keep giving grace, such as exists in the case of biblical "steadfast love" or "covenant love." Grace is therefore a free gift (Rom 3:24; Eph 1:6), but it differs from ordinary gifts in that it can be taken away. The Psalmist often cries out for the Lord's grace or favor, fearing that the Lord may have turned his face away in anger, will have forgotten him, or will not attend to his affliction (Ps 4:1; 6:2; 13:2; 25:16).

The grace of God can be *irrational*; that is, it can be given even when not deserved. It also does not need to be given in equal amounts. It can come as mercy. Such is not the case with judgment, which must be dispensed fairly and justly. We see this irrational grace of God in the following biblical texts:

1. Exod 33:19—the LORD God to Moses in a revelation of himself
2. Matt 5:38–48—Jesus's teaching about retaliation and love in the Sermon on the Mount
3. Matt 20:1–15—Jesus's parable of the Laborers in the Vineyard
4. Rom 5:20—Paul speaking about God's plan of salvation

The grace of God is meant to lead people to repentance, forgiveness, and reconciliation. In the reconciliation of Jacob and Esau (Gen 33:1–11), Jacob says to his brother: "To see your face is like seeing the face of God, with such favor have you received me" (v. 10, RSV). In Jesus's parable of the Lost (Prodigal) Son (Luke 15:11–32), the repentance of the son, the forgiveness of the father, and the reconciliation of father and son teaches us about the return of wayward children to God the Father. And Paul tells us that God's grace is given to lead people to repentance (Rom 2:4), and that his free gift of grace justifies sinful humanity through the redemption that is in Christ Jesus (Rom 3:24).

The Biblical Idea of Salvation / Liberation

Salvation, or liberation, in the Bible is not a ticket to freedom. It is a change of masters.[2] The primary act of liberation in the Old Testament is the exodus from Egypt, where God redeemed Israel from slavery and thus became her new master. The idea has its roots in the ANE (also in Africa) where slavery was practiced.

In ancient society a slave could be redeemed—and thus liberated—by a next of kin. It was indeed an obligation and point of honor for a father, brother, or other kinsman to act as redeemer. Money was paid to the slave owner, and the slave was freed. But he was not totally free. The redeemer became the new master, and the former slave was now under obligation to him. But the good news was that the new master would be much kinder than the old, because he was a relative, and so the new servitude would not be that difficult.

In the Old Testament the Lord acts to redeem his "son" from slavery (Exod 4:22–23), and this liberation becomes a change of masters: Pharaoh is the old master, the Lord is the new master. Israel is therefore under obligation from now on to serve the Lord, for which reason the Lord gives Israel the law at Mount Sinai. This law, as the Old Testament makes clear, is based on the Lord's prior grace (Exod 20:2–3; Deut 5:6–7), and because the new master is much kinder than the old (Exod 34:6), the new servitude will be easy to carry out (Deut 30:11–14).

Liberation in the New Testament is to be understood in similar terms. Jesus, by paying the price with his own life, redeems all people from slavery to sin and death. In so doing, Jesus becomes the new master. The old master is Satan and the power of sin; also, for Paul, a law that has grown to be an intolerable burden. People are now under obligation to serve Jesus. We are to take his yoke upon us (Matt 11:29; also the Sermon on the Mount in Matt 5–7), but this new servitude will not be hard like the old (Matt 11:28). Jesus says, "my yoke is easy and my burden is light" (Matt 11:30).

2. David Daube, *The Exodus Pattern in the Bible* (London: Faber & Faber, 1963).

Similarities between Old and New Testament:

1. Liberation is always based on God's grace.
2. Grace always comes before law.

Differences between Old and New Testament:

3. In the Old Testament oppression exists in the society; in the New Testament it is something within the individual person.
4. In the Old Testament we rejoice that the old master is defeated (Exod 15); in the New Testament we pray for our enemies and work for their liberation. We also forgive enemies
5. There is no confession of sin in Old Testament liberation (the exodus); in New Testament liberation, which is effected by Jesus's death on the cross, confession of sin becomes essential.

Biblical Covenants

Our Christian Bible is composed of an Old Covenant (Testament) and a New Covenant (Testament). The Old was made with the nation Israel; the New is made with all people through Jesus Christ.

A covenant is a formal agreement binding two parties together for mutual benefit. Some of the common types of covenant include 1) marriage covenants, 2) business contracts, and 3) international treaties.

In the ancient world international treaties were made between powerful kings and weaker subordinate kings, also between the nations over which both kings ruled. We have many examples of these now from the Hittites and Assyrians. They were often made following a war, to prevent future wars, or to set up alliances if wars were declared on either party by another nation. The stronger king drew up the treaty. The weaker king had to sign it and agree to its terms. The treaties had a common structure:

a. Preamble
b. Review of past history and relations between the parties
c. Stipulations
d. Arrangements for public readings and renewal
e. List of witnesses
f. Blessings and curses

God's covenant with Israel was given through Moses, and it is reported in the Old Testament books of Exodus and Deuteronomy. The parties to the covenant were God and the nation Israel. The covenant was made or renewed following a war (with Egypt in Exod 1–15; with the Canaanites in Deut 1). God drew up the covenant at Mount Sinai, and Israel had to agree to its terms (Exod 24:3–8). The structure of this covenant was much like the structure of international treaties of the time:

a. / b. Preamble and review of past history (Exod 20:2; Deut 5:6; also Deuteronomy 1–4);

c. Stipulations (Exod 20–23; Deut 5–26);

d. Public reading and renewal (Exodus 34; Deut 6:4–9; 11:18–20; 27; 31:10–13; Joshua 24);

e. Witness of heaven and earth (Deut 4:26; 30:19, 28; 32:1);

f. Blessings and curses (Deut 11:26–29; 28).

Israel was under obligation to keep this covenant. If it did not, the covenant would be declared broken, which happened many times, and would have to be renewed (see Deut 31-32; 2 Kgs 23:21–23). This covenant was concerned largely with the land. The curses in Deuteronomy stated that if the covenant was broken, the land would be lost. This happened in 586 BC, when nationhood for Israel came to an end. The Sinai covenant had become so broken that it could not be renewed. Jeremiah therefore announced for Israel and Judah a new covenant (Jer 31:31–34).[3]

The Old Testament contains other covenants, two of the most important being the covenants that God made with Abraham and David (Gen 12:1–3; 15; 17; 2 Sam 7). They were not like the international treaties, or the covenant made with Israel through Moses. God was the sole maker of these covenants, and they contained no obligations; they had only to be claimed (but see Gen 17:14). These covenants therefore could not be broken. Both were made with individuals, and both promised an unending line of descendants.

In the New Testament one finds both covenant types. Conditional covenants are said to exist with individual Jews and Christians (Matt 5–7; 23; John 14–15; Rom 11:1–24; Heb 10:26–31), and unconditional covenants are said to exist with Israel and the church (Rom 11:25–36; Matt 16:18). The unconditional covenant with Israel is based on the covenant made with Abraham, and the unconditional with the church is a fulfillment of Jeremiah's new covenant.

3. Jack R. Lundbom, *Jeremiah 21–36*, AB 21B (New York: Doubleday; and New Haven: Yale University Press, 2004), 464–82.

Hearing and Obedience

The Bible puts more weight on hearing than on seeing. The Greeks at their best used the eye; the Hebrews at their best used the ear. Israel's prophets were messengers of the Lord who heard the divine word and then delivered it to individuals, the nation, and foreign nations. They were in trouble if they heard the word but did not deliver it (Ezek 3:16–21). They were also in trouble if they delivered a word the Lord had not spoken (Jer 23:18, 21–22). Prophets began their messages with an introductory "Thus said the LORD," and the people were expected to hear this word (Jer 7:13). In the New Testament we hear Jesus saying, "He who has ears to hear, let him hear" (Matt 11:15).

Hearing in the Bible must be active hearing. In Hebrew the verb "to hear" also means "to obey." It is the kind of hearing you do when the drum sounds, calling you to assemble. Obedience is therefore an important biblical teaching. Abraham obeyed (Gen 12:1–4; Heb 11:8); the Old Testament covenant had to be obeyed (Deut 30:11–14), and Jesus's words in the Sermon on the Mount, which was a "new covenant," were to be obeyed (Matt 7:24–27). Following Jesus is also an act of obedience (Matt 8:18–23), and the New Testament teaches that obedience will come after repentance (Matt 21:28–32).

James teaches that "faith without works is dead" (Jas 2:26). It is so in life today:

a. The schoolboy who brings the teacher an apple must do his work.

b. The parishioner who brings his pastor food must at the same time follow biblical teaching and preaching.

c. The person who reads his Bible must be sure to care for his family, also for the poor and needy.

Faith *begins* with obedience. Abraham obeyed before he believed (Gen 12:4; 15:6). Dietrich Bonhoeffer, in his book *The Cost of Discipleship* said, "Only those who obey can believe."[4] We find out in the Christian walk that we often learn God's will only after we are on the way. Similarly, we find that often we believe—really believe—only after we are on the way.

Faith *is tested* by obedience. Abraham obeyed by making a sacrifice (Gen 22). Saul learned to his sorrow that "obedience is better than sacrifice"

4. Dietrich Bonhoeffer, *The Cost of Discipleship*, Macmillan Paperbacks (New York: Macmillan, 1963).

(1 Sam 15). The prophets Micah and Jeremiah taught also that obedience to the covenant demands is better than sacrifice (Mic 6:6–8; Jer 7:22–23).

The Biblical Idea of Wholeness

The Hebrew word for "person" (*nepesh*) does not mean a separated "soul," but rather a "whole self" that includes the body. Christians believe not in an "immortality of the soul," which is a Greek idea, but in "resurrection of the body."[5]

The Hebrew word for "peace" (*shalom*) is both active and positive. It means not simply an absence of conflict, although it does mean that, but more importantly health, wholeness, and well-being (Jer 6:14). *Shalom* is a greeting meaning, "I hope you are well," or "Have a good day." It carries with it a blessing. *Shalom* means health for the individual. Shalom is a family sitting together having a joyous time—talking, laughing, and showing consideration towards one another. Shalom is community well-being: It is a happy time at a village gathering; it is when there is no stealing or dishonesty in the village. Shalom is lost when there is no shame, no confession of wrongdoing.

Human life and human history are journeys toward wholeness. They are so for individuals gaining in maturity (1 Cor 13:9–12; Eph 4:13), and when Jesus brings to individuals peace and health (Mark 5:24–34). They are so for the local church (Rom 1:12; 1 Cor 1:10–13; 12), and for the church worldwide.[6] They are so for the country, where we must not just increase our weapons for defense, but work to help the poor, needy, and suffering. They are so for all creation (Rom 8:18–25; 11:1–36). Finally, let us remember that it is the Holy Spirit who brings peace and unity (John 14:26–27; Acts 2). Come Holy Spirit!

5. Oscar Cullman, *Immortality of the Soul; Or, Resurrection of the Dead?* (New York: Macmillan, 1964).

6. Russell A. Cervin, *Mission in Ferment* (Chicago: Covenant Press, 1977), 11.

Translation into Lingala—Rev. Richard Anderson

I. Ngolu Ejali Nini?

A. Na Kondimana na Kala liloba oyo ebongwani NGOLU ejalaki na ntina ete: KITOKO Tomoni na mokanda na Masese ete "kitoko" ekokisami na "ngolu." Tala oyo:

a. Kitoko na mwasi—na motindo malamu—Masese 11:16.
—na motindo mabe—Masese 31:30 (Tala Nahumu 3:4)

b. Kitoko na nyama—Masese 5:19

c. Kitoko na libanga na motuya—Masese 17:8

d. Kitoko na maloba na bato—Masese 22:11 (Na motindo mabe—Masese 26:25)

B. Liloba yango ekoki kolobama mpe mpo na motindo moto akosepela na eloko na kitoko. Soko moto akosepela na eloko na kitoko, yango ekomonana na elongi a ye mpe na miso na ye. Bongo soko moto abongi na miso na yo ejali lokola ajui ngolu na miso na yo.

1. Ekoki kojala ngolu mpo na mwa ntango—Genese 47:29; 50:4
2. Moto akoki kopɛsa matondi mpo na ngolu yango—Genese 47:25; I Samwele 1:18
3. Ngolu ekoki koumela ntango molai, mpe ekoki kosanganisa bato na lisanga na koumela.
    a. Yosefe abongaki na miso na Potifala—Genese 39:4
    b. Mose abongaki na miso na Yawe—Esode 33:17
    c. Dawidi amonani malamu na miso na Saulo—I Samwele 16:22

C. Na Mokanda na Biblia, Yawe ajali Njambe na ngolu. Akopɛsa ngolu na bato na Ye. Ejali motindo na Ye kojala na ngolu. Esode 33:19; 34:6.

D. Ngolu ekɛsɛni na bolingo. Bolingo ekoki kosangana na nkanda mpe na likamba. Kasi ngolu ekoki kosangana na nkanda tɛ; ekoki kosangana na etumbu to na likamba tɛ, to na ekateli tɛ. Mas. 3:12.

E. Ngolu na Njambe ejali seko kosala mosala (ejali "active"). Ngolu ekotikala bobɛlɛ na likanisi na Njambe tɛ, kasi ekomonana na mosala na Ye. Ndakisa: motindo Ye akosunga bajangi, akoleisa bato na njala, akobikisa bato na mawa, boye na boye.

F. Njambe akoki kopɛsa ngolu lokola likabo pelamoko elingi Ye. Soko alingi akoki kolongola yango lisusu. Njambe akopɛsa ngolu lokola nyongo tɛ. Akopɛsa ngolu mpo na mobeko tɛ. Akopɛsa ngolu bobɛlɛ soko Ye alingi. Ngolu ejali likabo (Baɛfɛsɛ 1:6; Baloma 3:24). Kasi ekɛsɛni na likabo mosusu mpo ete Njambe akoki kolongola yango soko alingi. Ata Dawidi abondɛlaki mbala na mbala mpo na ngolu na Njambe, ntango mosusu ayembaki pelamoko Njambe asili kobombela ye elongi. Tala Njembo oyo: 4:1; 6:2; 25:16; mpe 13:2.

G. Ntango mosusu ngolu na Njambe akomonana lokola ejali na ntina tɛ. Ekokɛsɛna na likanisi na bato; ekobilaka 'règlement' ntango yonso tɛ. Njambe akopɛsa ngolu na moto ata moto yango abongi kojua yango tɛ. Akoki kopɛsa moto mpko ngolu mingi, mpe moto mosusu bobɛlɛ mokɛ. Ejali lokola koyokela moto mawa. Bongo ngolu ekɛsɛni na nkanda mpe na etumbu (likamba) mpo ete kokata likambo ekoki kobila boyɛngɛbɛnɛ, kasi ngolu ejali boye tɛ.

Ndakisa:

1) Ngolu oyo Yawe atalisaki Mose—Esode 33:19
2) Na liteyo na Yesu na ngomba—Matai 5:38–48
3) Liteyo na Yesu na lisese na Lifuti na Basali—Matai 20:1–15
4) Motindo Njambe akobikisa bato na lisumu—Baloma 5:20

H. Ntina na ngolu na Njambe ejali ete ebenda bato mpo na kobongola mitema ete balimbisama mpe bajongisama na bondeko na Ye.

1. Pelamoko oyo na Yakobo na Esau—Genese 33:1–11
2. Oyo Yesu ateyaki na lisese na Mwana na Kilikili—Luka 15:11–32
3. Oyo Paulo alakisi mpo na motindo na kobikisama—Baloma 2:4; 3:24

II. Kobikisama Ejali Nini?

A. Na Mokanda na Njambe (Biblia) kobikisama ejali koloba ete moto alongwi na nse na nkolo moko mpe ajui nkolo mosusu na sika. Tomoni ndakisa monɛnɛ na yango na Kondimana na Kala na mokanda na Esode, wana baYisalaele balongwi na Ejipito. Njambe asikoli baYisalaele na boombo mpe Ye mpenja akomi nkolo na bango—nkolo na sika. Motindo yango ebandi kalakala na mikili na Proche Orient mpe na Afrique.

B. Motindo na Lisiko na bato na kalakala

1. Soko moto akangami moombo, moto mosusu akokaki kosikola ye. Ntango mosusu mosikoli ajalaki ndeko na ye, to moto na libota na ye to na etuka na ye. Batata mpe bandeko na ye bakokanisa ete kosikola ye ekopɛsa bango lokumu. Bakanisaki ete ekoki na bango komeka makasi kolongola ye na boombo.
2. Soko bafuti motuya yango, nkolo na moombo apɛsi ye njela.
3. Bongo mosikoli yango akomi nkolo na sika.
4. Moombo yango ayebaki ete ajali na nyongo epai na mosikoli.
5. Kasi nkolo na sika akɛsɛni na nkolo na kala. Boboto na ye eleki mpo ete ajali ndeko. Bongo boombo na sika ejali nkaka tɛ.

C. Motindo na Lisiko na Kondimana na Kala

1. Yawe asikolaki "mwana" na ye na boombo. —Esode 4:22–23
2. Falo ajalaki nkolo na kala. Yawe ajali nkolo na sika.
3. Sikawa Yisalaele bajali na nyongo epai na Njambe. Mpo na yango Mibeko mipɛsami na Sinai. Njokande yonso euti na ngolu na Njambe liboso—Esode 20:2–3; Dutɛlonomɛ 5:6–7
4. Boboto na nkolo na sika (Yawe) eleki oyo na nkolo na kala—Esode 34:6

   Bongo boombo na sika ejali nkaka tɛ—Dutɛlonomɛ 30:11–14

D. Motindo na Lisiko na Kondimana na Sika

1. Yesu ajali kosikola bato yonso na boombo.
2. Yesu apɛsi bomoi na Ye kofuta lisiko yango.
3. Yesu ajali Nkolo na sika. Nkolo na kala ajalaki Satana, lisumu, mpe mobeko.
4. Sikawa tojali na nyongo kosalela Yesu. Tokokamata ekanganelo na Ye. Matai 11:29

   Tokoosa mateyo na Ye lokola oyo na Matai 5–7.
5. Kasi kosalela Yesu ejali nkaka tɛ. Ekɛsɛni na boombo na kala. Ekanganelo na Ye ejali motau, bojito tɛ. Matai 11:28, 30

E. Motindo Lisiko na Kondimana na Sika ejali *pelamoko* oyo na Kondimana na Kala

1. Lisiko euti seko na ngolu na Njambe (ejali "fondation" na yango)

2. Ngolu ebimi seko liboso, mobeko ebimi nsima na yango.

F. Motindo Lisiko na Kondimana na Sika *ekɛsɛni* na oyo na Kondimana na Kala

1. Na Kondimana na Kala boombo euti na bato mosusu. Na Kondimana na Sika boombo ejali eloko na kati na moto mpenja.
2. Na Kondimana na Kala tokosepela soko nkolo na kala akwei. (Esode 15) Na Kondimana na Sika tokobondɛla mpo na bayini na biso mpe tokolimbisa bango. Tokolinga ete basikwa, bongo tokomeka kosala ete balongwa na boombo lokola.
3. Na Kondimana na Kala tomoni tɛ ete bato babongoli mitema na motindo na koyambola masumu mpo na kojua lisiko. Na Kondimana na Sika ekoki ete mota ayambola masumu mpo na kojua lisiko.

III. Kondimana Ejali Nini?

A. Mokanda na biso Baklisito ejali Biblia. Yango ejali na kondimana mibale: oyo na *Kala* mpe oyo na *Sika*. Kondimana na Kala esalami na Yisalaele. Kondimana na Sika ekosalama na bato yonso kati na Yesu Masiya.

B. Kondimana esalami soko bato mibale, to bituka mibale, bandimani mpo na ntina mosusu oyo ekosunga bango mibale yonso. Ndakisa: (1) kondimana na libala, (2) endimaneli (contrat) na mombongo, (3) kondimana na kati na mabota to mikili (pays), lokola "traité international."

C. Kalakala mabota mosusu bajalaki na kondimana kati na ese na ese, lokola ba-Hiti mpe ba-Asulia.

1. Kondimana isalami kati na bakonji mpe kati na mabota (nations)
2. Ntango mosusu ejalaki na ntango etumba esukaki.
3. Mokonji oyo esili kolonga alekaki na nguya. Ye moto apɛsaki kondimana na mokonji mosusu oyo akwei na etumba mpe ajangi nguya.
4. Mokonji ajangaki kolonga ekoki na ye kondima mpo yango yonso.
5. Mikanda na Kondimana na bango na kalakala ekojala na makambo motoba na kati:
   a) Maloba na ebandeli

b) Ekaniseli na makambo na kala (histoire) mpe motindo likambo ebandi
c) Mibeko mpe "règlements"
d) Motindo na kotanga kondimana yango mbala na mbala mpo na ekaniseli
e) Nkombo na batatoli (témoins)
f) Mapamboli mpe kolakelama mabe

D. Kondimana na Njambe oyo apɛsaki na ba-Yisalaele na maboko na Mose (Esode mpe Dutɛlonomɛ)
1. Esalami na kati na Njambe mpe Yisalaele
2. Epɛsami na nsuka na etumba (Esode 1–15 mpe Dutɛlonomɛ 1)
3. Njambe apɛsaki yango na Sinai
4. Ekokaki ete Yisalaele bandima yango mpe maloba yonso na kati. Esode 24:3–8
5. Maloba majalaki na kati na yango:
a) Maloba na ebandeli mpe ekaniseli na makambo na kala (histoire) Esode 20:2 Dutɛlonome 5:6 mpe chap. 1–4
b) Mibeko—Esode 20–23 Dutɛlonomɛ 5–26
c) Motindo bakotanga yango mbala na mbala ete bamipɛsa lisusu na yango—Esode 34 Dutɛlonomɛ 6:4–9; 11:18–20 mpe chap. 27; 31:10–13; Yosua 24
d) Batatoli: lola mpe mokili—Dutɛlonomɛ 4:26; 30:19, 28; 32:1
e) Mapamboli mpe kolakelama mabe—Dutɛlonomɛ 11:26–29; mpe chap. 28
6. Yisalaele bajalaki na nyongo—etali bango kobatela kondimana yango. Bayisalaele bakokaki kobuka yango mpe basalaki boye mbala na mbala. Bongo ejalaki likambo na bango kojonga mbala na mbala komipɛsa lisusu kotosa yango. Dutɛl. 31–32; II Mikonji 23:21–23
7. Ntina na kondimana yango etali mokili na elaka.

E. Kondimana na Njambe epai na Abalayama mpe na Dawidi Genese 12:1–3; 15; 17; II Samwele 7
1. Ekɛsɛni na endimaneli kati na ese na ese. Ekɛsɛni na kondimana epɛsami na Yisalaele.
2. Njambe Ye moko asalaki kondimana yango
3. Moto akoki koyamba kondimana yango ata asali eloko tɛ (obligations tɛ, "conditions" tɛ)

4. Kondimana oyo ejali bobɛlɛ na bato mpe bana na libota na bango seko
5. Moto akoki kobuka kondimana yango tɛ

F. Kondimana na ndenge mibale oyo ijuami na Kondimana na Sika
1. Kondimana na "conditions" ekosalama na moYuda mpe na Moklisito. Matai 5–7; Matai 23; Yoane 14–15; Baloma 11:1–24; Baɛbɛlɛ 10:26–31
2. Kondimana oyo ejangi "conditions" esalami na Ekelesia mpe na Yisalaele. Matai 16:18; Baloma 11:25–36

IV. Koyoka Mpe Kotosa

A. Koyoka ejali na ntina monɛnɛ na kati na Mokanda na Njambe. Bongo na Biblia tomoni ete KOYOKA eleki KOMONA na ntina. Baɛla bakanisaki mingi na ntina na *miso* na bango, kasi Baɛbɛlɛ (Bayuda) bakanisaki mingi na ntina na *matoi*.
1. Basakoli bajali bantoma na Yawe. Lotomo na bango ejali ete *bayoka* maloba mpe bapɛsa yango na bato.
   a) Soko bayoki maloba kasi bajangi kosakola yango, bajui likambo. Ejekiele 3:16–21
   b) Soko bameki kosakola maloba mosusu oyo Njambe atindi tɛ, bajui likambo. Yilimia 23:18, 21, 22
2. Basakoli babandi na maloba oyo: Yawe alobi boye ete.
3. Ekoki ete bato bayoka maloba oyo etindami na Yawe. Yilimia 7:13
4. Yesu alobi ete: "Ye oyo ajali na matoi, ayoka." Matai 11:15

B. Bongo ekoki ete *koyoka* esala mosala. Na likota na Liɛbɛlɛ, *Koyoka* ejali na ntina na *Kotosa*. Ejali lokola oyoki ngonga na losambo mpe osimbi njela noki kokɛnda kosambela.
1. Abalayama atosaki. Genese 12:1–4; Baɛbɛlɛ 11:8
2. Njambe alingaki ete baYisalaele batosa kondimana na Ye. Dutɛlmiomɛ 30:11–14
3. Yesu alingi ete totosa kondimana oyo na sika. Matai 7:24–27
4. Ntina na kobila Yesu ejali *kotosa*. Matai 8:18–23
5. Nsima na kobongola motema, moto akotosa. Matai 21:28–32
6. Kondima oyo ejangi misala esili kokufa. Yakobo 2:26

   Ndakisa:

a) Soko moyekoli na kelasi apɛsi molakisi na ye likabo (lokola likei to ananasi) tika abosana tɛ kosala devoir na ye na kelasi lokola.

b) Soko moto na lingomba apɛsi pasteur na ye bilei, ekoki na ye kotosa liteyo na pasteur lokola.

c) Moto oyo asepeli kotanga Mokanda na Njambe abosana tɛ kobokola libota na ye mpe kosunga babola mpe bajangi.

C. Kondima ekobanda na kotosa

1. Abalayama atosaki liboso mpe andimaki na nsima. Genese 12:4; 15:6

2. "Bobɛlɛ batosi bakoki kondima," elobi Dietrich Bonhoeffer

a) Okoyeba mokano na Njambe wana ejali yo na njela.

b) Okondima solo bobɛlɛ soko ojali na njela kokɛnda.

D. Kondima ekomekama na kotosa

1. Abalayama atosaki mpe atalisaki kondima na ye wana akei kopesa mwana na ye na mbɛka na kotumba. Genese 22

2. Njambe alakisi Saulo ete kotosa eleki mbɛka na kotumba. I Samwele 15

3. Yilimia asakoli mpe boye ete kotosa eleki mbɛka. Yilimia 7:22, 23

V. Bolamu Mobimba

A. Na lakota na Liɛbɛlɛ liloba mpo na *moto* (nephesh) ejali koloba mpo na *molimo* elongo na *njoto*. Ejali koloba tɛ mpo na molimo ekabwani na njoto. Ntina na liloba yango na Liɛbɛlɛ ejali ete mo!imo na moto mosangani na njoto na ye. Ndakisa: Molimo + Njoto = Moto Mobimba. Bongo biso baKlisito tokotiya kondima na biso na lisekwa na njoto. Bato mosusu bakondima ete molimo mokoumela libela kasi njoto ekosila.

B. Na lakota na Liɛbɛlɛ liloba mpo na *kimia* ejali Shalom. Ntina na yango ejali "kojanga etumba" soko "kosila na etumba," njokande ntina mosusu ejali na kati na yango lokola. Ejali koloba ntina na "njoto malamu, kolongonu, bolamu." Yilimia 6:14

1. Shalom ejali losako. Ntina na losako yango: "Najali na elikia ete ojali malamu," soko "Jala malamu lɛlo." Ntina na !ipamboli ejali na kati na yango.

2. Shalom ejali koloba "njoto malamu" (kolongonu) mpo na moto na moto.
3. Shalom ejali lokola libota malamu wana bato bajali kofanda elongo kosepelana, kosololana, kosɛkana, kokumisana.
4. Shalom ejali bolamu na mboka- ejali "mboka malamu."
   a) Ejali esɛngo ekomonana na ntango bato na mboka bakoyangana.
   b) Ejali wana mboka ejangi moyibi mpe lokuta mpe kokosa.
5. Soko Shalom ekosila mpe ekojanga
   a) Bato bakojala na nsoni mpo na yango tɛ
   b) Bato bakoyambola bikweli na bango tɛ

C. Bomoi na biso bato na mokili ejali lokola mobembo. Ejali lokola tojali koluka kokɛnda na mboka oyo tokotanga yango Bolamu Mobimba. Ejali oyo biso yonso tojali koluka.

1. Biso moko na moko tokolukaka kojala malamu mobimba
   a) Wana ejali biso kokola ete moto na moto akoma mokolo mobimba. I Bakolinti 13:9–12; Baɛfɛsɛ 4:13
   b) Wana Yesu apɛsi kimia mpe njoto malamu. Malako 5:24–34
2. Ekelesia na mboka ekoluka kojala mokolo mobimba. Baloma 1:12; I Bakolinti 1:10–13; I Bakolinti 12
3. Ekelesia mobimba na mokili bakosungana lokola elobi M. Russell Cervin.
4. Na ese na biso (pays na biso), Soko tolingi mokili na biso kojala mokili na kolongonu mpe mokili malamu, ekoki ete tokanisa bobɛlɛ koselingwa komibatela na ntango na etumba tɛ, kasi tokanisa kosunga babola, bajangi mpe bato na mawa.
5. Mpo na mokili mobimba oyo Njambe ajalisaki. Baloma 8:18–25; 11:1–36
6. Tobosana tɛ ete Molimo Mosanto akopɛsa kimia mpe bomoko. Yoane 14:26–27 Misala na Bantoma 2

5

Deuteronomy[1]

DEUTERONOMY, THE FIFTH BOOK of the Pentateuch, is the preeminent document on law and ethics in the Hebrew Scriptures / Old Testament (OT). Emanating from the late eighth or early seventh century BC, the major portion of the book (Deuteronomy 1–28) updates, supplements, and sermonizes on the Decalogue and Covenant Code of Exodus 20–23. Deuteronomy also differs in content from the so-called Priestly laws in Exodus, Numbers, and Leviticus, as well as the Holiness Code of Leviticus 17–26. The book has recognized parallels to preaching of the eighth-century prophets, particularly Amos and Hosea, stating climactically in a final edition that Moses was prophet *non pareil* (Deut 34:10). Deuteronomy also betrays influence from Wisdom literature in Israel and texts of the ANE. A supplement includes two old poems, the Song of Moses (Deut 32:1–43) and the Blessing of Moses (Deut 33). The book closes with a brief account of Moses's death (Deut 34). Deuteronomy later becomes an important source for the teachings of Jesus and virtually every writer of the New Testament (NT).

Law and Covenant

Ethics in ancient Israel was anchored not in philosophical thought, as in other cultures. The moral value of human conduct, the principles governing it, and the rationale for right living were defined in the main by a divinely initiated covenant naming Israel as Yahweh's holy (= set apart) people, and

1. *The [Oxford] Encyclopedia of Bible and Ethics* (New York: Oxford University Press, forthcoming).

mandating that Israel worship Yahweh alone as God. Israel's election and what it meant for the nation are articulated more clearly in Deuteronomy than anywhere else in the OT. The covenant made at Mount Sinai, called (Mount) Horeb in Deuteronomy, included a law that had to be obeyed. The core of this law was the Decalogue, or Ten Commandments (Deut 5:1–21; cf. Exod 20:1–17), which in Deuteronomy was supplemented by another code given to Israel in the plains of Moab, just prior to Moses's death and Israel's crossing of the Jordan to enter Canaan (Deut 12–26; 28).

Yahweh could lay this law upon Israel because he acted to liberate Israel from Egyptian slavery. The Decalogue begins: "I am Yahweh your God, who brought you out of the land of Egypt, out of the house of bondage. You shall have no other gods before me . . ." (Deut 5:6–7; cf. Exod 20:2–3).

This act of liberation was not simply a granting of freedom; it consisted rather of a change of masters: Pharaoh was the old master, Yahweh the new master.[2] A similar change was later affirmed by the nascent church—where the old master was Satan and the power of sin, the new master Jesus the Christ, who saved humankind from sin by his death on the cross.

Yahweh's liberation in the exodus was modeled on a practice known to exist in ANE law. If someone fell into slavery, a kinsman could pay the redemption price that the enslaved was unable to pay. The freed individual would then be required to serve the kinsman who had paid the release. The good news, however, was that this new servitude would be considerably easier because the kinsman would treat the redeemed more kindly. Yahweh, acting similarly, said the law now being laid upon Israel would not be difficult, but rather easy to carry out (Deut 30:11–14). Once again, the idea was carried over into the NT, where Matthew reports Jesus as saying, "Take my yoke upon you . . . for my yoke is easy and my burden is light" (Matt 11:29–30).

The Decalogue in Deuteronomy

The book of Deuteronomy intends primarily to present Israel with statutes and ordinances of the covenant Moses brokered with the nation in the plains of Moab (Deut 1:1–5; 29:1), but before the statutes and ordinances can be expounded, hearers must become familiar once again with the core law of the covenant made at Horeb (= Sinai). This comes in Deut 5, where

2. David Daube, *The Exodus Pattern in the Bible* (London: Faber & Faber, 1963).

we are told that only the Decalogue was given to the people at Horeb (Deut 5:22). The Deuteronomic Code was vouchsafed to Moses (Deut 5:30–31), who only now was presenting it to Israel in the plains of Moab. But the new generation, says Moses, should think of itself as standing with the older generation at the foot of the fiery mountain, entering into the covenant made there with the prior generation (Deut 5:1–5). The defining law of this covenant was commandment number one: Israel must have no other gods besides Yahweh (Deut 5:7).

Deuteronomy's presentation of the Decalogue does not differ substantially from the version appearing in Exodus, containing only minor word changes and a different rationale for keeping the fourth commandment (on Sabbath rest: Deut 5:12–15; cf. Exod 20:8–11); and in the tenth commandment (on coveting), containing only minor word changes and a different ordering of the coveted items (Deut 5:21; cf. Exod 20:17).

The Decalogue—except for the fourth commandment, on keeping the Sabbath, and the fifth, on honoring one's father and mother—is apodictic law,[3] characterized by the use of the second singular "you" together with an emphatic and unconditional "not." No punishments are prescribed. Alt says: "The categorical prohibition lays down the law in a much more absolute fashion than the provision of the severest punishment . . . the Decalogue, more than the other lists, refrains from naming actual individual cases, but tends rather to lay down principles, without getting lost, however, in abstractions."[4] The "you" is directed to every man and woman, except in the tenth commandment, where the beginning is directed only to every man. No parallel to apodictic law is known to exist in law codes of the ANE. Parallels occur in other ANE texts, but they are rare.

Other legislation in Deuteronomy, the Book of the Covenant, and known law codes of the ANE (e.g., the Laws of Ur-Nammu, the Lipit-Ishtar Code, the Laws of Eshnunna, the Code of Hammurabi, and the Middle Assyrian, Hittite, and Neo-Babylonian law codes) are casuistic in form: If someone does such and such, then such and such will be the punishment. Casuistic law, says Alt, is suited for normal jurisdiction in a court of law.

3. Albrecht Alt, "The Origins of Israelite Law," in *Essays on Old Testament History and Religion*, trans. R. A. Wilson (Oxford: Blackwell, 1966), 79–132.

4. Ibid., 122.

Deuteronomy Is Preached Law

Deuteronomy is preached law,[5] seen especially in chapters 6–11 where the priest, assuming the speaking voice of Moses, aims at driving home the importance of obeying commandments 1 and 2: no other gods, and no idols. Framing this discourse is a liturgical piece admonishing Israel to love Yahweh, keep the law in one's heart, teach it to one's children, and display it in conspicuous places (Deut 6:4–9; 11:18–21). In its first occurrence it is preceded by the Shema, which becomes Israel's bedrock confession: "Hear O Israel, Yahweh our God, Yahweh is one" (Deut 6:4).

Deuteronomy contains three defining doctrines: 1) Israel's election as a holy people, 2) Yahweh's gift of land to Israel, and 3) the conduct of holy war. Yahweh chose Israel not because it was a large people, for it was small, but because of his love for Israel and because of a prior oath made to the Fathers (Deut 7:6–8). Election is thus a divine mystery, known only to God. The idea appears in rudimentary form in the Blessing of Moses, where it says that Yahweh left three mountainous abodes in the southland to cast in his lot with "peoples," specifically the people of Israel, over whom he came to reign as King (Deut 33:2–5). It was because of a love for the peoples of earth that Yahweh left behind myriads of holy ones on mountains of the southland.

The prophet Isaiah teaches the holiness of Yahweh (Isa 1:4; 6:3), but in Deuteronomy the holiness of Israel gets the emphasis (Deut 7:6; 14:2, 21; 28:9). Israel's holiness is given renewed emphasis in Leviticus 17–26, where the point is made that Israel is to be holy because Yahweh is holy (Lev 19:2). Israel becomes holy by doing the commandments and not going after other gods; this in turn translates into loving Yahweh, fearing (= revering) Yahweh, walking in Yahweh's way, and joyfully serving Yahweh (Deut 6:4–9, 13–14; 8:6; 10:12–13, 20; 11:1, 13, 22; 13:4).

The second doctrine of Deuteronomy is Yahweh's gift of land to Israel, which again was to make good on a promise to the Fathers and on Yahweh's determination to cast out the prior inhabitants, who were wicked (Deut 9:4–6). The land was given, not because of Israel's righteousness, for Israel was a rebellious and stiff-necked people (Deut 9:6), its rebellion seen already at Horeb and at other times in the wilderness (Deut 9:7–29). Yahweh's gift of land receives mention also in the Song of Moses, where it

5. Gerhard von Rad, *Studies in Deuteronomy*, trans. David Stalker, Studies in Biblical Theology 1/9 (London: SCM, 1953).

says that in hoary antiquity the Most High parceled out to each nation an inheritance, and Israel became Yahweh's own portion (Deut 32:7–9).

The third doctrine of Deuteronomy is that of holy war, the means by which Israel will obtain the land of promise (Deut 7:1–2). Yahweh will lead the people in battle, for he is "Lord of hosts," meaning the "Lord of the (heavenly) army." Cities will be taken, and captured inhabitants—sometimes also beasts and other spoil—will be "devoted to destruction" (i.e., they will be presented as a sacrificial offering to Yahweh). Holy war was carried out against Sihon and Og, the Amorite kings of Transjordan: captured men, women, and children were put to death under the holy-war ban (Deut 2:34–35; 3:6–7). The land was then resettled with Israelite tribes. Deuteronomy envisions the same for cities in Canaan. In battles subsequently fought, the holy-war ban was applied (Josh 6:21; 10:28–40; 11:10–20). If Israel was fighting a distant city, however, women, children, and spoil would not be subject to the ban (Deut 20:10–15), and captured women could be taken by Israelite men as wives (Deut 21:10–14). But before Israel conducted its first holy war, it undertook an "unholy war" in trying to take Canaan against Yahweh's command,[6] and was roundly defeated (Deut 1:19–46).

Problematic ethical behavior for any people is going to war, and a Yahweh-led holy war is particularly offensive to modern sensibilities. Deuteronomy's holy-war commands were mitigated already by the rabbis, their uneasiness made explicit in the Talmud. Christians, for their part, have always had great difficulty reconciling holy war with gospel teaching. Even in the church's doctrine of a just war, nations are to go to war only as a last resort.

The *ḥerem* law of Deuteronomy, whereby every living person and animal is put to death and devoted to God (Deut 20:16; cf. Josh 10:40) seems even in the ancient world unnecessarily severe on Yahweh's part, particularly with Israel emerging the victor and other peoples being exterminated. Seeds are present for an extreme form of nationalism. Of course one might simply say that other nations were also doing it. The term *ḥrm* appears on the ninth century Moabite Stone (line 17), where Mesha says he "devoted" seven thousand Israelite men, boys, women, girls, and maidservants to Ashtar-Chemosh. Other examples have been cited from the ancient world.

6. William L. Moran, "The End of the Unholy War and the Anti-Exodus," *Biblica* 44 (1963) 333–42; reprinted, Duane L. Christensen, ed., *A Song of Power and the Power of Song*, Sources for Biblical and Theological Study 3 (Winona Lake, IN: Eisenbrauns, 1993), 147–55.

However, if Israel is to occupy the higher moral ground, and Yahweh is to be morally superior to other gods, such an explanation will hardly do.

Deuteronomy's reason for engaging in holy war is that Yahweh had to root out the worship of other gods. If the Canaanites were permitted to remain in the land, their abominable religious practices would become a snare to Israel (Deut 7:1–5, 16; 18:12; 20:16–18). But it should be noted that in Deuteronomy the same *ḥerem* law is applied to Israelite cities found chasing after other gods (Deut 13:12–18). And later on, we find Yahweh declaring unambiguous holy war against the rump state of Israel, bringing nationhood to an end (Jer 6:4–5; 22:7). Even beasts came under the ban (Jer 7:20; 21:6; 36:29) and were destroyed (Jer 32:43; 33:10, 12). Today the *ḥerem* law—practiced by any people—is taken to be immoral. People everywhere were horrified over the Nazi Holocaust of the Jews during last century, roundly condemning it.

The Deuteronomic Code

The Deuteronomic Code (Deut 12–26; 28) contains two collections of laws and preaching on laws: chapters 13–18, and chapters 19–25. The legal material in chapters 19–25 is casuistic, although not all laws specify punishment. Worship at a single sanctuary is mandated in an introduction (Deut 12:5–14), supporting a date for Deuteronomy 1–28 in connection with Hezekiah's reform, ca. 712–706 BC (2 Kgs 18:4, 22; 2 Chr 29–31). Following the legal material are two rituals to be performed at the central sanctuary: one for the presentation of the firstfruits, the other attesting to a proper distribution of the third-year charity tithe (Deut 26). The code closes with blessings and curses for covenant obedience and disobedience (Deut 28). Deut 27, a fragment from an old covenant-renewal festival at Shechem, is a later interpolation.

The Deuteronomic Code contains laws and preaching regarding

- Tests to be applied for going after other gods (Deut 13:1–18)
- Clean and unclean foods; holiness in lamenting and eating (Deut 14:1–21)
- Tithes, remissions, and offerings (Deut 14:22–15:23)
- Keeping the feasts (Deut 16:1–17)
- Office holders in Israel (Deut 16:18–18:22)
- Judicial procedure (Deut 19:1–21)

- War and preparation for war (Deut 20:1–20)
- Expiation for an unsolved murder (Deut 21:1–9)
- Marriage to a woman war captive (Deut 21:10–14)
- Rights of the firstborn (Deut 21:15–17)
- Death for a rebellious son (Deut 21:18–21)
- Hanged bodies of executed criminals (Deut 21:22–23)
- Lost property, treatment of animals, dress and building codes (Deut 22:1–8)
- Mixtures and the tassel exception (Deut 22:9–12)
- Chastity and marriage (Deut 22:13–30)
- Purity, cleanliness, and hospitality to runaways (Deut 23:1–18)
- Loans, vows, and theft (Deut 23:19–25)
- Marriage, divorce, remarriage, and the newlywed deferment (Deut 24:1–5)
- Pledges, kidnapping, and scale disease (Deut 24:6–13)
- Justice and benevolence to the poor and needy (Deut 24:14–22)
- Limit on flogging (Deut 25:1–3)
- No muzzle on a threshing ox (Deut 25:4)
- Levirate marriage (Deut 25:5–10)
- Wives interfering in a fight (Deut 25:11–12)
- Just weights and measures (Deut 25:13–16)
- Wiping out any remembrance of Amalek (Deut 25:17–19)

The Covenant Code in Exodus has more laws dealing with personal injury (Exod 21:18–27) and liabilities relating to animals, personal goods, and property (Exod 21:28—22:15). Deuteronomy does not deal with damages or civil suits, which occupy a large part of the Covenant Code. Its concern is rather with protecting human individuals, particularly individuals who have little or no means of protecting themselves. The Deuteronomic Code contains only two laws on property: the law prohibiting removal of a landmark (Deut 19:14) and the law concerning just weights and measures (Deut 25:13–16).

When the whole of Deuteronomy is examined, unmistakable parallels to vassal treaties of the ANE emerge, specifically those drawn up by the Hittite and Assyrian kings.[7] The treaties of Esarhaddon date from the seventh

7. George E. Mendenhall, *Law and Covenant in Israel and the Ancient Near East* (Pittsburgh: Presbyterian Board of Colportage of Western Pennsylvania, 1955); reprinted from two articles in *BA* 17 (1954), 26–46, 49–76; D. J. Wiseman, "The Vassal Treaties of Esarhaddon," *Iraq* 20 (1958) 1–99; Dennis J. McCarthy, *Treaty and Covenant*, AnBib 21

century (680–669 BC), making them contemporary with Deuteronomy. These treaties obligated the vassal king to keep the terms set forth by his suzerain. Six typical treaty elements with parallels to Deuteronomy are the following: 1) preamble introducing the speaker (Deut 1:1–5); 2) historical prologue (Deut 1–4); 3) stipulations (Deut 5; 12–26); 4) provisions for depositing the document in the temple and a periodic reading (Deut 31:9–13, 26); 5) a list of gods as witnesses (no parallel); and 6) blessings and curses (Deut 27–28). Deuteronomy, to no one's surprise, has no list of gods as witnesses. In the Song of Moses, witnesses to what is there called "law" (Deut 31:24; 32:46) are heaven and earth (Deut 32:1).

From within the OT we see that the Horeb (Sinai) covenant was unlike other biblical covenants made with Noah, Abraham, Phinehas, and David, which were covenants of divine commitment. The covenant with Israel was a covenant of obligation,[8] meaning it was conditional. Yahweh gave it freely and was committed to keeping it, but Israel's obedience was required for it to remain in tact. If Israel disobeyed its terms, the covenant would be declared broken, and would have to be renewed. In the end, renewal was not possible; the curses of Deut 28 fell, and the nation was destroyed. Jeremiah therefore announced for Israel and Judah a new and eternal (or everlasting) covenant (Jer 31:31–34; 32:40), which, like other OT covenants, contained no conditions and would last forever.

Deuteronomy and the Prophets

Earlier scholars saw the prophets as the ones who gave Israel its high ethical and spiritual teaching, believing also that Deuteronomy must have originated among heirs to the eighth-century prophets, particularly Amos and Hosea.[9] Some called Deuteronomy a "prophetic law code," in which Moses

(Rome: Pontifical Biblical Institute, 1963), 68–79; Moshe Weinfeld, *Deuteronomy and the Deuteronomic School* (Oxford: Clarendon, 1972), 59–157; Weinfeld, *Deuteronomy 1–11*, AB 5 (New York: Doubleday, 1991), 6–9.

8. David Noel Freedman, "Divine Commitment and Human Obligation," *Int* 18 (1964) 419–31; reprinted in John R. Huddlestun, ed., *Divine Commitment and Human Obligation*, vol. 1, *History and Religion* (Grand Rapids: Eerdmans, 1997), 168–78.

9. Julius Wellhausen, *Prolegomena to the History of Ancient Israel* (New York: Meridian, 1957); S. R. Driver, *A Critical and Exegetical Commentary on Deuteronomy*, ICC 5 (Edinburgh: T. & T. Clark, 1895); H. Wheeler Robinson, *Deuteronomy and Joshua*, Century Bible (Edinburgh: T. C. & E. C. Jack, 1907), 33–43; Robert Pfeiffer, *Introduction to the Old Testament*, rev. ed. (New York: Harper, 1948), 179–80; E. W. Nicholson,

was established as a prophet (Deut 18:15–18). By the time the book was completed, Moses had become the greatest of the prophets (Deut 34:10–12).

Deuteronomy knows the election of Israel about which Amos speaks (Amos 3:2). Judah's indictment by Amos for rejecting Yahweh's law and not keeping his statutes (Amos 2:4) could be background for Deuteronomy's recurring admonition that Israel be sure to keep the commandments, statutes, and ordinances once it becomes settled in the land. Amos's indictment of Israel for injustice and oppression of the poor (Amos 2:6–8) could also be background for Deuteronomy's teaching of justice, especially toward the poor. Yahweh's moral government of the world (Amos 1:3—2:3), and a recall of Yahweh's having destroyed the Amorites (Amos 2:9), could have informed Deuteronomy's view that Yahweh was determined to drive out Canaan's prior inhabitants because of their wickedness.

Deuteronomy's greater debt appears to have been to Hosea, however, given that Deuteronomy echoes both diction and ideas of this prophet and contains legislation that could have been a response to his preaching.[10] Language about "forgetting Yahweh" and "going after other gods" (Hos 2:5, 13; 3:1; 8:14) is precisely what turns up in Deuteronomy, appearing also in the Song of Moses. For Driver too Deuteronomy was the spiritual heir of Hosea, repudiating as it does nature worship, and acknowledging Yahweh to be the true giver of earth's bounty (Hos 2:5, 8, 12). The Deuteronomic preacher agreed with Hosea in giving prominence to the emotional side of religion: love, affection, and sympathy—but particularly love.

Hosea preached that there was no God but Yahweh (Hos 13:4), which in Deuteronomy became bedrock teaching. Israel, says Hosea, was in gross violation of Yahweh's law and covenant (Hos 4:6; 8:1), particularly the Ten Commandments (Hos 4:2; 6:9). Israel's princes were like those who remove landmarks (Hos 5:10), which became prohibited in the Deuteronomic Code. The nation was behaving like a trader with false balances (Hos 12:7), a situation issuing forth in another Deuteronomic law.

Hosea speaks against Israel's multiple sanctuaries (Hos 4:15; 9:15; 12:11); high places (Hos 4:13; 10:8); feasts occurring there (Hos 2:11, 13; 9:5); and sacrifices connected with feasts (Hos 4:13; 6:6; 9:4). Yahweh has no delight in any of these, says Hosea, and will put an end to Israel's feasts (Hos 2:11, 13; 8:13). Hosea censures Israel's many altars (Hos 8:11; 10:1–2,

Deuteronomy and Tradition (Philadelphia: Fortress, 1967), xi.

10. H. Louis Ginsberg, *The Israelian Heritage of Judaism* (New York: Jewish Theological Seminary of America, 1982), 19–24.

8; 12:11); pillars by the altars (Hos 10:1–2); and priests officiating at the altars (Hos 4:6; 5:1; 6:9), saying the latter will be punished (Hos 10:5). Deuteronomy's response to all this was a single sanctuary for the worship of Yahweh.

Deuteronomy and Wisdom

Wisdom is commonly defined as an intellectual capacity or quality of the mind enabling one to live well in the world, to succeed, and to counsel others in the way of success. Its opposite is foolishness, usually reduced to a lack of good sense or good judgment. Wisdom deals not so much with God as with matters of earth, for which reason Israelite wisdom occupies common ground with other wisdom in the ancient world. Important here are such extrabiblical texts as the Instruction of Amen-em-opet,[11] the Sefire Stele,[12] and the Vassal Treaties of Esarhaddon.[13] Yet Israelite wisdom is deeply religious (Ps 111:10: "The fear of the Lord is the beginning of wisdom").[14] Deuteronomy is now recognized as having been much influenced by Israelite wisdom,[15] balancing off any debt it might owe to Israelite prophecy.

Wisdom has at least three defining characteristics: 1) wisdom builds on knowledge; 2) wisdom requires discrimination, or discernment; and 3) wisdom resides in individuals who utilize the knowledge and discernment they possess. Wisdom is something you do (Deut 4:6).

In Deuteronomy Moses is the great teacher, teaching Israel the commandments, statutes, and ordinances of the covenant (Deut 4:1, 5, 14; 5:31), also giving people a song that will witness against them in future days (Deut 31:19–22). People are admonished to learn them, remember them, and lay them to heart (Deut 6:6; 11:18; 32:46). The same must be taught to their children (Deut 4:9–10; 6:7, 20–25; 32:46). The Hebrew verb "teach" (*lmd* piel), which occurs in no other book in the Pentateuch, occurs ten times in Deuteronomy, and the verb "learn" (*lmd* qal) seven times.

11. *ANET*^{3}, 421–25.

12. Joseph A. Fitzmyer, "The Aramaic Inscriptions of Sefire I and II," *JAOS* 81 (1961) 178–222; Fitzmyer, *The Aramaic Inscriptions of Sefire*, BibOr 19 (Rome: Pontifical Biblical Institute, 1967); McCarthy, *Treaty and Covenant.*

13. *ANET*^{3}, 534–41.

14. David Daube, "The Culture of Deuteronomy," *Orita* 3 (1969) 28.

15. Ibid., 51–52; Weinfeld, *Deuteronomy and the Deuteronomic School.*

Deuteronomy expects people to discern between the worship of Yahweh and worship of other gods: Deut 30:15–29 lifts up the celebrated wisdom teaching of the "two ways": one leading to life, the other to death. People must know what sacrifices are to be offered at the central sanctuary and what other animal slaughterings can be performed in towns where they live (Deut 12). People are required to discriminate between false prophets and true prophets, to know what tests are to be employed in making the discrimination (Deut 13:1–5; 18:21–22). Also, judges in Israel are to be men of wisdom (Deut 1:15–17; 16:19).

In Deuteronomy, hearing, learning, and remembering the commandments are not enough; people must do them, and blessings will accrue, which in Deuteronomy are the material rewards of health, life, multiplication, goodness, and longevity in the land (Deut 7:12–16; 8:1, 6–10; 32:46–47).

Four Deuteronomic themes are commonly attributed to wisdom influence, with parallels existing in Proverbs, other OT Wisdom literature, and varied texts of the ANE: 1) a humanitarian concern for people, especially the poor, and for animals; 2) justice for society's poor and needy; 3) benevolence to orphans, widows, sojourners, and Levites, the latter having no inheritance (= landed property) and in the late eighth and early seventh century being jobless because of the closure of local sanctuaries; and 4) how to avoid shame.

Many laws of Deuteronomy betray a humanistic concern: parapets (low walls on flat roofs) are to be constructed on new houses to keep people from falling off (Deut 22:8); women taken in foreign wars for wives are to be treated humanely, especially if their husbands want later to be rid of them (Deut 21:10–14); asylum must be given to slaves escaping to Israel, and slaves must not be oppressed once they come to live in Israelite towns (Deut 23:15–16); debt remission must be given to the poor Israelite in the seventh year (Deut 15:1–11); Hebrew slaves—male and female—must be manumitted in the seventh year (Deut 15:12–18); men must not discriminate against an unfavored wife and her firstborn in liquidating their estates (Deut 21:15–17); loans to fellow-Israelites are to be without interest (Deut 23:19–20); hand-mills and upper millstones must not be taken from the poor as security for a loan (Deut 24:6); creditors must not enter one's house to collect a pledge, but must wait outside (Deut 24:10–11); garments taken in pledge from the poor must be restored before sundown (Deut 24:12–13); the poor laborer or sojourner must receive his wages the same day (Deut 24:14–15); and a widow's garment must not be taken as a pledge under any circumstances (Deut 24:17). Blessings will accrue to Israelites who obey these laws.

Two laws in Deuteronomy deal with cruelty to animals: 1) a prohibition against taking the mother bird with her eggs or her young from a nest happened upon by chance (Deut 22:6–7); and 2) a prohibition against muzzling an ox treading grain (Deut 25:4).

Deuteronomy teaches that justice not be perverted toward the sojourner, orphan, and widow (Deut 24:17; 27:19), for Yahweh loves them and treats them justly (Deut 10:17–18). In other societies, too, special care was taken to protect and treat justly the orphan, widow, and outcast. In the "Instruction for King Meri-ka-Re," a ruler gives this advice to his son and successor: "Do justice while you endure on the earth. Quiet the weeper; do not oppress the widow."[16] The Laws of Ur-Nammu (LUN 162–168) mandate protection for the orphan, widow, and the poor.[17] King Hammurabi in the epilogue to his Lawcode (lines 30–90) boasts that he "promoted welfare in the land . . . in order that the strong might not oppress the weak, that justice might be dealt the orphan and the widow in Babylon."[18] In the "Keret Legend," King Keret is reprimanded by his son Yaṣṣib for neglecting the orphans and the widows, and told to step down so Yaṣṣib can reign.[19] Finally, in the "Tale of Aqhat," it is the good Daniel who judges the cause of the widow and the orphan.[20]

Benevolence is to be shown toward widows, sojourners, orphans, and Levites, who are invited to join families and their servants in annual pilgrimages to the central sanctuary, and to eat there and be glad (Deut 16:10–11, 13–14). The same are entitled to the third-year charity tithe in the towns where they live (Deut 14:28–29), and at harvest time the sojourner, orphan, and widow are accorded gleaning rights (Deut 24:19–21).

Deuteronomy is also seen to contain a strong shame element. Daube says that while the guilt mechanism in Israel is vigorous, and may still predominate, especially when one has succumbed to wrongdoing, attention must nevertheless be paid to shame, or our picture of Deuteronomy will be

16. *ANET*^{3}, 415.
17. Ibid., 524.
18. Ibid., 178.
19. Ibid., 149.
20. Ibid., 151, 153.

distorted.[21] Deuteronomy permits shaming, but its greater aim is to teach people to avoid shame.

A shame element can be discerned in a number of Deuteronomic laws. The officer recruiting the militia concludes his speech before the assembly by saying that fearful and weak-hearted souls should depart and not go to battle, which appeals to a man's sense of shame (Deut 20:8). Disgrace awaits anyone who slips away due to fear and weak-heartedness.

A cluster of directives in Deut 22:1–4 warns against "hiding oneself" from awkward situations, none of which has a parallel outside Deuteronomy. One must not hide oneself from another's animal that has wandered off, or when one finds someone's lost object, or from another's animal that has fallen. The Deuteronomic writer assumes that one will be embarrassed at an unseemly object and try to escape without being noticed.

The law concerning a bride charged by her husband of coming to him and not being a virgin is promulgated with shame in mind (Deut 22:13–21). Bedclothes of the wedding night are displayed in public for all to see. If the charge proves false, the groom must pay the bride's father a hefty fine (100 shekels of silver) and cannot divorce her—a rough justice, needless to say, for the wife. If the charge is true, the bride is stoned at the door of her father's house where she lived and misbehaved. Her conduct has brought shame on all Israel.

Wages of a cult prostitute—male or female—are not to be brought into the assembly of Yahweh (Deut 23:18); they are tainted by the disgraceful way in which they were received.

The divorce-and-remarriage law of Deut 24:1–4 reflects a preoccupation with shame. A wife's losing the favor of her husband in a shame culture is a terrible misfortune. The great aim in a shame culture is to find favor in the beholder's eyes.

The law regarding leprosy (scale disease) in Deut 24:8–9 recalls what Yahweh did to Miriam when Israel came out of Egypt. Miriam questioned Moses's authority and was smitten with leprosy. Moses interceded on her behalf, but Yahweh replied: "If her father had but spit in her face, should she not be shamed seven days?"

Where a pledge is required in giving a loan, the creditor may not go into the house to seize the pledge but must remain outside and have the pledge brought to him (Deut 24:10–11). If the creditor were to enter the

21. Daube, "The Culture of Deuteronomy," 51–52.

house and seize whatever pledge he desired, it would be a great dishonor to the debtor and his family.

A wrongdoer sentenced to whipping must not be given more than forty stripes (Deut 25:1–3). If he is subjected to a wild, unlimited bastinado, he will lose his dignity and be degraded forever.

A man refusing to perform the duty of a levirate marriage is publicly shamed (Deut 25:5–10). The widow of the dead man, in the presence of city elders, will pull off his sandal, spit in his face, and shame him with a degrading word.

If a woman intervenes in a fight involving her husband, and grabs hold of the opponent's "shameful parts," she is punished in having her hand cut off, bringing her permanent disfigurement and eternal shame (Deut 25:11–12).

While many Deuteronomic laws were doubtless beneficial in their ancient context, rising above lawlessness or traditions vastly more severe, some by the Second Temple (NT) period were mitigated by the rabbis or set aside entirely: The holy-war ban was mitigated; eunuchs banned from Yahweh's assembly (Deut 23:1) were allowed entrance in the postexilic period (Isa 56:4–5). Jesus later refused to judge them (Matt 19:12), and the early church was willing to baptize them (Acts 8:26–39); and Jewish law eventually did away with the maiming prescribed in Deut 25:12, substituting in its place monetary compensation. In the modern day more changes still are made to Deuteronomic law in light of our own understanding of what makes for ethical and right behavior in individuals, the community, and the larger world.

6

Yahweh Comes to Be King on Earth

Deuteronomy 33:2–5

Deuteronomy, before reporting the death of Moses in a final chapter (34), has included a Blessing of Moses (33), one of two old poems in a second supplement to the book (31–34), the other being the Song of Moses (32:1–43). The Song of Moses is a strident rebuke of Israel for chasing after other gods. With a concluding blessing on the twelve tribes (excluding Simeon), the book of Deuteronomy can now end on a calming note before Moses dies and Joshua replaces him as Israel's leader. The book of Genesis similarly ends with a Blessing of Jacob on the Israel's twelve tribes (Gen 49:1–27).

The Blessing of Moses contains a prologue and epilogue lifting up the glorious and majestic name of Yahweh (33:1–5, 26–29). In the prologue Israel is told how Yahweh left three mountainous abodes in the southern desert to cast in his lot with peoples, specifically the tribes of Israel, over whom he would reign as king. There is none like this God, the helper and protector of Israel, and one who makes Israel a people like none other on the face of the earth. My concern in the present chapter is to lift up some key ideas in the prologue to this blessing, that not only determine early Israelite theology, but also appear to anticipate the later doctrine of Incarnation in the Christian church.

Yahweh Becomes King in Israel

Moses begins his blessing in Deut 33:2–5:[1]

> 2 And he said:
> Yahweh from Sinai came
>   and rose up from Seir for him
> He shone forth from Mount Paran
>   and went from the thousands of holy ones
>   from his southland slopes for him
> 3 Yes, one who loves peoples
>   all his holy ones were at your hand
>   and they, they were assembled at your foot
> Each executed your words
> 4 A law Moses commanded to us
>   a possession of the assembly of Jacob
> 5 And he became King in Jeshurun
>   when the heads of the people gathered
>   all together, the tribes of Israel.

Yahweh, like other gods of the ancient world, was believed early on to reside atop lofty mountains.[2] Yahweh enjoyed the luxury of three mountainous abodes: Sinai, Seir, and Paran. Sinai, known in the Bible also as Horeb (particularly in Deuteronomy), became the best known, for there Yahweh met Israel after delivering the people from Egyptian slavery, made a covenant with them (Deut 5:2–3), and gave them the core law of the Ten Commandments (Exod 20:1–17; Deut 5:6–21). Horeb was called "the mountain of God" even before Yahweh's defining revelation to Moses in the burning bush (Exod 3:1). Num 10:33 called it "the mountain of Yahweh." But according to this ancient poem above,[3] Yahweh had other mountain abodes at Seir and Paran. Seir was Mount Seir ("Hairy = Wooded Mountain"; cf. Gen 25:25), located in Edom, west of the Arabah and northeast of the Wilderness of Paran. Seir and the "mountain of Seir" are mentioned in the Amarna Letters (mid-fourteenth cent. BC) and in the Egyptian texts of

1. The translation is that in Jack R. Lundbom, *Deuteronomy* (Grand Rapids: Eerdmans, 2013), 913–14.

2. Richard J. Clifford, *The Cosmic Mountain in Canaan and the Old Testament*, HSM 4 (Cambridge: Harvard University Press, 1972).

3. The poem is dated by Frank Moore Cross and David Noel Freedman to the eleventh cent. BC, and said to have been written down in the tenth cent.; cf. Lundbom, *Deuteronomy*, 916–17.

Ramses II (ca. 1290–1224 BC) and Ramses III (ca. 1183–1152 BC).[4] Mount Paran is a specific peak or mountain range in the Wilderness of Paran, the main desert of the east-central Sinai Peninsula. Another old poem in the book of Habakkuk says that "the Holy One (i.e., the God of Israel) came from Mount Paran" (Hab 3:3). All three holy mountains were in the southland, in the desert wilderness of the Sinai Peninsula.

At Mount Paran Yahweh is said to have resided in brilliant splendor (Deut 33:2; cf. Hab 3:3–4), which was doubtless the case in his two other lofty abodes. Later, Yahweh was said to shine forth in Zion (Ps 50:2). Our poem goes on to say that Yahweh left behind thousands of "holy ones" on these mountains to throw in his lot with the people of earth, specifically the people of Israel, over whom he would become king. In these mountainous abodes holy ones were ever ready to serve him, at his hand and assembled at his feet, then going forth to execute his word on command.

Scholars in recent times have missed the main point of the prologue by reading divine-warrior ideology into the text, assuming that Yahweh was taking his entourage on a holy-war venture.[5] One does find divine-warrior imagery in the epilogue (Deut 33:26–29), but in the prologue it is not there. Yahweh is simply said to have left his dwelling places on high, and his myriads of devoted holy ones, to come to earth and be proclaimed king in "Jeshurun," a poetic name for Israel, meaning "The Upright One" (vv. 5, 26). Verse 3 tells us why: It was because he loved people, specifically the people of Israel (cf. Deut 7:7–8).

Our poem gives important insight into the origins of the early Israelite theology, in which Yahweh was said to be enthroned over the nation as King (Exod 15:18; Num 23:21; Judg 8:23). This bedrock idea was called into question when Israel asked for an earthly king like other nations had, and Samuel (overlooking the incompetence of his own sons) objected in the strongest of terms, saying that Yahweh was King (1 Sam 12:12). He unloaded his burden to Yahweh, and Yahweh answered by saying that the people were not rejecting Samuel, but rather himself as King (1 Sam 8). Israel got the king it asked for; nevertheless, the idea that Yahweh was (still) King survived the establishment of a monarchy, in Psalms (Pss 24:7–10; 68:25[24]; 93:1; 95:3; 96:10; 97:1; 98:6; 99:1, 4), and in the Prophets (Isa 6:1–5; 33:22).

4. EA 288; *ANET*[3], 488; cf. Lundbom, *Deuteronomy*, 183–84.

5. Lundbom, *Deuteronomy*, 923–24.

The Incarnation in Christian Theology

In Christianity the doctrine of the incarnation refers to God taking on human form in Jesus Christ. The word *incarnation* (Lat. *caro*, "flesh") means "enfleshment," or the taking on of (human) flesh.[6] The doctrine is not developed in the New Testament, but a key supporting text is John 1:14: "And the Word became flesh and dwelt among us," where the "Word" is God (John 1:1) and "flesh" denotes a "human person," who is Jesus (synecdoche). The doctrine also builds on the "virgin birth" account in Matt 1:18–25. The Nicene Creed (AD 325) states:

> Who, for us men for our salvation, came down from heaven, and was incarnate by the Holy Spirit of the virgin Mary, and was made man . . .

The doctrine of the two natures of Christ—fully divine and fully human—was worked out at the Council of Chalcedon (AD 451). Other NT texts supporting the incarnation doctrine are Phil 2:5–11 and Col 1:15–20.

The Blessing of Moses does not contain such a doctrine, for there is no suggestion that Yahweh took on human flesh in becoming King over Israel. But it does anticipate the doctrine at certain points. In the Blessing, Yahweh leaves a holy abode on high (not a distant heaven, as in the New Testament, but a mysterious abode high above the goings-on of earth, and inaccessible to the people of earth) and comes to earth to reign as King over people. He does this because he loves people, which has a nice parallel in John 3:16: "*For God so loved the world* that he gave his only Son, that whoever believes in him should not perish but have eternal life." The NT also teaches the coming of the kingdom of God (Matthew has "kingdom of heaven")—which is God's rule—in Jesus. This notion is strikingly similar to Yahweh's coming to earth to be King. The Lord's Prayer says, "Your Kingdom come, your will be done, on earth as it is in heaven" (Matt 6:10; cf. Luke 11:2).

6. See James D. G. Dunn, "Incarnation," in *ABD* 3:397–404; E. A. Weis, "Incarnation," in *The New Catholic Encyclopedia*, 2nd ed. (Detroit: Thomson/Gale, 2003), 7:373–75.

7

And the Word of the Lord Came to Huldah[1]

"And she said to them, 'Thus said the LORD, the God of Israel.'"
(2 Kgs 22:15)

MY MATERNAL GRANDMOTHER'S NAME was Hulda: Hulda Ohlson. During my early years she stood before me as a towering figure. Forceful in word and deed, she had no identity crisis so far as I can tell. She knew who she was. Hulda also had what you would call presence—that is, you knew when she was in the room, just as you always knew when she was merely around the corner.

Hulda was a strong but not overpowering wife to my grandfather. Their marriage was dynamic—plenty of give and take, plenty of mutual help, plenty of love. There was also enough open display of emotion. Hulda was a strong family person. To be with her, as I was so much of my growing up years, was to be "in process." You knew you were going somewhere, that things were being done, that life was important.

Hulda was a grand hostess. At her home in Chicago she held frequent parties for as many as twenty to thirty people. I was often present on such occasions, since we lived in the same building. Limited entry was granted provided I kept a low profile. My job was usually to answer the door and welcome the guests. Hulda had a wide circle of friends—many within the

1. *The Covenant Companion* 73/6 (June 1984) 26–27.

North Park Covenant Church, and many from outside. Covenant leaders were commonly in the home, as were missionaries from various parts of the world. Seminary students lived in her front bedroom while my aunt Virginia was in Japan. Pastors too could be seen sitting at the kitchen table during the day, drinking coffee with her.

Hulda was a leader in her church; also in the Covenant Women's Auxiliary, as Covenant Women was then called. At one time she was CWA national vice president.[2] The Free Bed Fund at Swedish Covenant Hospital was her idea. She campaigned for it and saw it come into being.

Hulda was a deep Christian, and was steeped—as many Mission Friends were—in the Bible. It was from her that I first learned the great biblical stories. She liked the colorful figures of the Old Testament, particularly Elijah.

Strange that I should remember her telling me about Elijah, that mighty prophet of the Lord. Strange, too, that I should recall her social concern (for example, her awareness of the need to provide hospital care for those who could not afford it).

Sometimes her words had trajectories into the future. At her first meeting with my grandfather in Colorado Springs, she said to him, "So you're the man I'm going to marry!" Grandpa Otto, by no means any less endowed with inner strength and self-worth than she, perceived fully the truth of those words, and not long after, they were married.

Whether it ever occurred to him that Hulda might be a prophet incognito, I do not know. But I will say this: that thought has crossed my mind. When I was still a young boy, it was she who spoke to me about my being a minister. On one level it was but a personal hope. But on another it was God's word coming through her word. I am thankful today that she conveyed this word to me fearlessly and lovingly.

Today we are caught up in a movement that aims to raise the standing of women. Its roots are deep in American history—indeed in all of modern Western history, where democracy, equal rights, and the lifting of women and men to new heights of value have been championed.

At the same time this movement has upset accepted patterns of church life. Women now in many of our churches may fill any leadership position, may sit on any church board, may serve Communion, and may usher. The Covenant denomination has approved ordination and licensure for women, and women are serving as pastors in some of our conferences. The step has

2. *Covenant Weekly* (August 30, 1957) 10.

been a big one for many to take. Others are as yet unable to take it. "God did not intend," they say, "that women should preach his Word, shepherd his flock, and dispense the holy sacraments."

Still, we have sent some mighty women to foreign mission fields. I think of Edla Matson, Mildred Nordlund, Signe Berg, Viola Larson, Millie Nelson, and Martha Dwight in China and Taiwan; of Vanette Thorsell, Helen Bergquist, and Fern Wickstrom in Zaire (Congo), just to name a few I have known. They were only commissioned—not ordained. Nevertheless on the field they stood side by side with the men, and it is hard to see how their ministries can be substantively less in the sight of God than the ministries of men. These women have all had strength and possessed great spiritual gifts.

Looking into the Old Testament. we see that there were no women priests, but there were some prophetesses. A certain Huldah surfaced in the great Josianic Reform, during which she played an important role. According to the writer of 2 Kings, this reform began with the finding of an old scroll, perhaps a torah of Moses. When the king heard its contents, he was cut to the heart. He sensed an immediate need for a current word from the Lord. The high priest was summoned to get that word, and he complied by going straightaway to the Second Quarter of Jerusalem where he found Huldah. Were there no men in Jerusalem to exegete and preach for the king? At any rate, Huldah heard the scroll read, or else read it herself, after which she delivered a thunderous judgment on the inhabitants of Jerusalem.

Huldah was preaching. She was bringing Yahweh's ancient word into the present with urgency and power. There was all the authority of an Amos, Isaiah, or Jeremiah. The standard formula of the divine messenger was used: "Thus said Yahweh." The king received special mercy because he tore his robe in contrition. Nevertheless, his portion remained bittersweet, for only by death would he be kept from seeing the chaos to come. Things happened pretty much as Huldah said. Josiah died prematurely.

The prophetic word was thus accepted, one that had come in this case by way of Yahweh's servant Huldah. She therefore joins a venerable line of women prophets, beginning with Miriam and Deborah, and continuing on after her with Anna, who was on hand to witness the birth of Jesus (Luke 2:36–38).

Scripture is thus seen to have an affirming word for women who today feel called to preach, teach, and pastor Christ's church. Salvation-history, the term we use to describe history as seen from the perspective of God's economy, is moving climactically toward the time when *all* people—men and women, young and old, slave and free—will be empowered by God's Spirit to give prophetic utterance (Joel 2:28–29). This same vision is reiterated in only slightly different terms by Paul in Gal 3:28.

But a word should be given to women who are not called to speak after the manner of Huldah. God wants you, nevertheless, to be strong. But this does not mean you are to reject the strength you find in men, whether in your husband or in other men. The women's movement is misguided any time it champions naked power and hubris. It is misguided if it leads women away from men instead of into healthy interchange with them. It is misguided whenever it tells women, "Get your own way regardless of the cost and the opposition: if you don't, then ride off by yourself into the sunset!"

There is enough good in the women's movement to bring profit for all of us. Strong women make strong wives and mothers; they make strong citizens in the community; they make strong persons in the church. Men unable to see this, who demean their wives, who treat them and other women as objects instead of as full persons, who help them remain weak instead of helping them to become strong, destroy those women, and (what is just as tragic) they destroy also themselves in the end.

8

Jeremiah and the Created Order[1]

ONE MAY WELL POSE the question whether Jeremiah had any thoughts at all on creation, living as he did on the eve of a calamitous destruction—people dying from sword, famine, and disease; the land he loved becoming an uninhabitable ruin; and the nation he loved tumbling headlong into inglorious demise. How much more we might learn from Second Isaiah, whose eloquence on creation compares with writers of Gen 1, Ps 104, and a handful of other biblical texts on the subject (Isa 40:21–31; 42:5–9; 43:1–7; 44:1–5, 21–28; 45:12–18; 51:12–16). It is Second Isaiah who speaks about a new heaven and a new earth (Isa 65:17), which gets ultimate and climactic expression at the close of the New Testament (Rev 21:1–22:5). Jeremiah's eloquence appears at first glance to be saved for the undoing of creation, on the one hand (Jer 4:23–26), and for the prophecy of a new covenant, on the other (Jer 31:31–34).

Jeremiah, as it happens, has a good deal to say about Yahweh and the created order, but we must begin by taking a look at pronouncements about creation's undoing, including a vision the prophet received about creation returning to primeval chaos. The undoing of creation is Jeremiah's concern in the early and middle years of his preaching. We need also to know the reasons Jeremiah gave for destruction on such a grand scale, spoken to those who lived through it, but which can also inform those of us for whom the fragility of the created order is a topic of daily conversation.

1. *Jeremiah Closer Up*, HBM 31 (Sheffield: Sheffield Phoenix, 2010), 42–57.

Visions of Cosmic Destruction

Jeremiah's Vision of Cosmic Destruction in chapter 4, for which the prophet is perhaps best known, describes a return of the created order to primeval chaos:

> I saw the earth, and look! it was waste and void
>   and the heavens, their light was not there
> I saw the mountains, and look! they were quaking
>   and all the hills were tossing about
> I saw, and look! no human was there
>   and all the birds of the skies had fled
> I saw, and look! the garden land was a desert
>   and all its cities were ruined
>   before Yahweh
>   before his burning anger. (Jer 4:23–26)

The vision contains unmistakable echoes of the creation account in Gen 1, reproducing its characteristic language ("waste and void"), balancing terms ("heaven" and "earth"), and strong cadences, yet possessing a rhetorical quality all its own. It is unparalleled in the prophetic corpus, perhaps in all literature, ancient and modern. The repetitions ("I saw . . . and look!") and balancing terms ("earth" and "heavens," "mountains" and "hills," "quaking" and "tossing about," "human" and "birds," "garden land" and "cities") are supplemented by diminution to a couple terse, climactic lines ("before Yahweh / before his burning anger"), simulating creation's undoing. If creation was a gift of Yahweh God, and it was, its undoing is the result of Yahweh's burning anger.

On another occasion, Jeremiah sees creation coming apart—burned-out mountains, meadows empty of people, no cattle, no wild animals, no birds overhead—and he is reduced to tears:

> Over the mountains I make weeping and lament
>   and over pastures of the wild a dirge
> For they are burned, without a person passing through
>   they do not hear the sound of cattle
> From birds of the skies to the beasts
>   they have fled, they are gone. (Jer 9:10–11)

Portrayals mixing vision and metaphor with real-life scenarios occur all throughout the prophetic writings. The return to darkness routinely describes Yahweh's day of judgment (Amos 5:18–20; 8:9; Isa 13:10; Joel 2:2), a day when the land will become dry, and the mountains and hills will shake violently (Amos 1:2; Nah 1:4–6). Joel 1 stresses drought and famine, the prophet in this instance seeing a veritable garden of Eden turned into a desert wilderness (Joel 2:3). Beasts, birds, and fish will disappear on that day (Hos 4:3), and so will humans in the vision of Zephaniah (Zeph 1:2–3). There's no talk here of sparing innocent civilians, women and children, animals, trees, or fruit of the ground (Jer 7:20; 21:6; 36:29; cf. Deut 32:22). The divine wrath will descend on all creation, and it did (Jer 32:43; 33:10, 12). In the Battle of Gettysburg during America's Civil War (July 1–3, 1863), it was not only fallen soldiers who lay dying on the battlefield: the Peach Orchard and surrounding land was ruined, and thousands of horses lay dead, waiting to be buried. Other wars have witnessed destruction on an even greater scale.

Jeremiah's vision, like those of the other prophets, is only a vision, and as bad as things became, the creation never returned to primeval chaos. Still, the impact of his words is stunning. Jeremiah tells us that he sees more chaos than creation, more endings than beginnings, and more of Yahweh tearing down than of Yahweh building up. Gunkel said the "end times" are a return to "beginning times" (*Endzeit gleicht Urzeit*),[2] and for Jeremiah this return would be a return to the beginning of creation itself.

This is a different picture, surely, from the one given by Isaiah of Jerusalem, who reaches back not quite so far for his typology, only to the time when creation was in perfect harmony. The end times for this prophet would be a felicitous return to harmony after eons of disharmony, a day when

> The wolf shall live with the lamb
>   and the leopard shall lie down with the kid
> and the calf and the lion and the fatling together
>   and a little child shall lead them
> The cow and the bear shall graze
>   their young shall lie down together
>   and the lion shall eat straw like the ox
> The nursing child shall play over the hole of the asp
>   and upon the adder's den
>   the weaned child shall put his hand

2. Hermann Gunkel, *Schöpfung und Chaos in Urzeit und Endzeit* (Göttingen: Vandenhoeck & Ruprecht, 1895; English: *Creation and Chaos in the Primeval Era and the Eschaton*, trans. K. William Whitney Jr. The Biblical Resource Series (Grand Rapids: Eerdmans, 2006).

They will not hurt and they will not destroy
on all my holy mountain
For the earth will be full of the knowledge of Yahweh
as the waters cover the sea. (Isa 11:6–9)

Jeremiah is called to act out symbolically the message of a creation slated for destruction by not taking a wife and having children (Jer 16:2). Marriage in ancient Israel was regarded as having been built into the created order (Gen 2:18–24); children were considered to be a great blessing (Gen 22:17; Ps 128). God's command from creation on was "to be fruitful and multiply" (Gen 1:28; 8:17; 9:1, 7). Celibacy therefore was highly unusual (Deut 7:14). But now in light of the imminent distress, the command to procreate is suspended. The Apostle Paul in his day similarly counseled a suspension of the procreation command when writing to the Corinthian church (1 Cor 7:26–31; cf. Luke 23:29).

In a brilliantly crafted poem among the oracles against Babylon, Jeremiah employs mythic imagery, first to record Lady Jerusalem's lament over treatment it received from Nebuchadnezzar, then to describe Yahweh's eventual destruction of mighty Babylon—of its celebrated rivers, canals, and artificial lakes, and climactically of Bel Marduk, its powerless god (Jer 51:34–45). The sea will roar in upon Babylon as a chaotic force, leaving her and daughter-cities as dusty, dried-up ruins:

The sea has come up upon Babylon
with its roaring heaps she is covered
Her cities have become a desolation
a land of drought and desert
A land in which no person shall dwell
and a human shall not pass through
So I have reckoned with Bel in Babylon
and taken out what he has swallowed from his mouth.
(Jer 51:42–44a)

A Good Creation Gone Bad

Gerhard von Rad and others have made the point that God's work of creation does not stand in the Old Testament as an independent doctrine, but occurs in tandem with God's work of redemption and salvation, specifically his redemption and salvation of Israel.[3] As for Jeremiah and the

3. Gerhard von Rad, "The Theological Problem of the Old Testament Doctrine

prophets, they too have no interest simply in affirming Yahweh's creation or lamenting its undoing, although Jeremiah does a considerable amount of both. At issue for Jeremiah is Israel's sinfulness, which at root comes down to covenant violation. The created order suffers a reversal because Israel has been unfaithful to Yahweh, his word, and his covenant.

Deuteronomy states that Yahweh is giving Israel an exceedingly good land. Moses tells the people:

> For Yahweh your God is bringing you into a good land
> a land with flowing streams, with springs and underground waters welling up in valleys and hills
> a land of wheat and barley, of vines and fig trees and pomegranates
> a land of olive trees and honey
> a land where you may eat bread without scarcity, where you will lack nothing
> a land whose stones are iron, and from whose hills you may mine copper
> You shall eat your fill and bless Yahweh your God for the good land he has given you. (Deut 8:7–10)

But in Jeremiah Yahweh says the following about his gift of land and Israel's taking possession of it:

> Then I brought you into a garden land
> to eat its fruit and its goodness
> But you came in and polluted my land
> and my heritage you made an abomination. (Jer 2:7)

The view that things began to go bad with settlement in the land comes from the Song of Moses (Deut 32:10–18), and Jeremiah shows a clear familiarity with this Song (Jer 2:2–9).

---

of Creation," in *The Problem of the Hexateuch and Other Essays*, trans. E. W. Trueman Dicken (London: SCM, 1984), 131–43; reprinted in Bernhard W. Anderson, ed., *Creation in the Old Testament* (Philadelphia: Fortress, 1984), 53–64; von Rad, *Old Testament Theology*, vol. 1, *The Theology of Israel's Historical Traditions*, trans. D. M. G. Stalker; Edinburgh: Oliver & Boyd, 1962), 124, 136–39; Walther Eichrodt, "In the Beginning," in Bernhard W. Anderson and Walter Harrelson, eds., *Israel's Prophetic Heritage: Essays in Honor of James Muilenburg* (New York: Harper, 1962), 8, reprinted in Bernhard W. Anderson, ed., *Creation in the Old Testament*, 70–71; Dennis J. McCarthy, "'Creation' Motifs in Ancient Hebrew Poetry," in Bernhard W. Anderson, ed., *Creation in the Old Testament*, 75–76; H. H. Schmid, "Creation, Righteousness, and Salvation," in Bernhard W. Anderson, ed., *Creation in the Old Testament*, 103, although Schmid goes on to say that creation is the fundamental theme of biblical theology (111).

On another occasion, Jeremiah says that Yahweh hoped that his gift of a good land to daughter Israel would lead to faithfulness on her part, but to his sorrow, the exact opposite occurred. Yahweh says,

> And I said to myself,
> "How will I treat you among the children?
> I will give you a fine land
> a heritage—beauty of beauties—among the nations"
> And I said, "You will call me 'My Father'
> and will not turn back from following me"
> Surely as a woman faithless with her companion
> so you have been faithless to me, house of Israel. (Jer 3:19–20)

Ezekiel echoes this in calling Israel's heritage "a beauty of all the lands" (Ezek 20:6, 15).

Jeremiah may also have learned from the Song of Moses that Yahweh was a Father to Israel (Jer 3:4; 31:9). The Song Moses berates the wilderness generation for dealing corruptly with its God, whose created work is perfect, and whose ways are just (Deut 32:4–6). Moses says:

> Do you repay Yahweh thus?
> O people foolish and unwise!
> Is not he your father who created you?
> He made you and set you up to last! (Deut 32:6)

An early Jeremiah oracle berates the covenant people. Yahweh says they are a people

> Who say to a tree, "You are my father"
> and to a stone, "You gave me birth"
> For they face me with the back of the neck,
> not the face. (Jer 2:27ab)

The words are ironic, reversing the gender of Canaanite fertility symbols. The tree (or wooden pole) is the female fertility symbol, the Asherah; the stone (pillar) is the male fertility symbol. Two deliberate mismatches.

In another Jeremiah oracle (2:20–22), Yahweh says that Israel herself has gone bad, and he wonders how such a thing could have happened. Jeremiah knows about good and bad vine stock, perhaps recalling the portrayal of Israel's enemy in the Song of Moses as a strange vine yielding poisonous grapes (Deut 32:32–33). Jeremiah completes the contrast: Yahweh planted

Israel as a good vine, but now she has become something else. Yahweh says to the nation:

> But I, I planted you a choice vine
>   perfectly good seed
> How then have you become something putrid
>   a strange vine? (Jer 2:21)

The *sorek* vine was high-quality stock, producing grapes dark red in color (Gen 49:11; Isa 5:2). Jeremiah's usage continues to be metaphorical, with Yahweh referring once again to Israel's settlement in the land and its becoming like the former inhabitants, the very thing Deuteronomy inveighed against in the strongest of terms (e.g., Deut 12). Israel broke the covenant yoke and took to whoredom "on every high hill and under every leafy tree" (Jer 2:20). Hosea, using the vine metaphor, gave a similar indictment of northern Israel (Hos 10:1–2), and Isaiah embellished the metaphor for Judah in his memorable Song of the Vineyard (Isa 5:1–7). In the natural order such things do not happen. Good vines remain good, and bad vines remain bad. All the same, in another Jeremiah oracle Yahweh calls for alien vines and trailing branches to be stripped away (Jer 5:10).

Regular Creation, Irregular Judah

Jeremiah took particular notice of regularity within the created order, and cited examples of this regularity for the purpose of making a contrast with the irregular behavior of the covenant people. At times the irregular behavior stretched into incredulity.

Creation and wisdom themes combine in one Jeremiah oracle in order to focus attention on stability and rebellion (Jer 5:20–25). Jeremiah noted the control Yahweh exercised over the ever worrisome sea, having made the sandy shore a border over which it could not pass (Jer 5:22–23; Pss 104:9; 148:6; Prov 8:29; Job 26:12; 38:8–11). In this oracle, Yahweh asks first whether people fear him, and then contrasts his turbulent yet controlled sea with a covenant people who turns and goes its own way:[4]

4. See Hans-Jürgen Hermission, "Observations on the Creation Theology in Wisdom," in Bernhard W. Anderson, ed., *Creation in the Old Testament*, 130; John Barton, "History and Rhetoric in the Prophets," in Martin Warner, ed., *The Bible as Rhetoric*, Warwick Studies in Philosophy and Literature (London: Routledge, 1990), 59.

Me do you not fear—oracle of Yahweh
in my presence do you not writhe?
In that I made the sand a border for the sea
an ancient prescribed limit it does not go past
They shake themselves but do not prevail
its waves roar but they do not go past
But this people has a wayward and rebellious heart
they turn and go their way. (Jer 5:22–23)

In the same oracle Jeremiah answers that people do not fear Yahweh, who gives seasonal rains and the prescribed weeks of harvest:

They did not say in their heart
"Let us now fear Yahweh our God
Who gives showers and early rain
and latter rain in its season
The weeks prescribed for harvest
he maintains for us." (Jer 5:24)

The oracle concludes by saying that sins of the people have turned these away (v. 25). Sinful behavior disrupts the regularity of the created order.

On another occasion, Jeremiah contrasts a consistently fresh well with a people consistently evil, embellishing his contrast with a wordplay in the Hebrew:

As a well keeps fresh its water
so she keeps fresh her evil. (Jer 6:7)

Judah is as consistently bad as a fresh well is consistently good.

Jeremiah's contrast of the covenant people with migratory birds focuses on the question of knowledge, or in this instance, the lack thereof. From Hosea Jeremiah may have learned that people could be sadly lacking in knowledge (Hos 4:1, 6; 5:4; 6:6; Jer 4:22), and in concluding this oracle (Jer 8:4–7) Jeremiah says that it comes down to a people not knowing the order of Yahweh:

Even the stork in the skies
knows her seasons
The turtledove, swift, and swallow
keep the time of their coming
But my people do not know
the order of Yahweh. (Jer 8:7)

Migratory birds bear witness to an ordered creation under Yahweh's control, knowing instinctively when to fly south and when to fly north. But Yahweh's covenant people, with whatever capacities they possess, do not know Yahweh's order for them. Saint Jerome, in commenting on this verse, recalls the words of Isaiah: "The ox knows its owner and the ass its master's crib, but Israel does not know, my people does not understand" (Isa 1:3).

Jeremiah observed regularity in the snow and streams of mountainous Lebanon, and in one oracle (18:13–17) he contrasted this trustworthy natural wonder to a forgetful and idolatry-driven people. A pair of rhetorical questions sets up the contrast:

> Can it leave the mountain highland
>   the snow of Lebanon?
> Can foreign waters dry up
>   the cool flowing streams?
> But my people have forgotten me
>   they burn incense in vain. (Jer 18:14–15)

Human sinfulness goes against the natural order; more than that, the natural order becomes profoundly disturbed because of sinful human behavior (5:24–25). The effect of human sin on the created order is a major motif in Jeremiah's preaching. In Jer 3:2–3, the prophet notes that on dusty, dry hills, people are polluting the land with sexual improprieties. He says,

> So the showers were withheld
>   and the latter rains did not come. (Jer 3:3)

Yahweh was widely confessed by the Israelite people as the one who sends rain (Deut 11:11–12; Hos 6:3; Jer 5:24; 14:22; Pss 104:10–16; 147:8; Job 5:10), but when people buy into Canaanite whoredom, Yahweh withholds it. Amos recalled Yahweh's withholding of rain that still had no appreciable effect on the people (Amos 4:7–8), Hosea saw the land mourning because of covenant infidelity (Hos 4:1–3), and Isaiah linked covenant infidelity with a mourning creation (Isa 24:4–7). Not surprisingly, Jeremiah repeats these same ideas (Jer 4:28; 12:4, 11; 14:1–10; 23:10). The drought described in Jer 14:1–6 was particularly severe; it left farmers and nobles covering their heads, wild asses losing their eyesight, and does in the field forsaking their young. All Judah lay prostrate in mourning, said Jeremiah, while the cry of Jerusalem went up. Rain was a covenant blessing, and drought a covenant curse. Deuteronomy stated that covenant obedience would bring about rain and abundant crops (Deut 11:13–15; 28:12), but if people turned to the worship of other gods, the heavens would become brass and the earth hard as iron (Deut 28:23). Without crops, the covenant people would then perish (Deut 11:16–17; 28:24).

Humans Taking On the Behavior of Animals

Jeremiah appears to presuppose a hierarchy in creation, which is transparent in Gen 1, but which is stated somewhat differently in the Yahwistic account of creation in Gen 2, where humans—male and female—rank higher in the created order and are given more responsibility than the animals, birds, and other living beings (Gen 1:26–28; 2:18–23; cf. Matt 6:26). This hierarchy, says Jeremiah in metaphor and simile, shows signs of having broken down. Humans, whether in denial, flagrant wrongdoing, or just unknowingly, have taken on the behavior of animals. In an early oracle (Jer 2:23–25a), Jeremiah compares a people chasing the Baals to a dancing young camel or a wild ass in heat:

> How can you say, "I am not defiled
> after the Baals I have not gone?"
> Check your way in the valley
> know what you have done
> A swift young camel crisscrossing her tracks
> a wild ass used to the wilderness
> in her desirous craving sniffing the wind
> in her season who can bring her back? (Jer 2:23–24)

On another occasion, Jeremiah compares a well-fed people to sex-crazed horses. Satiated men are committing adultery and cutting paths to the whorehouse. Yahweh therefore asks,

> Why should I pardon you?
> your children have forsaken me
> and have sworn by 'no-gods'
> When I fed them to the full they committed adultery
> and to a whorehouse they cut a path
> well-endowed early-rising horses they were
> Each man neighing for his neighbor's wife. (Jer 5:7–8)

The Song of Moses says that Israel, after settling in the land and enjoying its good things, returned thanks by forgetting the Grand Provider and chasing after other gods (Deut 32:13–18). Hosea found the very same thing happening in his time (Hos 2:8; 13:6).

In Jeremiah's oracle contrasting the covenant people to migratory birds (8:4–9), a people unaware of evil is compared also to warhorses charging blindly into the fray:

> Everyone turns to their course
> like a horse plunging headlong into battle. (Jer 8:6)

On yet another occasion, Jeremiah compares the man accumulating illicit gain to the partridge who tends or incubates chicks he did not bring forth. In doing a bad job of things, both end up with substantial loss:

> A partridge that brooded but did not bring forth
> is one raking in riches but not by right
> In the middle of his days he will forsake it
> and at his end he will have become a fool. (Jer 17:11)

Yahweh Creator of Heaven and Earth

Jeremiah, despite an early preoccupation with covenant infidelity and creation's undoing, showed later, precisely at the time when events were spinning wildly out of control, a rock-solid belief in Yahweh as creator of heaven and earth. At midpoint in the First Edition of the Jeremiah book (chaps 1–20) are liturgical pieces praising the God of Israel and exalting him over the gods of the nations, who, in fact, are no gods (10:1–16). The first liturgy (vv. 1–10) acknowledges Yahweh as the one true, living God, incomparable to the inert idols that have been crafted and decked out by human hands. Coming next, sandwiched in between the two liturgies, and exercising a climactic function in the larger compilation, is a playful verse debunking the gods who did not make the heavens and the earth. This verse, written in Aramaic, has perhaps been left untranslated because it preserves a pun on the words "make" and "perish":

> The gods who did not make the heavens and the earth
> these shall perish from the earth and from under the heavens.
> (Jer 10:11)

The second liturgical piece (vv. 12–16) is a hymn, basically, repeated a second time amid the Foreign Nation Oracles (51:15–19). Verse 13 is a near quotation of Ps 135:7, and vv. 12–13 have turned up in a hitherto unknown psalm from Qumran.[5] The hymn could derive from Jeremiah, or else be of unknown provenance, having simply been added to the Jeremiah book in the compilation process. Von Rad noted that "the creation and preservation of the world by Jahweh was certainly one of the principal subjects of the hymns of the Old Testament,"[6] and so it was (Pss 89:12[11]; 102:26[25]; 104:2–9; 148:5–6; Amos 4:13; 5:8–9; 9:5–6). The present hymn celebrates the greatness of Yahweh, who created the world and is the portion of Jacob:

> The Maker of the earth by his strength
> the Establisher of the world by his wisdom
> and by his understanding he stretched out the heavens
> When he utters his voice—a roar in heaven's waters
> clouds come up from the ends of the earth
> Lightning bolts for rain he made
> and he brought forth the wind from his storehouses
>
> Every human is stupid without knowledge
> every smith is very ashamed because of the idol
> For his cast image is a lie
> and no breath is in them
> They are nothing—a laughable work!
> at the time of their visitation they shall perish
>
> Not like these is the Portion of Jacob
> for the one forming everything is he
> And Israel is his tribal heritage
> Yahweh of hosts is his name. (Jer 10:12–16)

Again we see that belief in Yahweh's creation of heaven and earth goes hand in hand with a belief in Yahweh's covenant with Israel.

In an oracle to foreign envoys, spoken in connection with Jeremiah's wearing the yoke bars, Yahweh says that because he made the earth and its inhabitants by his great strength, he can and will give them over to Nebuchadnezzar, who for a time will be his servant. Yahweh says:

> I, I made the earth, human and beast that are on the face of the earth, with my great strength and with my outstretched arm, and I give it to whoever seems right in my eyes. And now I, I have given all these lands into the hand of Nebuchadnezzar, king of Babylon, my servant; and even the beasts of the field I have given him, to

5. James A. Sanders, *The Dead Sea Psalms Scroll* (Ithaca: Cornell University Press, 1967), 129–31.

6. Von Rad, *Old Testament Theology*, 1:361.

> serve him. So all the nations shall serve him and his son and his grandson until the time of his land comes—even he! Then many nations and great kings shall make him serve! (Jer 27:4–7)

In the questioning prayer that follows Jeremiah's purchase of the field at Anathoth, Yahweh is confessed by the prophet to be the matchless creator of heaven and earth. Jeremiah says: "Ah, Lord Yahweh! Look, you, you made the heavens and the earth with your great strength and with your outstretched arm. Nothing is too difficult for you" (Jer 32:17). Following immediately is a confession of Yahweh as redeemer in the Exodus and giver of the land. Jeremiah continues in his prayer:

> You have shown signs and wonders, in the land of Egypt—up to this day—and in Israel and among humankind, and you made for yourself a name, as at this day. And you brought your people Israel out from the land of Egypt with signs and wonders and with a strong hand and with an outstretched arm and with great terror, and you gave to them this land that you swore to their fathers to give to them, a land flowing with milk and honey. And they came in and took possession of it, but they did not obey your voice and in your law did not walk; everything that you commanded them to do, they did not do, so you made them meet up with all this evil. (Jer 32:20–23)

The paired confessions of Yahweh as creator of heaven and earth and as redeemer of Israel are foils for a concluding indictment of covenant disobedience. Something similar occurs early on in the Song of Moses (Deut 32:1–18). In both Genesis creation accounts we observe an intentional balancing of creation and fall. The Yahwist writer transparently juxtaposes creation and fall in Gen 2–3, and the Priestly writer, in framing the Yahwistic narrative, comes up with a creation and fall of his own in Genesis 1 and 6–9, the latter being his story of the flood.

Von Rad and others believed that creation theology developed late in ancient Israel, the earlier focus being on Yahweh's redemption of Israel from Egyptian slavery (Isa 45:12–13; Neh 9:6–15). According to this view, exodus faith was the prior faith in ancient Israel.[7] But it is now believed by many scholars that creation ideas were very old, entered Israel at an early time, and were well established in the preexilic period, probably by

7. Von Rad, "The Theological Problem of the Old Testament Doctrine of Creation," 131–43; and von Rad *Old Testament Theology*, 1:124, 136–39.

the early monarchy (1 Kgs 8:22–23; 2 Kgs 19:15).[8] Creation theology in Jeremiah, for this reason and for others, is assuredly not late.[9] It occurs in Jer 27:5 and 32:17, as we have seen, and exists elsewhere in the book.[10]

Yahweh Creator and Re-creator of Nations

In Jeremiah's early preaching is a striking oracle about Yahweh recreating nations—Israel first and foremost, but also other nations. This oracle, which came to the prophet in a visit to the potter's shop (Jer 18:1–10), draws on imagery from the Yahwistic account of creation, where the Divine Potter is said to have "formed" man out of clay from the ground, and then breathed into him the breath of life (Gen 2:7–8). From the clay Yahweh also "formed" the beasts of the field and the birds of the air (Gen 2:19). The same Hebrew verb occurs when Yahweh tells Jeremiah of having "formed" him in the womb of his mother (Jer 1:5), and denotes Yahweh's creative work elsewhere in the Old Testament (Amos 4:13; Jer 10:16[=51:19]; 33:2; Pss 94:9; 104:26).

In the potter's shop, Jeremiah sees the potter remaking a spoiled vessel. In the oracle that follows, Yahweh says, how much more does he exercise the same sort of control over nations, including Israel, remaking them if it becomes necessary? The divine action is not arbitrary. It depends on a prior divine word about Yahweh tearing down or building up, and nations responding by committing evil or repenting of evil. Yahweh says:

> Like this potter am I not able to do to you, house of Israel?—oracle of Yahweh. Look! Like clay in the hand of the potter, so are you in my hand, house of Israel. At one moment I will speak concerning a nation or concerning a kingdom to uproot or to break down or to destroy, and that nation against which I spoke turns from its evil, then I will repent concerning the evil that I planned to do to it. And at one moment I will speak concerning a nation or

8. Schmid, "Creation, Righteousness, and Salvation," 111; George M. Landes, "Creation and Liberation," in Bernhard W. Anderson, ed., *Creation in the Old Testament*, 136–37; Terence E. Fretheim, *God and World in the Old Testament* (Nashville: Abingdon, 2005).

9. Jeremiah's "Vision of Cosmic Destruction" in Jer 4:23–26 clearly presupposes the Genesis 1 creation account. The P material, following Y. Kaufmann, is now dated by many scholars to the preexilic period; cf. Jack R. Lundbom, *Jeremiah 21–36*, AB 21B (New Haven: Yale University Press, 2004), 451.

10. Lundbom, *Jeremiah 21–36*, 312–13.

> concerning a kingdom to build or to plant, and it does evil in my eyes, not hearing my voice, then I will repent concerning the good that I thought to benefit it. (Jer 18:6–10)

Here and throughout the Jeremiah book are references to building and planting. Yahweh not only uproots and breaks down, he builds up and plants (Jer 1:10; 12:14–17; 24:6; 31:28; 32:41; 42:10; 45:4). This realization of divine upbuilding may have dawned upon Jeremiah in the potter's shop, but more than likely it came earlier. Already in his call to holy office, the young Jeremiah is informed by Yahweh that his appointment over nations and kingdoms is

> to uproot and to break down
> and to destroy and to overthrow
> to build up and to plant. (Jer 1:10)

Baruch, Jeremiah's scribe and friend, learned to his sorrow that Yahweh was currently busy with the overthrowing and uprooting of nations (Jer 45:4; cf. 27:5–7). But the day would come when Yahweh would once again build up and plant, and the latter would be a work of re-creation.

Jeremiah tells the covenant people, at a time of painful uprooting, that in Babylon and later in the homeland it can look forward to once again being built up. Israel's re-creation is the dominant theme of Jeremiah's Letters to the Exiles (chap. 29), which are to be dated shortly after the first deportation in 597 BC. The two letters (29:1–23, 24–28) echo the "be fruitful and multiply" word of Gen 1:28:

> Build houses and live in them, and plant gardens and eat their fruit. Take wives and beget sons and daughters, and take for your sons wives, and your daughters give to husbands, and let them bear sons and daughters. Yes, multiply there, and do not decrease . . . Build houses and live in them; and plant gardens and eat their fruit. (Jer 29:5–6, 28)

In a couple other future-oriented oracles, Jeremiah speaks of Yahweh building up a united Israel and Judah in the homeland. In the first, the verb "sow" is used, an echo of Hos 2:23:

> Look, days are coming—oracle of Yahweh—when I will sow the house of Israel and the house of Judah with the seed of human and the seed of beast.

> And it will be, as I have watched over them to uproot and to break down and to overthrow and to destroy, also to bring evil, so I will watch over them to build and to plant—oracle of Yahweh. (Jer 31:27–28)

Jeremiah along with other prophets is clear about Israel multiplying in its own land after Yahweh's destructive work is completed (Jer 3:16; 23:3; 30:19; cf. Hos 1:10; Ezek 36:8–11; Isa 49:20–21; 54:1–3). Re-creation will occur also in other nations. Jer 12:14–17 says that Israel's enemies, after their own uprooting, will be returned to their land and will be built up if they learn Yahweh's ways and swear by Yahweh's name.

Yahweh's Covenant with Creation

Some oracles in the book of Jeremiah speak of Yahweh as a God who keeps covenant with his creation, an idea that appears to develop from the Noachian covenant in Gen 9:8–17. The Noachian covenant is unconditional and everlasting, like the covenants made with Abraham (Gen 15:5; 17:7, 13–14), David (2 Sam 7:12–16), and Phinehas the priest (Num 25:11–13).[11] Each of the latter, not surprisingly, finds a place in one or more of the present oracles. The Noachian covenant was made with every living creature on earth; Yahweh promised never again to destroy them as he did in the flood. This effectively puts a cap on Yahweh's destructive work for all future time.

Jeremiah in a couple brief oracles first affirms Yahweh's eternal covenant with creation (the Noachian covenant), then in a protasis-apodosis argument Yahweh's covenant with the seed of Israel (the Abrahamic covenant). If the former cannot cease, neither can the latter:

> Thus said Yahweh
>   who gives the sun for light by day
> statutes of the moon and stars
>   for light by night
> Who stirs up the sea so its waves roar
>   Yahweh of hosts is his name
>
> If these statutes depart
>   from before me—oracle of Yahweh

11. David Noel Freedman, "Divine Commitment and Human Obligation," *Int* 18 (1964) 419–31; reprinted in John R. Huddlestun, ed., *Divine Commitment and Human Obligation* (Grand Rapids: Eerdmans, 1997), 168–78.

> Then the seed of Israel shall cease
> from being a nation before me—all the days.
> (Jer 31:35–36)

The mention here of "statutes" puts the emphasis not upon Yahweh's initial creation but upon Yahweh's regulation of creation over time (cf. Jer 5:24; 33:20, 25).

Another oracle argues along similar lines. In it Yahweh says he has established an eternal covenant with day and night, which must refer to what is stated in Gen 8:22 (Rashi):

> As long as the earth endures
> seedtime and harvest, cold and heat
> summer and winter, day and night
> shall not cease. (Gen 8:22)

This covenant is apparently another that cannot be broken, making it like the covenants with Noah, David, and the Levitical priests. The covenant with the Levitical priests is the covenant of peace made with Phinehas. The present Jeremiah oracle reads as follows:

> Thus said Yahweh: If you could break my covenant of the day and my covenant of the night, so daytime and night would not come at their appointed time, then could my covenant be broken with David, my servant, so there would not be for him a son reigning on his throne, also with the Levitical priests, my ministers. (Jer 33:20–21)

The continuance of the Davidic covenant is argued on the basis of Yahweh's (prior) covenant with creation in Ps 89:19–37.

A final oracle in the expanded Book of Restoration (chaps. 30–33) uses another protasis-apodosis argument to assert Yahweh's eternal covenants with creation, Abraham, and David:

> Thus said Yahweh: If indeed I have not established my covenant of daytime and night—statutes of heaven and earth—then the seed of Jacob and David, my servant, I will reject, not taking from his seed rulers unto the seed of Abraham, Isaac, and Jacob, for I will surely restore their fortunes, and I will show them mercy. (Jer 33:25–26)

Yahweh and a New Creation

For the grand prophecies of creation and a new creation we must wait until Second Isaiah, who digs deeper than Jeremiah into hoary antiquity to resurrect mythical ideas about the creation of the world. In Isa 51:1–10 this lyrical prophet of the exile combines creation motifs with remembrances of Abraham and Sarah, then Israel's deliverance through the Sea.

The cryptic remark by Jeremiah in Jer 31:22b, which concludes the core poetry in an early Book of Restoration (chaps. 30–31), is not a serious statement on the new creation, although it was given literal and positive interpretation in Targum Jonathan and the LXX, also by Jerome and Kimḥi, among others.[12] It is rather gentle irony from the prophet, expressing incredulity at the weakness of Judah's soldiers in defeat. As such, it represents a reversal of the created order. Jeremiah says,

> For Yahweh has created a new thing on earth
> the female protects the man! (Jer 31:22b)

Language here comes straight out of Gen 1 ("create" and "female" in Gen 1:1 and 27).

Another cryptic word spoken by Jeremiah while he was shut up in the court of the guard just before Jerusalem fell to the Babylonians, does anticipate a new creation. Yahweh speaks here about hidden things held in store for the future; Jeremiah in an embellished messenger formula uses language straight out of Gen 2–3 ("make" and "form" in Gen 2:4b, 7–8, 19; 3:1):

> Thus said Yahweh who made it
> Yahweh who formed it to establish it
> Yahweh is his name
> Call to me and I will answer you
> and let me tell you great and hidden things
> you have not known. (Jer 33:2–3)

The great New Testament scholar Johannes Weiss, commenting on the obscure beginnings of the nascent church, said that all of God's great works begin in secret (cf. Ps 139:13–16).[13] Here we learn from Jeremiah

12. Lundbom, *Jeremiah 21–36*, 452.

13. Johannes Weiss, *Earliest Christianity*, vol. 1, trans. Frederick C. Grant (New York: Harper, 1959), 14.

that Yahweh is holding in store for the covenant people secret things that will constitute a wonderful new creation.

9

The Confessions of Jeremiah[1]

The Confessions Are Mostly Laments

In Jeremiah we are accustomed to speak of the prophet's confessions, so named because of their likeness to the *Confessions* of Saint Augustine. These are a singular legacy of Jeremiah, for in them the prophet is not so much speaking Yahweh's word with power and passion, although some of this is definitely to be found in them, but rather telling us how he feels about what is going on, and what impact his preaching is having on him personally. We see in these confessions the other side of Jeremiah's role as mediator and divine messenger, which is to bring concerns of the people along with some of his own before Yahweh. The confessions are then a legacy of Jeremiah's prayer life.

No other prophet bares his soul to the extent Jeremiah does. Since most all the confessions are in poetry, we are probably closer to the prophet's own words than is the case in compositions of prose. The Old Testament preserves prayers, personal utterances, and dialogues of other covenant mediators, the most prominent being Moses, Samuel, Elijah, and Amos, but all are embodied in narrative. Elijah makes complaints like those of Jeremiah (1 Kgs 19:10, 14), but from him and the literate prophets coming later we have nothing even approaching the corpus of Jeremianic confessions. The only Old Testament discourse that can be compared to the confessions are the Psalms, which are

1. *Jeremiah Closer Up: The Prophet and the Book*, Hebrew Bible Monographs 31 (Sheffield: Sheffield Phoenix, 2010), 75–103.

also in poetic verse, and convey similarly an intimacy that has made them an unrivaled spiritual and human treasure down through the ages.

Most all the Jeremianic confessions are laments, basically, precisely the sort of which we find in the Psalter. Only one confession expresses confidence in besting an enemy (20:11–12), and only one is a ringing word of praise (20:13). From Jeremiah come also a few communal laments, which again have their prototypes in the Jerusalem psalm book.

Scholars of the early nineteenth century noted the similarity between Jeremiah's confessions and the Psalms, attributing certain psalms to Jeremiah, such as we find in some LXX and Vulgate manuscripts. But the scholar responsible for the pioneering work in comparing psalms in the Psalter to the confessions of Jeremiah was Hermann Gunkel (1862–1932), who was followed by Walter Baumgartner and an important monograph of 1917, titled *Jeremiah's Poems of Lament*.[2] Baumgartner demonstrated in copious detail that Jeremiah's laments were little different from laments in the Psalter. More recent studies have been done on the Jeremianic laments, but none advances significantly the work of Baumgartner, except to show occasional literary features not examined by Gunkel and his form-critical colleagues.[3]

In speaking here about individual and communal laments we are not talking about laments that mourn the dead, which are dirges, basically—a different type of composition entirely. Karl Budde is credited with the important work on the *qînâ* genre,[4] shown to be a carefully crafted dirge (3:2 rhythm) sung mainly but not exclusively by women leading people in mourning the dead (cf. Jer 9:17–22). According to the Chronicler, Jeremiah uttered a dirge over King Josiah (2 Chr 35:25), but it is not included in the book. Other compositions of this type, however, are (Jer 22:10, 18–19, 28–30).

2. Walter Baumgartner, *Jeremiah's Poems of Lament*, trans. David E. Orton, Historic Texts and Interpreters in Biblical Scholarship (Sheffield: Almond, 1988).

3. A. R. Diamond, *The Confessions of Jeremiah in Context*, JSOTSup 45 (Sheffield: JSOT Press, 1987); Kathleen M. O'Connor, *The Confessions of Jeremiah*, SBLDS 94 (Atlanta: Scholars, 1988); Mark S. Smith, *The Laments of Jeremiah in Their Contexts*, SBLMS 42 (Atlanta: Scholars, 1990).

4. Karl Budde, "Das hebräische Klagelied," *ZAW* 2 (1882) 1–52.

Individual and Communal Laments in the Psalter

After completing two major works on Genesis,[5] Gunkel turned his attention to the Psalms and a study of literary genres. His first book on selected psalms was published in 1904;[6] a year earlier some essays were translated into English.[7] In 1926 Gunkel published a Psalms commentary,[8] which was followed in 1930 by an important article on the Psalms in *RGG*².[9] The latter was translated into English and appeared in the little Facet book, *The Psalms: A Form-Critical Introduction.*[10] Gunkel's major work on the Psalms, completed by Joachim Begrich, was published posthumously in 1933.[11]

Considerably more important than Gunkel's early articles on selected Psalms were his essays outlining a program of "form-criticism" for Old Testament study.[12] This program sought to identify literary "forms" or "types" (*Gattungen*; genres). Gunkel's larger goal was to write a history of Israelite literature. This never got done, but the many and various literary genres

5. Hermann Gunkel, *Schöpfung und Chaos in Urzeit und Endzeit*; English: *Creation and Chaos in the Primeval Era and the Eschaton*, trans. K. William Whitney Jr., Biblical Resource Series (Grand Rapids: Eerdmans, 2006); Gunkel, *Genesis*, trans. Mark E. Biddle, Mercer Library of Biblical Studies (Macon, GA: Mercer University Press, 1997).

6. Gunkel, *Ausgewählte Psalmen übersetzt und erklärt*, 3rd ed. (Göttingen: Vandenhoeck & Ruprecht, 1911).

7. Psalms 1, 8, 19:1–6, 24, 42, 43, 46, 103, and 137 appeared in *Biblical World* for 1903.

8. See Muilenburg's "Introduction" to Gunkel, *The Psalms: A Form-Critical Introduction*, Facet Books, Biblical Series 19 (Philadelphia: Fortress, 1967), vii.

9. *RGG*² 4 (1930) 1609–27; Gunkel wrote an earlier article on the Psalms in *RGG*¹ 4 (1912) 1927–49.

10. Gunkel, *The Psalms: A Form-Critical Introduction.*

11. Gunkel, *Introduction to Psalms*, completed by Joachim Begrich, trans. James D. Nogalski, Mercer Library of Biblical Studies (Macon, GA: Mercer University Press, 1998).

12. Gunkel, "Die Grundprobleme der israelitischen Literaturgeschichte," *DLZ* 29 (1906) 1797–1800; 1861–66. [English: "Fundamental Problems of Hebrew Literary History," in Gunkel, *What Remains of the Old Testament and Other Essays*, trans. A. K. Dallas (London: Allen & Unwin, 1928), 57–68; Gunkel, "Israelite Literary History," in Gunkel, *Water for a Thirsty Land*, ed. K. C. Hanson (Minneapolis: Fortress, 2001), 31–41]; Gunkel, "Die israelitische Literatur," in Paul Hinneberg, ed., *Die Kultur der Gegenwart: Die orientalischen Literaturen* I. 7 (Berlin Teubner, 1906), 51–102; Gunkel, "Die Religionsgeschichte und die alttestamentliche Wissenschaft," in Max Fischer und Friedrich Michael Schiele, eds., *Fünfter Weltkongress für freies Christentum und religiösen Fortschritt, Berlin 5. bis 10. August 1910, Protokoll der Verhandlungen* (Berlin: Protestantischen Schriftenvertriebs, 1910), 169–80 [English: *The History of Religion and Old Testament Criticism* (Berlin: Protestantischer, 1911)].

preserved in the Old Testament were identified, with extraordinary results for both Old and New Testament study. In the Psalms, Gunkel found the main genres to be the hymn, community and individual lament, thank offering, song of the individual, and royal psalm. Other minor types and some mixed types were also recognized. Psalm genres were then compared to similar genres elsewhere in the Bible, also to similar genres outside the Bible (e.g., to the Babylonian psalms).

Gunkel sought to identify the *Sitz im Leben* ("situation in life") for each of the genres. Hymns, he said, were sung in the temple; lawsuits originated in the city gate; prophetic oracles were uttered in the outer courtyard of the temple; victory songs were sung by the conquering hero returning from battle; dirges were intoned over the bier of the dead; priestly rituals and liturgies were recited in the sanctuary.[13] Communal laments were recited at times of crop failure or pestilence, or when danger from an enemy threatened.

Gunkel took particular note of typical vocabulary in each genre, having been influenced here by Eduard Norden,[14] who believed that people in antiquity were more tied to convention than people today. The hymn, e.g., begins with "Sing to Yahweh" (*šîrû layhwh*); the dirge begins "Ah How!" (*hôy*); and the prophetic invective "Woe to those" (*hôy* + participle).[15] Gunkel cited for comparison modern examples of conventional beginnings, e.g., the fairy tale begins: "Once upon a time"; the letter begins: "Dear Sir"; and the sermon begins: "Beloved in the Lord."[16]

Stereotyped opening phrases were an aid to delimiting literary units, although Gunkel and subsequent form-critics more often delimited units on the basis of content. In the Psalms content and later chapter numbers made beginnings and endings fairly straightforward. But things were more difficult in the Prophets, where the most form-critical help in delimiting oracles came from messenger formulas when they were present: "Thus said Yahweh," and "oracle of Yahweh."[17] These occur most often at the beginning or end of the prophetic oracle, occasionally at both beginning and end. Rarely, at least in Jeremiah, do they come in the center.

13. Muilenburg, "Introduction," in Gunkel, *The Psalms: A Form-Critical Introduction*, v–vi.

14. Eduard Norden, *Die Antike Kunstprosa*, 1–2 (Stuttgart: Teubner, 1958).

15. Gunkel, "Israelite Literary History," 33.

16. Gunkel, *Introduction to Psalms*, 17.

17. Ludwig Köhler, *Deuterojesaja (Jesaja 40–55) stilkritisch untersucht*, BZAW 37 (Giessen: Töpelmann, 1923).

Gunkel, being primarily interested in the preliterary stage of Israelite literature, believed that oral literature was characterized by loose connections, an idea he apparently got from Johann Herder, who spoke of prophetic utterances as being like "pearls on a string."[18] The observation is basically a sound one, for we now know the importance of key words and catchwords in Hebrew composition—oral and written. Both occur in individual psalms and in psalm compilations. Martin Buber said, "The recurrence of key words is a basic law of composition in the Psalms."[19]

Gunkel believed that in laments of the individual, as well as in other songs of the individual, the *I* of the poet represented the individual. He therefore disagreed with Rudolph Smend,[20] who claimed that the *I* in the Psalter was a personification of the community. In Gunkel's view, the community would be personified only in cases of intense suffering (Lam 1:9; 11:16, 18–19), in places where the poet explicitly said so (Ps 129:1), or where it was clearly demanded by the sense (Mic 7:7–10; Isa 21:10; *Ps Sol* 1). Unless these indications were present—and they are infrequent—the *I* is the poet himself. Gunkel thought Smend's view was a remnant of the allegorical interpretation of Scripture prevailing earlier.[21] The debate was renewed in the past century, with Henning Reventlow arguing for a collective *I* in the Jeremiah confessions,[22] and John Bright arguing that the *I* is Jeremiah expressing his own personal distress.[23] The view of Gunkel and Bright, in my opinion, is more likely.

Gunkel believed the Hebrew Psalter contained a rich collection of poetry of the individual, calling it "the imperishable treasure in the Psalter." These songs, in his view, are the prototypes of Protestant hymnody.[24] The main parts of the Individual and communal lament are the following:[25]

18. J. G. Herder, *The Spirit of Hebrew Poetry*, trans. James Marsh (Burlington, VT: Smith, 1833), 1:81.

19. Martin Buber, *Good and Evil*, trans. Ronald Gregor Smith and Michael Bullock (New York: Scribner, 1953), 52.

20. Rudolf Smend, "Ueber das Ich der Psalmen," *ZAW* 8 (1888) 49–147.

21. Gunkel, *The Psalms: A Form-Critical Introduction*, 15–17.

22. Henning Graf Reventlow, *Liturgie und prophetisches Ich bei Jeremia* (Gütersloh: Mohn, 1963).

23. Bright, "Jeremiah's Complaints: Liturgy, or Expressions of Personal Distress?," in John I. Durham and J. R. Porter, eds., *Proclamation and Presence: Essays in Honour of G. Henton Davies* (Richmond: John Knox, 1970), 189–214.

24. Gunkel, *The Psalms: A Form-Critical Introduction*, 33.

25. Ibid., 34–35.

a. the lament proper, depicting the suffering of the poet, the purpose of which is to move Yahweh to compassion. The laments are very emotional. They often complain about enemies who are mocking the poet in his misery and waiting for his death. The poet, for his part, either expresses his innocence and tries to persuade God to recognize the same (Pss 17 and 26) or confesses his sin and asks for forgiveness (Ps 51).[26] Gunkel noted individual laments protesting innocence in both Jeremiah and Job.[27]

b. an entreaty to Yahweh to remove the calamity, whatever it may be. Often is a plea for divine revenge. All kinds of arguments are used. Expressions of confidence may be included. Gunkel noted the moving alternation of passionate laments and entreaties, on the one hand, and confident hope on the other (Pss 3, 123, 130).

c. certainty of a hearing (Ps 22). In some cases the answer of certainty may have been proclaimed by the priest in God's name.[28]

Individual laments in the Psalter include Pss 3, 5, 6, 7, 13, 17, 22, 25, 26, and others. Communal laments include Pss 44, 74, 79, 80, 83, 89:38–51, 94:1–7, and others. In Jeremiah, Gunkel identified Jer 3:22b–25 and 14:7–9, 19–22 as communal laments, containing confessions of sin. The communal lament in Jeremiah 14 was recited during a severe drought (Jer 14:2–6).

Rhetoric and Composition in the Psalms

More recent work in the Psalms has focused on rhetoric and composition. Mitchell Dahood, for example, found many examples of inclusio in individual psalms.[29] Some examples:

Psalm 1 "the assembly of sinners" (v. 1) and "the assembly of the wicked" (v. 6)

Psalm 17 "a righteous (cause)" (v. 1) and "in righteousness" (v. 15)

26. Ibid., 13–15, 19–22.

27. Ibid., 36.

28. Ibid., 14–15.

29. Mitchell Dahood, *Psalms 1–50*, AB 16 (Garden City, NY: Doubleday, 1966); Dahood, *Psalms 51–100*, AB 17 (Garden City, NY: Doubleday, 1968); *Psalms 101–150*, AB 17A (Garden City, NY: Doubleday, 1970).

Psalm 16 "I have trusted in Yahweh" (v. 1) and "I will bless Yahweh" (v. 12)

Psalm 30 "O Yahweh my God" (v. 2) and "O Yahweh my God" (v. 12)

Psalm 69 "Save me" (v. 1) and "God will save Zion" (v. 35)

Psalm 70 "O Yahweh . . . help me" (v. 1) and "my helper . . . O Yahweh" (v. 5)

Psalm 84 "O Yahweh of hosts" (v. 1) and "O Yahweh of hosts" (v. 12)

In Psalm 8 is a hymnic inclusio:

> O Yahweh, our Lord
> how majestic is your name in all the earth. (v. 1)
>
> O Yahweh, our Lord
> how majestic is your name in all the earth. (v. 9)

Psalms 106, 135, and 146–150 begin and end with "Praise Yahweh," likewise Psalm 105, if the "Praise Yahweh" ending 104 is placed where it belongs at the beginning of 105, since Ps 104 is a "Bless Yahweh, O my soul" psalm. Pss 103 and 104 have "Bless Yahweh, O my soul," at both beginning and end.

Key words link psalms in composition. Pss 1 and 2 are linked by the term *'ašrê* ("Blessed / Happy") in Pss 1:1 and 2:12. Muilenburg[30] showed too how Pss 20 and 21 have been linked by key words. In Ps 20:4 the king, departing for battle, is blessed with the words:

> *May he give you* according to *your heart*

Then in Ps 21:2, after returning victorious, the king praises Yahweh, saying,

> *You have given him his heart's* desire

Individual and Communal Laments of Jeremiah

Gunkel believed that prophets used lyric poetry and other literary forms to give expression to their feelings or to make an impression on people who

30. Muilenburg, "Psalms 20–21" (unpublished paper read at the 1956 Annual Meeting of the Society of Biblical Literature).

were receptive to such forms.[31] In his view, the laments of Jeremiah—both individual and communal—were imitations of genres from the cult. Since Jeremiah carried out his entire ministry in Jerusalem, he would doubtless have been influenced by temple worship, and would have known lament forms intimately. Gunkel thought prophets prepared confessions in anticipation of the day when Israel would repent (Hos 6:1–3; 14:2–3; Jer 14:7–9, 19–22), or they would compose a hymn of joy to be sung when people were delivered from some present distress. In prophetic material, Gunkel found the lament usually to have two parts: 1) a passionate appeal; and 2) a divine response. Many of the Jeremiah laments are joined with divine responses, but not all of them are. There are other combinations: for example, some laments appear in dialogues containing multiple speakers (Jer 8:18–21; 17:13–16a), and in other configurations. In Jer 20:7–13 a lament is followed by a hymn of confidence and a final word celebrating deliverance.

While Gunkel and Baumgartner made observations on typical vocabulary and phraseology in the lament, greater insights into style, rhetoric, and composition have come from rhetorical criticism carried out by Muilenburg and others.[32] Rhetorical criticism looks not so much for typical features in biblical discourse as for features that make it unique.[33]

Delimitation of the Jeremianic compositions, as we have said, is considerably more difficult than delimitation of the Psalms. Here both rhetorical and nonrhetorical criteria must be used, which for the Jeremiah laments would be the following:

a. shifts from poetry to prose, or prose to poetry
b. rhetorical structures delimiting laments and giving internal structures (repetitions, inclusio, chiasmus)

31. Gunkel, *The Psalms: A Form-Critical Introduction*, 1–2.

32. Muilenburg, "Form Criticism and Beyond," *JBL* 88 (1969) 1–18, reprinted in Thomas Best, ed., *Hearing and Speaking the Word: Selections from the Works of James Muilenburg*, Scholars Press Homage Series (Chico, CA: Scholars, 1984), 27–44; and in Paul R. House, ed., *Beyond Form Criticism: Essays in Old Testament Literary Criticism*, Sources for Biblical and Theological Study 2 (Winona Lake, IN: Eisenbrauns, 1992), 49–69; Jack R. Lundbom, *Jeremiah: A Study in Ancient Hebrew Rhetoric*, SBLDS 18 (Missoula, MT: Society of Biblical Literature, 1975); 2nd ed.: Winona Lake, IN: Eisenbrauns, 1997; Lundbom, *Jeremiah 1–20*, AB 21A (New York: Doubleday, 1999; New Haven: Yale University Press, 2004); Lundbom, *Jeremiah 21–36*, AB 21B (New York: Doubleday; New Haven: Yale University Press, 2009); Lundbom, *Jeremiah 37–52*, AB 21C (New York: Doubleday; New Haven: Yale University Press, 2004).

33. Muilenburg, "Form Criticism and Beyond," 4–5.

c. section markings (*setumah* and *petuḥah*)
d. content, including personal pronouns for individual and communal laments, and vocabulary typical of the lament form
e. divine answers, and the presence of the divine *I* and messenger formulas in the prophetic oracles ("Thus said Yahweh" and "oracle of Yahweh")

What follows are brief descriptions of seventeen—perhap nineteen—laments in the book of Jeremiah. Most but not all have been identified by Gunkel and Baumgartner. Three laments are communal, and all are penitential. Individual laments in almost every case contain a protestation of innocence, although in one Jeremiah pleads for divine correction.

Jeremiah 3:21–25

Here is a prophetic word calling people to repentance (vv. 21–22a), followed by a communal lament with a confession (vv. 22b–25). The latter brings to a quiet end the harsh oracles on apostasy and repentance in chapters 2–3. The lament is identified as communal by the "we" in v. 22b (Gunkel), and by "our God" in vv. 22b and 23. The prose of vv. 24–25 expands the confession. Key words link the call for repentance with the communal lament, also the communal lament with its expansion in vv. 24–25 (in small caps). The communal lament and expansion both have internal key-word balance (in italics). Section markings delimit the larger unit of vv. 21–25 at top and bottom. At the end of v. 25 is also the chapter division.

Prophetic call to repentance:

21 A cry on the bare heights is heard
the weeping supplications of ISRAEL's children
For they have perverted their way
they have forgotten YAHWEH THEIR GOD

22a Return, turnable children
I will heal your turning away

Communal lament with confession:

22b Look we, we have come to you
for you are YAHWEH OUR GOD

[23]*Surely*, The Lie is from the hills
Noise of the Mountains
Surely, in **YAHWEH OUR GOD**
is the salvation of **ISRAEL**.

[24]The Shame has consumed what *our fathers* worked for, *from our youth*—their flocks and their herds, their sons and their daughters. [25]Let us lie down in our shame and let our dishonor cover us, for against **YAHWEH OUR GOD** we have sinned—we and *our fathers, from our youth* unto this day. We have not obeyed the voice of **YAHWEH OUR GOD**.

The prophetic word was recited by a liturgist, perhaps even Jeremiah, with the communal lament intended for recitation by the congregation. The prophetic word alternates speakers: The liturgist speaks in v. 21 ("they have forgotten Yahweh their God"), and Yahweh speaks in v. 22a: ("I will heal your turning away"). Gunkel believed that Jeremiah in the communal lament was anticipating the day when Israel would see her waywardness and repent.[34]

Jeremiah 4:19–22

Here two poetic compositions appear to go together as an individual lament (vv. 19–21) and a divine response (v. 22). Commentators routinely treat the passages together. Gunkel does not discuss the lament, but Baumgartner says that vv. 19–21 echo the lament style.[35] Artur Weiser identified vv. 19–21 as a lament (*Klage*).[36] The lament is delimited by section markings at both top and bottom. No section marking, however, is present after v. 22. The divine response lacks a messenger formula, but "my people" and "me" at the beginning indicate that Yahweh is speaking. Both the lament and the divine response have intricate key-word structures (in italics).[37]

Jeremiah's lament:

[19]My innards, my innards, let me writhe
the walls of *my heart*

34. Gunkel, *The Psalms: A Form-Critical Introduction*, 14; similarly Rashi and others.

35. Baumgartner, *Jeremiah's Poems of Lament*, 83.

36. Artur Weiser, *Das Buch Jeremia 1–25*, 8th ed., ATD 20 (Göttingen: Vandenhoeck & Ruprecht, 1981).

37. Lundbom, *Jeremiah 1–20*, 350–51.

it roars to me, *my heart*
I cannot be still

For the sound of the trumpet you hear
my soul, the *shout* of battle
[20]Crash upon crash resounds
for all the land is *devastated*
suddenly my tents are *devastated*
in a moment my curtains
[21]How long must I see the *flag*
must I hear the sound of the trumpet?

Divine response:

[22]For my people are fools
me *they do not know*
stupid children are *they*
not discerning are *they*
wise are they to do evil
but to do good, *they do not know*.

In this lament Jeremiah articulates his own hurt and the hurt of his nation. Both are sick. In the second part he converses with himself (v. 19c: "you hear / my soul"), and at the end he asks how long his suffering must go on. Yahweh in answering does not say how long; he only attests to the people's foolishness. Volz calls this "Yahweh's lament."[38] If Jeremiah has a hurt, so does Yahweh.

Jeremiah 8:18–21

This utterance from the prophet is a three-way dialogue between Jeremiah, the people, and Yahweh, who interrupts unexpectedly in the center. It is structured into a speaker chiasmus, with Jeremiah's lament coming at beginning and end, and the other voices speaking in between.[39] The upper limit is secured by a section before v. 18. The lower limit has been in doubt, with the next section coming after 9:3. Older scholars, including Baumgartner, extended the present unit to include 9:1, which is not correct. The unit

38. Paul Volz, *Der Prophet Jeremia*, 2nd ed., KAT 10 (1928; reprinted, Leipzig: Deichert, 1983).

39. Lundbom, *Jeremiah 1–20*, 528–29.

is 8:18–21 (RSV, NRSV). The following poem, another individual lament, is delimited as 8:22—9:2. Baumgartner does, however, correctly discern the sequence of speakers in vv. 18–21.[40] Gunkel does not discuss the present verses as a lament.

Jeremiah: 18My joy is gone
    grief is upon me
    my heart is sick

People: 19Listen! a voice (a cry of my dear people from a land far off):
    "*Is* Yahweh not in Zion?
    Is her King not in her?"

Yahweh: *So why* have they provoked me to anger with their images
    with their foreign nothings?

People: 20The harvest is past
    the summer is ended
    and we are not saved!

Jeremiah: 21For the brokenness of my dear people
    I am broken, I mourn
    desolation has gripped me.

In v. 19 is a threefold rhetorical question in the "Is . . . Is . . . So why . . ." form, a signature of the prophet. Its use here differs from elsewhere in the book, with Yahweh interrupting two questions from the people with a third of his own. The first-person pronouns in vv. 18 and 21 are the prophet lamenting. The people in their laments speak directly to the calamity at hand, their questions in v. 19a and desperation statement in v. 20 indicating hopelessness in the face of a menacing enemy. There is no divine response to these multiple laments. Yahweh has spoken climactically in the center, indicting the people with a question they would just as soon not answer.

Jeremiah 8:22—9:2

This individual lament is spoken entirely by Jeremiah. In a larger chiasmus of 8:22—9:11, it balances another individual lament (with divine response) in 9:10–11. At the midpoint in this rhetorical structure are divine oracles

40. Baumgartner, *Jeremiah's Poems of Lament*, 84.

on reckless use of the tongue.[41] Since this structure appears to be editorial, no correlation is evident between the laments and the divine oracles. The limits of the present lament are determined by a rhetorical structure consisting of interlocking ending and beginning repetitions (in italics). The very last line is later expansion. Gunkel does not identify these verses as a lament, except to say that 9:1 uses language of the individual lament.[42] Baumgartner includes the first two verses with the lament in 8:18–21.[43]

> 22*Is* there no balm in Gilead?
>   *Is* there no healer there?
> Indeed *so why* has it not arisen
>   healing for *my dear people?*
>
> 1*Who can make* my head waters
>   and my eyes a well of tears
> So I might weep day and night
>   for the slain of *my dear people?*
>
> 2*Who can make* for me in the desert
>   a traveler's lodge
> So I might forsake my people
>   and go away from them?
>
> For all of them are adulterers, a faithless bunch.

This lament also employs the threefold rhetorical question, "Is . . . Is . . . So why . . . ," which we just saw in 8:19. Jeremiah complains because there appears to be no healing for Judah. He can only weep over the slain, wishing he could abandon his people by escaping into the wilderness.

Jeremiah 9:10–11

This individual lament (v. 10), as was just mentioned, balances the lament in 8:22—9:2, where two laments frame divine oracles in an editorial chiasmus. This lament, however, has a divine response (v. 11), to which it is linked by key words (in small caps). The response has no messenger formula, but the *I* in this verse has to be Yahweh speaking. The lament and divine response are delimited by section markings at top and bottom. Gunkel says v. 10

41. Lundbom, *Jeremiah 1–20*, 534–36.

42. Gunkel, *Introduction to Psalms*, 155.

43. Baumgartner, *Jeremiah's Poems of Lament*, 84.

is a communal lament heard somewhere in the city.[44] Baumgartner says Jeremiah is alluding to or making use of the dirge.[45]

Jeremiah's lament:

[10]Over the mountains I make weeping and lament
  and over pastures of the wild a dirge

For they are burned, **WITHOUT A PERSON** passing through
  they do not hear the sound of cattle
From birds of the skies to the beasts
  they have fled, they are gone

Divine response:

[11]I will make Jerusalem a heap of stones
  a den of jackals
And the cities of Judah I will make a desolation
  WITHOUT INHABITANT.

In 9:1 Jeremiah wept over the slain of Judah. Here he weeps over a burned and desolate land. Yahweh says in his response that Jeremiah can expect more of the same. Not only is the countryside desolate, but Jerusalem and neighboring cities will also become a wasteland.

Jeremiah 10:19–21

This Jeremianic lament, delimited by section markings at top and bottom, is without a divine response. In form and content it is similar to 4:19–22, only there the lament gets a divine answer (4:22). Here Jeremiah judges the foolish individuals himself (v. 21). Gunkel took 10:19–22 as an individual lament placed in the mouth of Zion. In his view, the *I* was spoken originally by an individual at a lament occasion of the entire community.[46] Commentators otherwise agree that in v. 20 a personified Jerusalem (or Judah) is speaking ("my children"), and that Jeremiah is speaking in v. 21. In my view, Jeremiah also speaks the lament of v. 19.[47] The whole is then a three-stanza poem in which Jeremiah and Jerusalem alternate laments. Stanzas 2 and 3 have their own internal rhetorical structures (italics).

44. Gunkel, *Introduction to Psalms*, 83.

45. Ibid., 113 n. 35.

46. Ibid., 87, 122.

47. Lundbom, *Jeremiah 1–20*, 603.

[19]Woe to me, at my brokenness
    my blow is incurable
Then I, I said to myself:
    "But this is suffering
    and I must bear it"

[20]***My tent*** is devastated
    and all ***my cords*** are torn away
    my children have gone from me and are no more
There is no one now who spreads ***my tent***
    and who sets up ***my curtains***

[21]For the ***shepherds*** are stupid
    they do not seek out Yahweh
Therefore they have not fared well
    and all ***their flock*** is scattered.

Jeremiah's lament opens with "Woe to me," which begins a lament also in 15:10. The prophet speaks again of his sickness and suffering, as in 4:19–21, a common motif in laments of the Psalms. In this lament, Jeremiah does not ask to be delivered from his suffering; he tells himself he simply must bear it. Jerusalem or Judah laments that towns and rural areas have been devastated by an enemy, and large numbers of people have been killed or taken into exile. At the end Jeremiah puts the blame on foolish kings and leaders of the nation. They do not seek Yahweh.

Jeremiah 10:23–25

These verses contain an individual lament in which Jeremiah asks for (gentle) correction (vv. 23–24). The lament brings to an end oracles and more general laments on the coming "foe from the north," and is followed by a separate word in which Jeremiah calls for Yahweh to take vengeance on his enemies (v. 25). The near identity of v. 25 to Ps 79:6–7 suggests that it is likely an add-on. The two compositions are linked by key words (in small caps). The first composition has its own key-word balance (in italics). The two compositions go well together, the call for vengeance being a common motif in laments of the Psalms. Also, section markings delimit the unit as vv. 23–25. Gunkel lists 10:23–25 as a communal lament.[48] Baumgartner

48. Gunkel, *Introduction to Psalms*, 82.

says these verses echo the communal song of lament, but thinks their authenticity is dubious.[49]

Jeremiah's lament:

> 23***I KNOW, YAHWEH***, that the person's way is not his
> it is not man who walks that determines his steps
>
> 24***Correct me, Yahweh***, but with justice
> not in your anger, lest you reduce me to nothing.
>
> 25Pour out your wrath on the nations
> **WHO DO NOT KNOW YOU**
> And on the families
> who do not call upon your name
> For they have consumed Jacob
> they have consumed him and brought him to an end
> his pasture they have made desolate.

Jeremiah begins by addressing Yahweh directly. Other Jeremiah laments either address Yahweh or name Yahweh at the beginning (11:18; 12:1; 14:7, 20; 15:15; 17:13; 18:19; 20:7). In the Hebrew text Jeremiah requests correction for himself personally, but in the LXX, "Correct me" is changed to "Correct us" (v. 24), making his plea one spoken on behalf of the nation.

Jeremiah 11:18–23

Here an individual lament in poetry (vv. 18–20) is followed by a divine response in prose (vv. 21–23). The divine response is preceded by an introductory word identifying the prophet's enemies as men of Anathoth (v. 21). Both Gunkel and Baumgartner treat these verses as an individual lament with a divine response.[50] The verses are delimited by section markings at both top and bottom. The lament is further delimited by a section marking after v. 20. There is also a section marking prior to v. 20, which could indicate the one-time independence of v. 20. This verse reappears with minor changes in 20:12. Another section after v. 21 sets off the introduction from the oracle following. We see here a repetition of "Yahweh" at beginning and end (italics).

49. Baumgartner, *Jeremiah's Poems of Lament*, 89.

50. Gunkel, *Introduction to Psalms*, 121; Baumgartner, *Jeremiah's Poems of Lament*, 41–46.

Jeremiah's lament:

[18]***Yahweh*** made me know and I knew
then you made me see their deeds
[19]I was like a trusting lamb led to the slaughter
I did not know that against me

They planned plans:
"Let us destroy the tree with its sap
Let us cut him off from the land of the living
that his name be remembered no more"

[20]***Yahweh of hosts***, who judges righteously
who tests the inner being and the heart
Let me see your vengeance upon them
when to you I have confided my case.

Divine response:

[21]Therefore thus said Yahweh concerning the men of Anathoth who are seeking your life, saying: "You shall not prophesy in the name of Yahweh, or you will surely die by our hand."
[22]Therefore thus said Yahweh of hosts:
Look I will reckon with them. The chosen ones will die by the sword, their sons and their daughters will die by famine, [23]and there shall not be a remnant of them, for I will bring evil upon the men of Anathoth in the year of their reckoning.

Jeremiah begins this lament by naming Yahweh rather than addressing Yahweh directly. Yahweh is addressed emphatically in v. 20 as "Yahweh of hosts." Jeremiah's major complaint is that he is being attacked by enemies, a common motif in laments of the Psalms. The lament contains an alternation of speaker, giving it the following structure:

I. Jeremiah addresses confidant (vv. 18–19a)

II. Enemies of Jeremiah speak (v. 19bc)

III. Jeremiah addresses Yahweh (v. 20)

Jeremiah here protests his innocence, saying he was like a trusting lamb led to the slaughter. Enemies wanted to kill him, and he did not know it. Jeremiah therefore puts out a call to Yahweh who judges righteously and truly discerns inner minds and passions, asking that Yahweh will take vengeance on his enemies. Yahweh in his divine response says that he will do just that.

Jeremiah 12:1–6

Here another individual lament (vv. 1–3) is combined with a divine response (vv. 5–6). The divine response has no messenger formula, but clarification about it being Yahweh's reply comes in the Targum. Verse 4 is later expansion reflecting on human evil and the land being ruined. In the divine response, the prose of v. 6 appears to expand the poetry of v. 5. Gunkel and Baumgartner both treat these verses as related to songs of lament in the Psalms.[51] The present lament is delimited by section markings at both top and bottom; another section at the end of v. 6 closes the larger unit. The lament and divine response in v. 5 have internal key word balance (italics).

Jeremiah's lament:

[1]Righteous are you, ***Yahweh***
when I make accusation to you
nevertheless judgments I will speak to you
Why does the way of the wicked prosper
and they live at ease, all who are faithlessly faithless?

[2]You plant them, what is more they take root
they grow, what is more they bear fruit
You are near in their mouth
but far from their inner being

[3]Now you, ***Yahweh***, you know me, you see me
and you test my heart toward you
Pull them out like sheep to the slaughter
dedicate them for the day of killing.

Divine response:

[5]If ***with*** men on foot you have run and they have wearied you
how then will you fare in a heat *with* horses?
And ***in*** a peaceful land you have fallen down
how then will you do *in* the pride of the Jordan?

51. Gunkel, *Introuction to Psalms*, 121; Baumgartner, *Jeremiah's Poems of Lament*, 63–71.

> [6]For even your brothers and the house of your father, even they, they have dealt faithlessly with you, even they, they are in full cry after you. Do not believe in them when they speak to you good things.

Jeremiah begins by addressing Yahweh, acknowledging Yahweh to be righteous despite the accusation he is about to lay before him. Here Jeremiah is not simply complaining; he is accusing. He is not wanting to talk over matters of judgment; he is speaking judgments. His burden is "the way of the wicked," an indication that the prophet is again having problems with enemies, as in 11:18–20. Jeremiah protests his innocence, and calls for vengeance on his enemies. Yahweh's answer in this case is largely a nonanswer. If Jeremiah is exhausted from a small battle, what will he do in a battle of greater magnitude? Things apparently are going to get worse. The add-on v. 6 identifies the enemies as family, presumably in Anathoth, but Yahweh does not say, as in 11:22–23, that they will get their just deserts.

This poem of lament in 12:1–3 is a companion poem to the lament in 11:18–20. Companion poems exist elsewhere in Jeremiah (6:1–7; 6:8–12). But the juxtaposition here is unique in that key words in each poem—which double as catchwords—make a large chiasmus.[52] The key words:

	[18]*Yahweh made me know and I knew*	
A	*you made me see*	
	[19]*like a lamb . . . to the slaughter*	
		its sap
	B	[20]*Yahweh . . . who judges righteously*
		the inner being
		when to you . . . my case rîbî
		[1]righteous . . . Yahweh
		when I make accusation to you 'ārîb
	B'	*judgments*
		[2]*fruit*
		their inner being
	[3]*Yahweh, you know me*	
A'	*you see me*	
	like sheep to the slaughter	

52. Lundbom, *Jeremiah: A Study in Ancient Hebrew Rhetoric*, 100–101; 2nd ed., 131–33.

Jeremiah 14:2–10

These verses have long been recognized as a drama, possibly a temple liturgy, in response to a severe drought (14:1). They contain a lament spoken by Jeremiah (vv. 2–6), a communal confession and petition that Yahweh will alleviate the suffering (vv. 7–9), and then a divine oracle rejecting the petition (v. 10). In a prose passage following (vv. 11–16), Jeremiah is rejected as covenant mediator. Gunkel and Baumgartner identify 14:2–6, 7–9 as a communal lament, with Baumgartner also recognizing v. 10 as a divine reply.[53] Gunkel believed the communal lament was written in anticipation of Israel's future repentance.[54] But it could have been spoken at the time of the drought, with Jeremiah or someone else leading the liturgy. Section markings delimit the lament and confession as a unit, and the divine response as a unit. Both the individual lament and communal confession have internal key word balances (in italics).

Jeremiah's lament:

2 ***Judah*** mourns
    her gates languish
    they are black to the earth
The cry of ***Jerusalem*** goes up

3 Their nobles send their young ones for ***water***
    they come upon the canals
They do not find ***water***
    their containers ***return*** empty

They are ashamed and disgraced
    and ***they cover their heads***
4 On account of the ground being cracked
    because there is not rain in the land

The farmers ***are ashamed***
    they cover their heads
5 ***Because*** even the doe in the field gives birth and forsakes
    because there is not grass

6 The wild asses stand on the bare heights
    they pant for air like jackals

53. Gunkel, *Introduction to Psalms*, 82; Baumgartner, *Jeremiah's Poems of Lament*, 88.

54. Gunkel, *The Psalms: A Form-Critical Introduction*, 14.

Their eyes fail
    because of no herbage.

Communal confession:

[7]Though our iniquities testify against us
    Yahweh, act for the sake of ***your name***
For our backslidings are many
    against you we have sinned

[8]The Hope of Israel
    its savior in time of trouble
Why will you become like a sojourner in the land
    and ***like*** a traveler turned aside to lodge?

[9]***Why will you become like*** a helpless man
    like a mighty man unable ***to save***?
But you are in our midst, ***Yahweh***
    and ***your name*** upon us is called
    do not leave us!

Divine response:

[10]Thus said Yahweh to this people:
So they loved to wander
    their feet they did not restrain
Thus Yahweh did not accept them
    now he will remember their iniquity
    and call to account their sin.

Jeremiah laments the severe drought. The canals have no water, people are overcome with shame, and animals are dying and forsaking their young. Because people are blanketed in shame, a communal lament follows. Yahweh is addressed directly, called the "Hope of Israel" and its savior in times of trouble. The people confess their sin and ask for deliverance and Yahweh's continued presence. But in the divine response Yahweh says the people have loved their waywardness. He therefore will not act as savior; rather he will punish the people for their sin.

Jeremiah 14:17—15:4

Here is another sequence just like the one preceding, containing a lament spoken by Jeremiah (14:17–19ab); a communal confession and petition that Yahweh not break the covenant (14:20–22); and a divine response in two oracles (15:2b–3). Gunkel took 14:19–22 to be a communal lament,[55] Baumgartner 14:17–18 as an individual lament and 14:19—15:2 as a communal lament.[56] The fragment of 14:19c, which repeats in 8:15, may be an add-on. Delimitation of the sequence as a whole is aided only by a section marking after 14:22, which separates the communal confession from the divine response. At top and bottom of the sequence are shifts from prose to poetry in 14:17 and 15:5, which give further aid in delimitation. This divine response differs from the one in the earlier sequence in that the oracles of answer are framed at the top by prose rejecting Jeremiah as covenant mediator (15:1–2a), and at the bottom by prose expanding the judgment and blaming King Manasseh for what he did in Jerusalem (15:4). In 14:11–16 the rejection of Jeremiah as covenant mediator came in prose at the end of the sequence. Both the lament and communal confession contain internal key word repetitions (italics).

Jeremiah's lament:

17And you shall say to them this word:
Let my eyes run down with tears
    night and day, and let them not stop
For a major shatter has been shattered
    my dear virgin people
    a most incurable ***stroke***

18***If I went out to the field***
    then look! those slain by the sword
And if I entered the city
    then look! the diseases of famine
For also prophet also priest
    wander to a land that they do not know

19aHave you utterly rejected Judah?
    Does Zion your soul abhor?
So why have ***you struck us down***
    that there is no healing for us?

Communal confession:

19cTo hope for peace—and no good!
    for a time of healing—and look, terror!

55. Gunkel, *The Psalms: A Form-Critical Introduction*, 14; Gunkel, *Introduction to Psalms*, 82.

56. Baumgartner, *Jeremiah's Poems of Lament*, 85, 88.

[20]We know, ***Yahweh***, our wickedness
the iniquity of our fathers
indeed we have sinned against you
[21]Do not spurn, for the sake of your name
do not disdain your glorious throne
Remember, do not break
your covenant with us

[22]Are there among the nothings of the nations rainmakers?
Or the heavens, do they give showers?
Are you not the one, ***Yahweh***, our God?
We are hoping for you
indeed you, you have made all these.

Divine response:

[2b]Thus said Yahweh:
Whoever is to death—to death, and whoever is to the sword—to the sword, and whoever is to famine—to famine, and whoever is to captivity—to captivity.

[3]And I will appoint over them four families—oracle of Yahweh—the sword to kill and the dogs to drag away; and the birds of the skies and the beasts of the earth to devour and to destroy.

Jeremiah in this lament expresses his grief over the effects of war, siege, and famine in city and country. He does not ask for deliverance, at least not directly. The lament ends with him asking whether Yahweh has utterly rejected Judah, since there appears to be no healing for the divinely inflicted blow. Jeremiah can only weep over his wounded people (cf. 8:22—9:2). The communal lament contains an acknowledgement of sin confessed directly to Yahweh. This is followed by a plea that Yahweh not break his covenant with the people, and an affirmation of Yahweh as the one who brings rain and is Israel's hope. Yahweh, in his response, remains unmoved. The people are told in two oracles that they can take their pick between death and exile.

Jeremiah 15:10–12

Here is an individual lament (v. 10) with a divine response (vv. 11–12), treated by Gunkel and Baumgartner as related to the individual lament.[57]

57. Gunkel, *Introduction to Psalms*, 121; Baumgartner, *Jeremiah's Poems of Lament*, 71–73.

Delimitation at top end is by a section marking. The dialogue concludes at v. 12.[58] Both lament and response have key-word repetitions (italics).

Jeremiah's lament:

> 10Woe to me, my mother because you bore me
>   ***a man*** of contention and ***a man*** of dispute
>   ***for the whole*** earth
>
> ***I have not loaned***
>   ***and they have not loaned to me***
>   ***all of them curse me.***

Divine response:

> 11Yahweh said:
> ***Have I not*** set you free ***for good***?
> ***Have I not*** stood by you
>   ***in time of evil***
>   and ***in time*** of distress with the enemy?
> 12Can ***iron*** break
>   ***iron*** from the north and bronze?

Jeremiah in this lament does not address Yahweh; he speaks rather to his mother ("because you bore me"), which may be apostrophe. A heavy "woe" is heaped on both himself and his mother. "Woe to me" begins the individual lament in 10:19. Yahweh, though not addressed, is nevertheless listening, and his response affirms Jeremiah as the ironclad prophet, given prior protection against all comers. Yahweh does not say that Jeremiah's suffering will end, but it must be concluded that Yahweh will continue to stand by his prophet and deliver him in the future.

Jeremiah 15:15–21

Here is another individual lament (vv. 15–18) with a divine response (vv. 19–21). Verse 21 may be a later add-on. Both the lament and divine response have internal key-word balance (in italics), and the two are linked by catchwords (in small caps). Gunkel and Baumgartner both treat the verses as an individual lament with a divine response.[59] The passage has

58. Baumgartner, *Jeremiah's Poems of Lament*, 71.

59. Gunkel, *Introduction to Psalms*, 121; Baumgartner, *Jeremiah's Poems of Lament*, 46–51.

also been discussed along with 15:10–12 by John Bright.[60] A. R. Diamond[61] points out that the lament and divine answer manifest a pattern of doublets, which are the following:

I. *you know*	v. 15
know	
II. *your words*	v. 16
your word (Q)	
III. *I sat not*	v. 17
I sat	
IV. *it has become*	v. 18
(will) you really be	

I. *If you return, then I will let you return*	v. 19
If . . . they, they will turn . . . you will not turn	
II. *to rescue you*	v. 20
I will rescue you	v. 21

Jeremiah's lament:

15 You, ***you know, Yahweh***
remember me and take account of me
and take vengeance for me on my pursuers
Do not in your slowness to anger take me away
know that on your account I bear reproach

16 ***Your words*** were found and I ate them
and ***your word*** was to me for joy
and for the gladness of my heart
For your name is called upon me
Yahweh, the God of hosts

17 ***I sat not*** in the happy crowd and acted jolly
because of your hand, all alone ***I sat***
for with indignation you filled me

18 Why ***has*** my pain ***become*** continual
and my blow desperate
refusing to be healed?
Will you ***really*** **be for me** as a deceptive stream
waters that are not sure?

60. Bright, "A Prophet's Lament and Its Answer: Jeremiah 15:10–21," *Int* 28 (1974) 59–74.

61. Diamond, *The Confessions of Jeremiah in Context*, 68.

Divine response:

[19]Therefore thus said Yahweh:
If you return, then I will let you return
before me you shall stand
And *if* you bring forth what is more precious than trash
AS my mouth YOU WILL BE
They, they will turn to you
but you, ***you will not turn*** to them

[20]And I will make you to this people
a fortified wall of bronze
They will fight against you
but will not overcome you
For with you am I
to save you and ***rescue you***
—oracle of Yahweh.

[21]Yes, ***I will rescue you*** from the hand of evildoers
and I will redeem you from the grasp of the ruthless.

Jeremiah's lament begins by invoking the divine name, as he does elsewhere (11:20; 12:1; 16:19; 17:14; 18:19; 20:7, 12). Here he asks Yahweh to "remember" him, using a word occurring often in the Psalms (Pss 25:6–7; 74:2, 18, 22; 89:47, 50). Being attacked once again by enemies, Jeremiah wants a speedy deliverance. If Yahweh delays, Jeremiah may become a victim. Jeremiah also wants Yahweh to take vengeance on his persecutors. Baumgartner sees in v. 18 lament vocabulary out of the Psalter: 1) the "why?" (*lāmmâ*) question (Pss 22:1; 42:9; 43:2; 88:14); 2) *neṣaḥ* ("continual / enduring"), which occurs equally often (Pss 13:2; 44:23 together with "why"; 74:1 together with "why," 3, 10, 19; 77:8; 79:5); and 3) *kĕ'ēb* ("pain"), which occurs only once (Ps 39:2).[62] Gunkel and Baumgartner believed that "pain" and "healing," both here and in Jer 17:14, are metaphorical, whereas the psalmist speaks of them in a real sense.[63] But Jeremiah may also be talking about real pain.

Jeremiah goes on in the lament to recall his joy at the finding of the temple law book in 622 BC, which he consumed with joy, and in so doing accepted Yahweh's call to be a prophet.[64] The lament closes with a complaint

62. Baumgartner, *Jeremiah's Poems of Lament*, 49.

63. Gunkel, *The Psalms: A Form-Critical Introduction*, 28; Baumgartner, *Jeremiah's Poems of Lament*, 91.

64. Lundbom, *Jeremiah 1–20*, 743–44.

about his present hurt not letting up (cf. Pss 38:5–8; 42:10), after which comes an ill-chosen remark about Yahweh being to him like a "deceptive stream." The divine answer is no less robust. Jeremiah receives not a word of consolation but is told he must return (= "repent"), and then he can once again stand before Yahweh. Jeremiah must abandon the worthless trash he has been preaching, get on with preaching Yahweh's precious word, and he can be again Yahweh's mouth. The promise given at the time of his commissioning is then renewed. Jeremiah will continue to be the "wall of bronze" he has been thus far against his enemies, from whom he will be delivered.

Jeremiah 17:13–18

Here is one poetic composition—perhaps two—that belong with Jeremiah's individual laments. Gunkel and Baumgartner treat 17:12–18 as a single poem of lament.[65] A section marking after v. 18 delimits the end of the unit. A rhetorical structure in the first composition (17:13–16a) sets it off from the second (17:16b–18), suggesting that perhaps two compositions have been joined together.[66] Like the structure of the speaker chiasmus in 8:18–21, the structure here is a three-way conversation between Yahweh, the people, and Jeremiah. Both poems have internal key-word repetitions (in italics), and key words linking them together (in small caps). The two have much in common with Psalm 17.[67]

Jeremiah: [13]The Hope of Israel, Yahweh
all who forsake you WILL BE SHAMED

Yahweh: Those turning from me will be written in the earth
for they have forsaken the spring of living water

Jeremiah: [14]Heal me, Yahweh, and I shall be healed
save me, and I shall be saved
for you are my praise

People: [15]Look, they are the ones saying to me,
"Where is the word of Yahweh? Let it come!"

Jeremiah: [16a]As for me, I did not insist on shepherding after you

65. Gunkel, *Introduction to Psalms*, 121; Baumgartner, *Jeremiah's Poems of Lament*, 51–56.

66. Lundbom, *Jeremiah 1–20*, 794–97.

67. Lawrence Boadt, *Jeremiah 1–25*, OTM 9 (Wilmington, DE: Glazier, 1982).

and **THE DAY OF DESPERATION** I have not desired!

16b *You*, you know what has gone out of my lips
it has come before your face!
17 Do not *become* to me a terror
my refuge *you* are in ***THE DAY OF EVIL***

18 ***Let my pursuers* BE SHAMED, *but let not me, me* BE SHAMED**
Let them, them be broken, but let not me, me be broken
Bring on them ***THE DAY OF EVIL!***
and a double breaking, break them!

Jeremiah begins the dialogue by addressing Yahweh, calling him the Hope of Israel. He says those who forsake Yahweh will be shamed. Yahweh speaks next, saying that those who turn away from him will be "written in the earth." In the center Jeremiah utters a lament. The prophet is again sick, asking to be healed and to be saved. The next stanza contains a taunt that has come to Jeremiah from his enemies. They ask that Jeremiah's word come to pass. Of course, they really do not want it fulfilled; they simply disbelieve Jeremiah's word. The dialogue ends with a complaint by Jeremiah that he did not seek the office to which he was called. Nor does he desire the dreadful day he has been preaching about.

In this second poem Jeremiah then protests his innocence to Yahweh, followed by a request that Yahweh not be a terror to him, but rather his refuge in the evil day. What he wants is Yahweh's vengeance on his enemies. This lament elicits no further reply from Yahweh.

Jeremiah 18:19–23

This lament by Jeremiah has no divine response. Gunkel and Baumgartner take 18:18–23 as a poem of lament,[68] which is delimited by section markings at both top and bottom. Verse 18 is a conspiracy speech announcing a plot laid against Jeremiah. The lament has striking affinities to Psalm 35, incorporating other stereotyped Psalm language. Key-word repetitions make a chiasmus (in italics).[69]

19 Give heed, ***Yahweh***, to me
and hear the voice of my adversaries:

68. Gunkel, *Introduction to Psalms*, 121; Baumgartner, *Jeremiah's Poems of Lament*, 56–59.

69. Lundbom, *Jeremiah 1–20*, 829.

[20]Should evil be repayment for good?
yet they ***dug a pit*** for my life
Remember how I stood in your presence
to speak good for them
to turn away your wrath from them?

[21]Therefore give over their ***sons*** to famine
(and pour them out to the power of the sword)
let their ***women*** become childless and husbandless
and their ***men***, let them be the slain by black death
Their ***young men*** sword-victims in battle

[22]A cry will be heard from their houses
for you will bring raiders upon them suddenly
for they dug a pit to catch me
and traps they hid for my feet

[23]But you, ***Yahweh***, you know
all their counsel against me for death.

Do not atone for their iniquity
their sin from your presence do not blot out
let them be stumblers in your presence
In the time of your anger deal with them.

Jeremiah here addresses Yahweh at both beginning and end. His request is that Yahweh listen to both him and his enemies, and then judge the rank evildoers. Jeremiah protests his own innocence, saying he has spoken good, not ill, of his enemies. He has even interceded on their behalf. But they have returned the favor by digging a pit to take his life (vv. 20, 22; cf. Ps 35:7). At the center Jeremiah curses his enemies and those related to them (v. 21), and at the end asks that the iniquity of these enemies not be atoned for, but that Yahweh act to make them stumble.

Jeremiah 20:7–13

Here an individual lament (vv. 7–10) is followed by a hymn of confidence and thankful praise (vv. 11–13). This time the response to Jeremiah's lament comes from the prophet himself after a crisis has passed. Gunkel and Baumgartner take vv. 7–9 as a poem closely related to the songs of lament, and vv. 10–13 as an actual song of lament.[70] But in my view, the lament is

70. Gunkel, *Introduction to Psalms*, 121; Baumgartner, *Jeremiah's Poems of Lament*,

best delimited to vv. 7–10, having as it does key words (in italics) making an inclusio.[71] Other balancing key words are also present (in italics). Gunkel sees in vv. 11–13 certainty of a hearing, which often occurs in laments of the Psalms.[72] Many psalms contain internal movement from complaint to confident assurance, e.g., Pss 6, 13, 22, 28, 30, 31, 35. The present lament has some striking affinities to Ps 31, e.g., v. 10 with Ps 31:13. But we seem to have two separate compositions joined by catchwords (in small caps).[73] Section markings delimit vv. 7–12 as a unit; v. 13 is delimited separately, and may be a later add-on. Verse 12 may also be an addition, since it is duplicated in 11:20.

Jeremiah's lament:

[7]***You enticed me***, **YAHWEH**, and ***I was enticed***
you laid hold of me, and **YOU OVERCAME**
I have become a joke ***all the day***
they all make fun *of me*

[8]*For* too often I speak, I cry out
violence and destruction, I proclaim
For the word of Yahweh ***has become for me***
reproach and ridicule ***all the day***

[9]Then I say, I will not mention him
I will not speak any longer in his name
But it becomes in my heart like a burning fire
shut up in my bones
I am weary from holding it in
and **I CANNOT OVERCOME**

[10]For I hear whispering in the crowd:
"Terror-on-every-side!
tell, let us tell on him!"
All my trusted friends watch for my fall:
'Perhaps ***he can be enticed*** **AND WE WILL OVERCOME HIM**
and we will take **OUR REVENGE** on him.'

Hymn of confidence:

[11]But **YAHWEH** is with me like a fearless warrior

59–62, 73–76.

71. Lundbom, *Jeremiah 1–20*, 853.

72. Gunkel, *Introduction to Psalms*, 181.

73. Lundbom, *Jeremiah 1–20*, 852–53.

therefore my pursuers will stumble
and **WILL NOT OVERCOME**
They are greatly shamed, for they did not succeed
eternal disgrace will not be forgotten!

12 Yahweh of hosts, who tests the righteous
who sees the inner being and the heart
let me see **YOUR VENGEANCE** upon them
when to you I have confided my case.

13 Sing to Yahweh
praise Yahweh
For he rescued the life of the needy
from the hand of evildoers!

Jeremiah begins this lament by complaining directly to Yahweh about his call to prophesy, alleging that Yahweh took advantage of his youth by forcing him into submission. He then cites reproaches and ridicule from enemies, saying they come all day long. He has tried keeping silent, but that does not work, for then he has a fire in his bones that he cannot contain. The lament ends with more complaining about taunts from enemies, who are would-be friends. There is no plea here for deliverance, but in the hymn that follows, Jeremiah is confident that will come. He is also confident that his enemies will not succeed. But just for good measure, v. 12 calls for Yahweh to take vengeance on the enemies. In v. 13 deliverance has come. Jeremiah refers here to himself as a "needy" soul, which Gunkel says is an identification made often in the Psalms.[74] Psalmists frequently paint themselves as the poor, distressed, humble, and silent faithful. The "Sing to Yahweh" of this final verse begins Pss 96:1–2; 98:1; and 149:1. The "praise Yahweh" following is likewise a common beginning in the Psalms (Pss 105[reconstructed]; 106, 111, 112, 113, 117, 135, 146–150).

Jeremiah 20:14–18; 1:5

Concluding the First Edition of Jeremiah (chaps 1–20) is the most moving lament in the book (20:14–18), delimited by content, a rhetorical structure, and section markings at top and bottom. Taken by itself, the lament is without a divine response. Von Rad says, "The God whom the prophet

74. Gunkel, *The Psalms: A Form-Critical Introduction*, 33–34.

addresses no longer answers him."[75] But in the larger compilation of the First Edition (chaps. 1–20), it receives an answer in 1:5. The tie-in is made by a key word inclusio (in small caps).

The lament needs reconstruction at the beginning of v. 17, since presently the curse on the day is not filled out and the curse on the man in v. 16 is disproportionately heavy.[76] The lament has extraordinary key-word balance, with a chiasmus of day / man / man / day upon reconstruction (in italics). Gunkel and Baumgartner both treat 20:14–18 as a poem related to the songs of lament.[77] Baumgartner thinks the poem is not directed to Yahweh, therefore not a song of lament in the strict sense. But v. 18, in my view, is addressed to Yahweh, and the whole a Jeremiah lament.[78]

Jeremiah's lament:

14 ***Cursed*** be ***the day***
    on which I was born
    the day ***my mother*** bore me
Let it not be ***blessed***

15 ***Cursed*** be ***the man***
    who brought ***my father*** the news:
"A male child ***is born*** to you"
    making him very glad

16 ***Let that man be like*** the cities
    which Yahweh overthrew and did not pity
Let him hear ***a cry in the morning***
    and ***an alarm at noontime***

17 [***Let that day be like . . .***]
    because he did not kill me ***in the womb***
So my mother would have been my grave
    and her womb eternally pregnant

18 Why this: **FROM THE WOMB CAME I FORTH**
    to see hard times and sorrow
    and ***my days*** end in shame?

75. Gerhard von Rad, *Old Testament Theology*, vol. 2, *The Theology of Israel's Prophetic Trditions*, trans. D. M. G. Stalker (Edinburgh: Oliver & Boyd, 1965), 204.

76. Lundbom, "The Double Curse in Jeremiah 20:14–18," *JBL* 104 (1985) 589–600.

77. Gunkel, *Introduction to Psalms*, 121; Baumgartner, *Jeremiah's Poems of Lament*, 76–78.

78. Lundbom, *Jeremiah 1–20*, 865.

Divine response:

1:5 Before I formed you in the belly I knew you
    and before **YOU CAME FORTH FROM THE WOMB**
        I declared you holy
    a prophet to the nations I made you.

In this lament Jeremiah curses the day of his birth and the man who brought the happy news to his father. Both mother and father are obliquely implicated in the malediction, but they are not cursed. Jeremiah knows they cannot be. The hapless friend of Jeremiah's father is compared to the proverbial cities of Sodom and Gomorrah, which Yahweh overthrew in his anger. But the man here will not die. He is simply condemned to hear human cries and war alarms day and night, which may be as bad as death, possibly worse. With reconstruction in v. 17 the day of Jeremiah's birth is compared to some other inauspicious day, no longer known, the reason being that Yahweh did not kill Jeremiah in the womb. Jeremiah concludes the lament by asking Yahweh why he was born to see hard times and sorrow and to end his days in shame.

The prophet's wrenching question receives an answer when the scribe compiling the First Edition ties v. 18 of the lament in with a word from Jeremiah's call in 1:5. The larger message is that Jeremiah came forth from the womb because Yahweh called him long before he came forth.

10

Psalm 23: Song of Passage[1]

One September evening after the nurse had gone out on an errand, I stood at George's bedside alone. His face against the pillow had a strange pallor, and all the color was drained from his lips. I knew that the end was near. I felt his hands. They were cold, icy cold, and I held them to my breast, trying to warm them. "George, can you hear me, darling?" I whispered, my lips close to his ear. His eyelids fluttered, and I knew he had heard me. "Shall I read to you, darling?" I asked. I reached for the Bible on his night stand, turned to the Twenty-third Psalm, and began reading aloud. "The Lord is my shepherd; I shall not want . . ."[2]

I

The minister knows this scene well. So do many other Christians who have stood watch at a time when the life of some friend or loved one is soon to be over. There is great comfort in knowing that the Divine Shepherd offers protection through the final "valley of the death-shadow"—reason enough, I suppose, why no other portion of Scripture is read as often as Ps 23 when life nears its end. The words just quoted were spoken by Pearl Kashishian, an Armenian woman of faith who looks back on sixty-five years of married life during which time goodness and mercy have pursued her and her husband. Ps 23 gives her the words to express her thanksgiving.

1. *Int* 40 (1986) 5–16.
2. Donita Dyer, *Pearl* (Wheaton, IL: Tyndale House, 1977), 252.

She continues after the psalm is read, "Truly, George, my cup runneth over with happiness."[3]

Death, however, is a life crisis, and psychologists tell us that the death of a spouse is *the* crisis above all others. If people are to negotiate this crisis with words of thanksgiving on their lips, they must be in possession of some resources. The story *Pearl*, as told by Donita Dyer, recounts how such resources are built up. As a child Pearl lived through the severe persecutions of 1894–1896 in Turkey when more than two hundred thousand Armenians died. By 1914–1915 the toll exceeded a million. As a young woman she left her town of Kayseri, lived through a "desert experience" across central Turkey, and came finally to America, which for her was the promised land.

Reflecting on her past life, Pearl appropriates not only language from Ps 23 but also other very familiar language from the Bible, language describing the central event of the Old Testament: Exodus, Wilderness Wanderings, and entry into the promised land. Countless immigrants to America have made a typology from the latter, but Pearl's story echoes the biblical theme more clearly than most because she lives through active persecution and survives a harrowing desert experience. Actually it is the desert experience across central Turkey that creates the coalescence of ideas. More than once the traveling party was without food or water. Miraculously they were led on the right paths to avoid danger. One night Turkish soldiers surrounded the group, bringing them well within the shadow of death, but a rod and staff quite literally protected them. This youthful experience becomes Pearl's resource now as she responds to her aged husband's final question about what she will do after he is gone. She says, "No, it won't be the same. But God is good, George. Remember how he protected me during the massacre, and brought me safely to America? Surely you can trust him to take care of me now."[4]

It is the spontaneous and seemingly natural combining of the exodus, wandering, and entry theme with themes from Ps 23 that suggests to me that Ps 23 is a song of passage. It speaks to the Christian about life's final passage, but it speaks too about other passages, passages that have been negotiated through the whole of life because help came from the Divine Shepherd. I believe further that this modern use of the psalm has a correlation with the psalm's use in antiquity. To show this, however, a tie-in between

3. Ibid., 253.

4. Ibid., 252.

the psalm and some ancient life passage will have to be established. That we will do later on in the essay. First we must be clear about what is meant by the term *passage*.

II

Current use of the term *passage* to describe life transitions or life crises derives from studies in anthropology and human development. In the field of human development, the groundbreaking work was Erik Erikson's *Childhood and Society* (1950), which identified eight basic stages through which all individuals pass.[5] Erikson does not use the term *passage*, nor does Daniel Levinson in *The Seasons of a Man's Life* (1978), which gives a developmental perspective on adulthood in men.[6] Yet both these works provide the underpinnings for Gail Sheehy's more popularized book, *Passages*.[7] Levinson talks about the "seasons" in the life of the adult male, but he is at the same time interested in the transitions between seasons, particularly the "mid-life transition." Erikson and Levinson both assume that human life reflects the rhythms of nature, rhythms that make life cyclical in character, though each uses the term *cycle* with some qualification. At any rate, Erikson's eight basic stages make up what is now called his life-cycle theory. A second assumption, most clearly stated in Erikson but present also in Levinson, is that individual development must be understood as taking place in the larger society.[8] Erikson's work is just now beginning to have some impact in the field of pastoral psychology.[9] An earlier effort along similar lines came from Paul Tournier who, in his own creative way, integrated the psychology of Freud and Jung with Christian thought in the little book, *The Seasons of Life*.[10]

5. Erik H. Erikson, *Childhood and Society*, 2nd ed. (New York: Norton, 1963).

6. Daniel J. Levinson et al., *The Seasons of a Man's Life* (New York: Ballantine, 1979).

7. Gail Sheehy, *Passages* (New York: Dutton, 1974). Her sequel to this, titled *Pathfinders* (New York: Morrow, 1981), is a more focused book, in my opinion, with a much clearer thesis.

8. Erikson (*Childhood and Society*, 16) calls it the "relation of the ego to society."

9. See, for example, Donald Capps, *Life Cycle Theory and Pastoral Care*, Theology and Pastoral Care Series (Philadelphia: Fortress, 1983; reprinted, Eugene, OR: Wipf & Stock, 2002), which contains by way of introduction an excellent summary of Erikson.

10. Paul Tournier, *The Seasons of Life*, trans. John S. Gilmour (Richmond: John Knox, 1963).

In the field of anthropology, Arnold van Gennep published his important *Les rites de passage* in 1908.[11] Van Gennep coined the term *rites of passage* to refer to the ceremonies that accompanied individual life crises, the most prominent being birth, puberty, betrothal, marriage, childbirth, fatherhood, and death. Other crises related only marginally to the growth cycle or not related at all were likewise studied, together with the ceremonies that accompanied them. Included here would be such things as the delivery of a second child, the adoption of a child, initiations of various sorts, advancement to a higher class in society, and the like. The partaking of a meal was called by van Gennep a "rite of incorporation"—merely a special type of the more general "rite of passage." Again the assumption was made that human life and the rest of nature contain an underlying unity; also that critical moments in individual lives are an inseparable part of societal life.

Of particular importance to the present discussion are what van Gennep calls "territorial passages." These include border crossings, the crossing of a river, the crossing of a mountain pass, and entrances as well as exits from houses or temples. Here van Gennep shows the influence of an earlier study by H. Clay Trumbull titled *The Threshold Covenant*, in which Trumbull documented the importance attached in many cultures to the crossing of a threshold.[12] Though van Gennep does not say it, passages of this sort are basically linear, having their locus of meaning not in the rhythms of nature but in movements through space. Still, the rites that accompany territorial passages are essentially no different from rites marking passage in the growth cycle, or rites of passage, say, for the New Year. Our family had a rite of territorial passage each summer as we came to the Menominee River that separated Wisconsin from Michigan. Driving across the river we would sing in Swedish a verse our grandparents taught us:

Nu vi är i Mifigan	Now we are in Michigan
Mifigan, Mifigan	Michigan, Michigan
Nu vi är i Mifigan	Now we are in Michigan
Mifigan idag	Michigan today.

11. Arnold van Gennep, *The Rites of Passage*, trans. Monika B. Vizedom and Gabrielle L. Caffee (Chicago: University of Chicago Press, 1960).

12. H. Clay Trumbull, *The Threshold Covenant*, 2nd ed., 1896; reprinted, New York: Scribner, 1906).

III

From the literature of Greek antiquity we have a classic case of passage in Homer's *Odyssey*, book 12. Odysseus, on his circuitous voyage home from Troy, must negotiate his ship through a narrow inlet on either side of which are imposing cliffs. Within these cliffs reside the devouring monsters Scylla and Charybdis. The divine word to Odysseus is that passage cannot be made here without a loss of some crew; still the risk of passing Scylla and Charybdis is less than if he should exercise his other option, which is to sail between the Moving Rocks.

What strikes fear into the hearts of all mariners passing through the Straits of Messina, and what keeps Scylla and Charybdis within our common fund of proverbial wisdom, is that the notion of passage so understood means inevitable crisis. The following all converge to make it so: 1) there is a transition being made; 2) there is an experience of restricted movement; 3) there is a situation presenting serious, hidden, and inescapable danger; and 4) the passage is unavoidable in the sense that it provides the only way open to the future and eventual freedom.

IV

The passage metaphor has not figured in any important way in Old Testament theology, though there is certainly broad acceptance of the idea that Israel's life as a nation is a journey with Yahweh. Little is drawn from the Old Testament in the modern studies just mentioned, and virtually nothing has been appropriated from them by Old Testament scholars and theologians. To be sure, van Gennep drew heavily from William Robertson Smith's *Lectures on the Religion of the Semites*[13] and Trumbull's *The Threshold Covenant*; yet he scarcely says more than that the Passover is a rite of passage, and he says it commemorates the passage from Babylon to Jerusalem. No mention is made of Egypt and the passage to Canaan.[14] The exodus, however, seems to me to be a classic example of passage. Israel passes through the Sea to escape the mighty Pharaoh. The song in Exod 15 points further to some ancient rite that celebrated this passage.

13. W. Robertson Smith, *Lectures on the Religion of the Semites*, 3rd ed., Library of Biblical Studies (New York: Ktav, 1969).

14. Van Gennep, *The Rites of Passage*, 40.

The entry into Canaan is another passage, this one through the River Jordan. The connection between this passage and the earlier one out of Egypt is made explicit in Josh 4:19–24, which records also a rite for subsequent commemoration:

> The people came up out of the Jordan on the tenth day of the first month, and they encamped in Gilgal on the east border of Jericho. And those twelve stones, which they took out of the Jordan, Joshua set up in Gilgal. And he said to the people of Israel, "When your children ask their fathers in time to come, 'What do these stones mean?' then you shall let your children know, 'Israel passed over this Jordan on dry ground.' For the LORD your God dried up the waters of the Jordan for you until you passed over, as the Lord your God did to the Red Sea, which he dried up for us until we passed over, so that all the peoples of the earth may know that the hand of the LORD is mighty; that you may fear the LORD your God for ever." (RSV)

In Deut 32 is a song which the context places just prior to the Jordan crossing (v. 47). Once again this points to an ancient rite celebrating the passage of entry, though in this instance the song has to be learned before the passage rather than after it.

The wilderness trek, while in one sense part of the larger exodus and entry experience, could nevertheless qualify as a passage in its own right. Despite its long duration, it is a transition between settlements, a time of continual danger, and a time of restriction—if not primarily of movement, certainly in terms of what food and water is available. The wilderness trek is also Israel's only way to the future, which is the promised land. Moses understands this better than the people, who would rather return to Egypt (Num 14:3–4).

The passage metaphor might also usefully describe later Old Testament theologies. I think, for example, of the court history (2 Sam 7, 9–20; 1 Kgs 1–2), which portrays David as caught within a series of crises relating to fatherhood. In Erikson's terms these would be crises over "generativity." So far as Israel is concerned, the crises involve royal succession. I have argued elsewhere that the Yahwist, building on perspectives from the court history, develops a "pilgrim theology" in the book of Genesis.[15] This theology—at certain points at least—might equally qualify as a theology of passage.

15. Jack R. Lundbom, "Abraham and David in the Theology of the Yahwist," in Carol L. Meyers and M. O'Connor, eds., *The Word of the Lord Shall Go Forth: Essays in Honor of David Noel Freedman*, Special Volume Series, ASOR 1 (Winona Lake, IN: Eisenbrauns,

The exile to Babylon and the return are also bona fide passages. In Isa 40:3–5 the return is typologized on the wilderness trek:

> A voice cries:
> "In the wilderness prepare the way of the LORD,
> make straight in the desert a highway for our God.
> Every valley shall be lifted up,
> and every mountain and hill be made low;
> The uneven ground shall become level,
> and the rough places a plain.
> And the glory of the LORD shall be revealed,
> and all flesh shall see it together,
> For the mouth of the LORD has spoken." (RSV)

Isa 51:10 builds a typology on the exodus:

> Was it not thou that didst dry up the sea,
> the waters of the great deep;
> That didst make the depths of the sea a way
> for the redeemed to pass over?

Later in the second century BC, Israel undergoes another passage under Antiochus Epiphanes. The folklorist Alan Dundes has recognized that in the book of Judith the passage into the city of Bethulia (Jdt 4:7) has an explicit function.[16] In this narrow entranceway the entire life-and-death struggle between postexilic Judaism and Hellenism is acted out. The enemy views the passage as the means for Israel's destruction, but it becomes instead the way of salvation. If Bethulia is a pseudonym for Shechem, as some have suggested, we can identify the narrow passage with the east-west corridor at Shechem. On the north of this corridor stands Mount Ebal and on the south the towering Mount Gerizim.

V

The foregoing is intended merely to suggest a further appropriation of the passage metaphor to Old Testament theology. My purpose in the present essay is to demonstrate that Ps 23 is a song of passage.

1983), 203–9.

16. Alan Dundes, "Response" to Luis Alonso-Schökel's *Narrative Structures in the Book of Judith* (Colloquy 11 of the Center for Hermeneutical Studies in Hellenistic and Modern Culture; Berkeley: Center for Hermeneutical Studies, 1975), 28.

So far as literary type is concerned, Ps 23 is a personal psalm of trust or confidence (Gunkel: *Vertrauenspsalm*).[17] The author affirms his trust in Yahweh, who is to him a good shepherd and a good host.[18] The psalm radiates childlike simplicity, yet commentators are quick to point out that in the background lies some deep struggle. Gunkel noted that the psalm had formal similarities to the individual lament. Mowinckel thought the psalm was either a "protective psalm" amid danger or else a "thanksgiving psalm" after an experience of salvation.[19] Weiser said this about the psalm:

> The sentiments of an almost childlike trust . . . are, however, by no means the product of a carefree unconcern characteristic of young people; on the contrary, they are the mature fruit of a heart . . . having passed through many bitter experiences and having fought many battles (vv. 4, 5).[20]

So despite a strong affirmation of faith and trust, there are indications that the psalm was born in travail. The psalmist mentions in verse 4 that he has walked through a "valley of the death-shadow." This would seem to suggest the negotiation of some important life passage.

The date and provenance of the psalm are not known. The superscription tells us that David is the author; but since superscriptions represent a later tradition, many do not credit the psalm to David.

In a recent study David Noel Freedman roots the psalm in the tradition of the exodus, wilderness wanderings, and entry into Canaan.[21] Freedman believes an unknown poet of the sixth century BC builds on this

17. Hermann Gunkel, *Einleitung in die Psalmen*, completed by Joachim Begrich, 2nd ed. (Göttingen: Vandenhoeck & Ruprecht, 1966), 172. English: *Introduction to Psalms*, trans. James D. Nogalski, Mercer Library of Biblical Studies (Macon, GA: Mercer University Press, 1998), 191.

18. Many scholars believe there are two separate themes here: 1) Yahweh as shepherd; and 2) Yahweh as host. Yet any division of such a short psalm is out of the question. Moreover, both themes can be subsumed under the one rubric of Yahweh as shepherd; see George Adam Smith, *Four Psalms* (New York: Dodd, Mead, 1896), 1–2; also Samuel Terrien, *The Psalms and Their Meaning for Today* (Indianapolis: Bobbs-Merrill, 1952), 228–29.

19. Sigmund Mowinckel, *The Psalms in Israel's Worship*, vol. 2 (New York: Abingdon, 1967), 41.

20. Artur Weiser, *The Psalms: A Commentary*, trans. Herbert Hartwell, OTL (Philadelphia: Westminster, 1962), 227.

21. David Noel Freedman, "The Twenty-Third Psalm," in Louis L. Orlin, ed., *Michigan Oriental Studies in Honor of George G. Cameron* (Ann Arbor: Department of Near Eastern Studies, University of Michigan, 1976), 139–66.

central tradition of Israelite faith in anticipation of the return from exile. It is the psalm's vocabulary and mental associations that point to a "wilderness experience." Of particular importance to Freedman is the phrase, "you prepare a table before me," which he interprets in light of Ps 78:19. The poet speaks as an individual, though at the same time he represents all Israel. The psalm is recited possibly at one of the great feasts such as Passover or Tabernacles.

This study represents an important advance in our understanding of the psalm, for it is now clear that a "wilderness experience" is being described. Our example of a modern usage earlier led us to the same conclusion. Nevertheless, in my opinion, the psalm is best understood in light of the David tradition. Whether David is the author or not remains uncertain.[22] What in any case is being reported in the psalm is that time when *David* had to make an exodus, when *David* was driven into the wilderness, and when *David*—by God's grace—would be returning to the promised land.

The full story is told in 2 Sam 15–19. David's troubles as a father come to a climax when his son Absalom rebels and proclaims himself king. David has to leave Jerusalem. Some faithful friends, including Zadok and Abiathar the priests, stay behind; but the greater number of David's companions accompany him on his trip into exile. Plans are made for the entourage to remain at the fords of the Jordan until word comes from the city reporting Absalom's activities.

David does not have to wait long for Yahweh to supply his needs. After passing the summit of the Mount of Olives, where he had paused to worship, he is met by Ziba, a servant of Mephibosheth who is a son of Jonathan and grandson of Saul. With Ziba are a couple of asses bearing two hundred loaves of bread, one hundred bunches of raisins, one hundred bunches of summer fruit, and a skin of wine. Ziba says to David, "The asses are for the king's household to ride on, the bread and summer fruit for the young men to eat, and the wine for those who faint in the wilderness to drink (2 Sam 16:2). Maybe the psalmist is thinking of this outpouring of kindness when he says, "I shall not want," or perhaps this is the table spread before him in

22. Earlier skepticism about the Davidic authorship of psalms attributed to him is reduced a good deal in Otto Eissfeldt, *The Old Testament: An Introduction*, trans. Peter R. Ackroyd (New York: Harper & Row, 1965), 448–50. Aubrey R. Johnson refused to rule out the possibility of Davidic authorship for Psalm 23 in his article, "Psalm 23 and the Household of Faith," in John I. Durham and J. R. Porter, eds., *Proclamation and Presence: Old Testament Essays in Honour of G. Henton Davies* (Richmond: John Knox, 1970), 271.

the presence of enemies (v. 5). Opposition was close at hand. No sooner had the food been received than a man by the name of Shimei, also from the house of Saul, appears to curse David loudly and throw stones at him (2 Sam 16:5–13).

Finally the weary pilgrims arrive at the Jordan. Here they rest, lying down in green pastures and refreshing themselves in still waters. Here David's "breath" or "life" (Heb *nephesh*) is restored (2 Sam 16:14).

As soon as Absalom enters Jerusalem, he makes plans to pursue his father. The pursuit begins, but Yahweh leads David in the "right paths" or "paths of deliverance" (Heb *ṣedeq* can also mean "deliverance" [cf. Isa 51:1, 5]; there are no moral overtones here such as "paths of righteousness" would suggest). Yahweh does all of this, not for David's sake, but for his own (cf. Pss 31:3[4]; 143:11; Jer 14:7; Ezek 20:9). When David walks through the "valley of the death-shadow"—a place where rocks and hills make shadows for enemies to hide—he is unafraid because Yahweh gives him the same promise given earlier to Isaac, Moses, and Gideon, and one that will later be given to Jeremiah: "I will be with you" (Gen 26:3, 24; Exod 3:12; Judg 6:12; Jer 1:8). Yahweh's club and staff "protect" or "vindicate" David (so Freedman).

David crosses the border into Ammonite country. The enemy, however, is not far away. Then at a place called Mahanaim Yahweh really spreads a table before David. One thinks here of the desert hospitality of the Bedouin who prepares for his guest a *mansef* (lamb and rice feast). We read in 2 Sam 17:27–29:

> When David came to Mahanaim, Shobi the son of Nahash from Rabbah of the Ammonites, and Machir the son of Ammi-el from Lodebar, and Barzillai the Gileadite from Rogelim, brought beds, basins, and earthen vessels, wheat, barley, meal, parched grain, beans and lentils, honey and curds and sheep and cheese from the herd, for David and the people with him to eat; for they said, "The people are hungry and weary and thirsty in the wilderness." (RSV)

Since David is the honored guest, custom dictates that he be anointed with oil. In Egypt a lump of scented ointment was placed on the heads of banquet guests;[23] here, however, as in Israel, it is oil (cf. Amos 6:6; Ps 45:7[8]; Eccl 9:7–8; and Luke 7:46). David's cup—whether of oil or water or wine we do not know—overflows.

23. A. M. Blackman, "The Psalms in the Light of Egyptian Research," in D. C. Simpson, ed., *The Psalmists* (London: Oxford University Press, 1926), 196.

In this life crisis the Lord showed himself to be David's shepherd. He left neither him nor his people in want. He gave them pleasant rest and refreshed their spirits by the waters of the Jordan. He led them in the right paths so the enemy could not find them. It was for his own sake, says the psalmist, so the glory would be his. Even when David was in dark and dangerous territory, he did not fear evil. The Lord was there to protect him. Indeed the Lord vindicated him, for the enemy was defeated. Twice the Lord spread a table in the presence of enemies. David's cup—which is probably symbolic of all the goodness he received—overflowed. Instead of the enemy pursuing him, it was goodness and mercy. At the end of the psalm the psalmist is confident that this will continue through the rest of life, and that David will again dwell securely in the Lord's domain (Heb *bêt YHWH*), that is, the promised land.[24] This will be for as long as he lives (RSV footnote and most commentaries).

VI

Set against this background, Ps 23 becomes a companion to Ps 3. The superscription to Ps 3 connects this psalm explicitly with the occasion on which David fled Absalom. We have then two psalms reflecting this important event: Ps 3, which is David's song of passage into exile, and Ps 23, which is David's song of passage back from exile. I would concur with the suggestion of Mowinckel that Ps 23 is a thanksgiving psalm after an experience of salvation. It is written from the perspective of the crisis being over, but David has not yet come to Jerusalem. The last line anticipates reentry and settlement there.

Pss 3 and 23 could well have been placed side by side in the Psalter, like Pss 20 and 21. James Muilenburg some years ago proposed that Pss 20 and 21 were deliberately juxtaposed because Ps 20 reflected a situation just before the king went to battle, and Ps 21 the situation after he returned victorious.[25] In Ps 20 the king is blessed with the words, "May he grant you your heart's desire" (v. 4). In Ps 21 the king praises Yahweh saying, "You have given him his heart's desire" (v. 2). Yet other considerations, it seems,

24. The translation "domain of Yahweh" for *bêt YHWH* is preferred by Freedman in "The Twenty-Third Psalm," 164.

25. The substance of Dr. Muilenburg's argument was conveyed to me personally, though I believe it was presented in his paper, "Psalms 20–21," to the 1956 Meeting of the Society of Biblical Literature.

determined the placement of Pss 3 and 23. In later worship Ps 3 is a morning psalm, and it has been juxtaposed to Ps 4 because that is a psalm for evening.[26] Ps 23, we may surmise, because of its strong affirmation of trust, was placed next to Ps 22 because that psalm contained a cry of deepest despair: "My God, my God, why have you forsaken me?" It is common to find complementary or contrasting materials intentionally juxtaposed in the biblical text (cf. Prov 26:4–5).

There is another contrast requiring some comment before we conclude. In 2 Sam 18–19 David is portrayed as being deeply troubled over Absalom's death. Yet here in Ps 23 his voice is raised in thanksgiving. Is it possible for such opposite moods to coexist in the David tradition? Yes, I believe it is. Moreover, I believe it is possible for them to coexist in a single individual. We need in the end to hear *both* expressions if we are to appreciate fully what the Absalom experience meant for David. David must grieve the loss of his son. At the same time, he must celebrate the preservation of his own life (in spite of his lament in 2 Sam 18:33[19:1]). How he does his celebrating is really the important thing to note. There is no gloating over the defeated foe, only thanksgiving to Yahweh for protection and deliverance. It is certainly the unusual dynamic of father and son locked in bitter struggle that makes for such a lofty expression in this psalm, one totally without recrimination or cries for vengeance.

Ps 23 is then best understood as a song of passage. Broadly speaking, it recounts David's passage out of Jerusalem. into the wilderness, and back to Jerusalem once again. There are other passages too, which 2 Sam 15–19 makes explicit. They are: a mountain crossing, two crossings of the Jordan, two important meals, and one passage at least through a valley of the death-shadow (2 Sam 18:6–8).[27] In terms of David's own development, there is a passage through a crisis with his rebellious son. A more precise analysis of this particular passage using human-development theory would be of value, I should think, but that will require another study.

26. So Eissfeldt, *The Old Testament: An Introduction*, 450.

27. Hans Wilhelm Hertzberg says of the "forest of Ephraim," where the decisive battle took place, "We are to imagine it as a mixture of deep undergrowth and rocks rather than as a forest land proper. The vast amount of cover quickly puts the host at a disadvantage and causes a great many casualties"; cf. Hertzberg, *I & II Samuel*, trans. John Bowden, OTL (Philadelphia: Westminster, 1964), 358–59.

VII

We said earlier it was the desert experience that brought about a coalescence of the exodus, wandering, and entry themes with themes from Ps 23 in the mind of Pearl Kashishian. The desert experience is also the bridge between ancient and modern understanding of the psalm. If this be so, it would seem to follow that the psalm deserves broader use, broader even than what Pearl makes of it. It is not simply for people on their deathbeds, though it is certainly for them. It is for parents who survive the folly of rebellious children, for people returning from war, for someone recently out of jail, or for someone passing through a divorce. It is for people crossing the Berlin Wall or the Green Line in Beirut. It is for anyone who has received unexpected outpourings of food and hospitality in time of need. It is for those recovering from a serious illness, for those who have lost a child or other loved one by death. It is for the person who is out of a job. It is for children and youth who are passing through the struggles peculiarly theirs. Broader use of the psalm will serve as a challenge to people who know the desert experience, and know it well, but who do not know the Good Shepherd—or perhaps know him only in more pleasant surroundings—to put the two together.[28] When this happens, a more authentic faith will result. Our world today needs to hear testimony from people who have plumbed the depth of human experience, but who have learned also to draw upon the infinite resources of the Good Shepherd and Gracious Host.

28. A helpful book for people in ministry who find themselves in the wilderness is James E. Dittes, *When the People Say No* (San Francisco: Harper & Row, 1970), especially chap. 3, "Ministry in the Wilderness, Not Beyond It" (pp. 37–52).

11

Mary Magdalene and Song of Songs 3:1–4[1]

Early on the first day of the week, while it was still dark, Mary Magdalene came to the tomb and saw that the stone had been removed from the tomb . . . Mary stood weeping outside the tomb. As she wept, she bent over to look into the tomb; and she saw two angels in white, sitting where the body of Jesus had been lying, one at the head and the other at the feet. They said to her, "Woman, why are you weeping?" She said to them, "They have taken away my Lord, and I do not know where they have laid him." When she had said this, she turned around and saw Jesus standing there, but she did not know that it was Jesus. Jesus said to her, "Woman, why are you weeping? Whom are you looking for?" Supposing him to be the gardener, she said to him, "Sir, if you have carried him away, tell me where you have laid him, and I will take him away." Jesus said to her, "Mary!" She turned and said to him in Hebrew, "Rabbouni!" (which means Teacher). Jesus said to her, "Do not hold on to me, because I have not yet ascended to the Father. But go to my brothers and say to them, 'I am ascending to my Father and your Father, to my God and your God.'" Mary Magdalene went and announced to the disciples "I have seen the Lord"; and she told them that he had said these things to her. (John 20:1, 11–18, NRSV)

1. *Int* 49 (1995) 172–75.

Was this woman, at some earlier time in life, as innocent and unknowing as she now appears? Perhaps she lived in some garden, some paradise, where flowers bloomed and love bloomed and life, she dreamed, was idyllic and beautiful.

Young Jewish women were not strangers to idealism, nor to beauty or songs of love. They could sing, surely, the greatest love song in the Bible, the Song of Songs, which Jewish tradition ascribes to King Solomon in his youth. The book was later taken to be allegory by both Jews and Christians, in the one case depicting the love existing between God and Israel, and in the other the love between Christ and the church. It remains, in any case, a love song. In it, a man and a woman sing alternately about their aspirations of love in a garden paradise.

Perhaps the Song of Songs was sung by the young Mary, who may have heard it at the synagogue in Magdala where, even in this early time, it may have been prescribed reading at Passover. We know Magdala had a synagogue, for one has been uncovered there as recently as 1971–73.[2] Let us imagine her singing the following lines:

> Upon my bed at night
> I sought him whom my soul loves;
> I sought him, but found him not;
> I called him, but he gave no answer.
> "I will rise now and go about the city,
> in the streets and in the squares;
> I will seek him whom my soul loves."
> I sought him, but found him not.
> The sentinels found me,
> as they went about in the city.
> "Have you seen him whom my soul loves?"
> Scarcely had I passed them,
> when I found him whom my soul loves.
> I held him, and would not let him go
> until I brought him into my mother's house
> and into the chamber of her that conceived me.
> (Song of Songs 3:1–4, NRSV)

When Jesus met Mary for the first time, she was certainly not the woman described here. We are told that she had, not one, but seven demons, which Jesus cast out of her (Luke 8:2; Mark 16:9). Her innocence was

2. James F. Strange, "Magdala," in *ABD* 4:464.

gone, her life in a former paradise—if there was one, real or imagined—is no more.

It is thought the demons were those of unchastity, for which reason a tradition has grown up around Mary that she was a harlot. That may or may not have been true. There is no evidence that she was a harlot, and some have suggested it is the city from which she came that compromised her character. But she did have seven demons, which would seem to indicate evil aplenty within her.

Magdala is situated on the west shore of the Sea of Galilee, one mile north of Tiberias. In Roman times it was a small fishing city, also a city of shipbuilding. The population was predominantly Greek; a hippodrome for horse-and-chariot races was there. The synagogue was small, only about 27 feet by 24 feet, indicating a Jewish population that was also small. Magdala, in any case, was a city of the fast life. When it was destroyed by the Vespasian in AD 67 the rabbis attributed the city's destruction to its licentiousness.

Mary is represented—as we all are—in that age-old story of the man and woman who lived in a garden, where flowers bloomed and love bloomed, until sin entered in and the harmony was broken. Then was the paradise lost and innocence lost, for the man and woman were sent out of the garden not to return (Gen 3:23–24). The punishment for outreaching themselves and for disobeying God was death. Eating the fruit of one tree denied them the fruit of the other.

But Mary has met Jesus. She has been set free from the seven demons that controlled her, and she is now his devoted follower. She is there at the cross (John 19:25), and early Easter morning we find her at the tomb.

She may not know, but we who look on from a distance do, that Easter morning for her is a paradise regained, a love rekindled, an innocence restored of the type that characterizes all those born anew in Christ Jesus. In Johannine theology, the garden—complete with its tree of life—reappears in heavenly Jerusalem (Rev 22:2) where death has given way to life, and separation from God has given way to reconciliation to God.

Whether or not Mary had sung the Song of Songs recently or at some earlier time is not the point I wish to make here. Rather, I believe it possible that the account of Mary's Easter morning experience in John 20 may deliberately have been shaped against the background of the woman singing her song and dreaming her dream in Song of Songs 3:1–4. It would be suitable enough if, in fact, the song was sung in the synagogue or temple during Passover.

Were Mary identified more clearly with the woman of this song, we might imagine her lying on her bed before dawn the past two nights, dreaming of the one who had captured her affection, but finding him not. She calls him, but he does not answer. Then she says, "I will rise and go in search of him." She goes into the city but cannot find him, whereupon a watchman—whose presence signifies the last watch of early morning—finds her. She asks him, "Have you seen him whom my soul loves?" Then, suddenly, she finds the one whom she loves. She takes hold of him, and will not let him go until she brings him to her mother's house.

In John 20, however, Mary regains her paradise somewhat differently. The details are altered just enough, on the one hand, to conform to the story of Easter morning and, on the other, so that we may know Mary is not the streetwise Mary of Magdala but the Mary who has regained a touch of innocence.

Mary is slow to believe after seeing the empty tomb and the angels; the beloved disciple, we are told, saw and believed (John 20:8). After the two disciples go home, she remains at the tomb, weeping. She does not know what has happened. She says the same thing to the angels she had said earlier to the disciples and will say once again to the supposed gardener when she talks to him about Jesus's body having been taken away. These are innocent questions. She also does not recognize Jesus when she sees him. Again, innocence fails to see things immediately.

Then Jesus finds her; she does not find him. He speaks, and she recognizes his voice. Her word to him, "Rabbouni," is a word of affection, yes, but also a word of respect. She does not say, "O my love!" She is not permitted to hold on to him. Does she want simply a bigger or longer hug? We do not know. The embrace, in any case, is over quickly. What we do know is that she cannot take him to her mother's house; instead he will take her—along with others—to the house of his Father. The text does not say this in so many words, but the point is made already in John 14:2–3. Also, if Song of Songs 3:1–4 is background for the account, this contrast can be implied.

By both word and action, Jesus raises their relationship to a level beyond that of ordinary love, where quite possibly it had been once the demons were exorcised and Mary was beholden to Jesus. That Mary understands this and accepts this seems clear from v. 18, where it is said that she went to the disciples and told them that she had seen the Lord but also what Jesus had said to her. These words she did not keep to herself.

In John's account, there is no suggestion of disappointment that Jesus will not let Mary hold him, nor any bitterness that she cannot have him all to herself. The governing mood—as in the Song of Songs—is one of joy, in this instance that although he will not come to her mother's house, Mary—along with others—will go to his, to a heavenly paradise where God is Father and Jesus is Son.

Mary, in this brief moment, has a taste of paradise regained. It is a paradise that will be fully realized later on. Mary has also regained her innocence, not in any pure sense, to be sure—just as she never had it in any pure sense to begin with—but enough that she becomes a woman of love and faith in the Christian community.

In the early centuries, Christians made pilgrimages to Magdala. They came to that village on the western shore of the Sea of Galilee to honor Mary.[3] And they came because they, like Mary, had experienced in their encounter with the living, resurrected Lord a paradise regained. Thanks be to God!

3. Ibid.

12

All Great Works of God Begin in Secret[1]

The Beginnings of the Church Took Place in Secret

THE GREAT NEW TESTAMENT scholar Johannes Weiss, in commenting on the dearth of information we possess about the beginnings of the Christian church, said, "It lies in the nature of things that the first beginnings of a religious movement are obscure, and hid from the eyes of contemporaries."[2] Put into theological terms, I would say that it lies in the very nature of God to begin all great works in secret. That is what I want to speak to you about this evening. Throughout the Bible, and also in our own day, we see that great works of God begin quietly, or in astonishing secrecy, with only a very few privy to what is happening, and remain hidden from the eyes of most everyone living at the time, becoming known and made clear in the economy of God only later when the beginnings are seen to bear much fruit.

The psalmist, addressing God about his own beginning, speaks these words:

> For you did form my inward parts
> you did knit me together in my mother's womb

1. Public Lecture given at the Lutheran Theological Seminary, Hong Kong, October 11, 2010; published in Simon Chow, et al., eds., *Exploring Bible, Church and Life: Essays in Celebration of the 100th Anniversary of Lutheran Theological Seminary, Hong Kong*, Theology and Life 36 (Hong Kong: Lutheran Theological Seminary, 2013), 289–99.

2. Johannes Weiss, *Earliest Christianity*, vol. 1, trans. Frederick C. Grant (New York: Harper, 1959), 14.

I praise you, for you are fearful and wonderful
    wonderful are your works!
You know me right well
    my frame was not hidden from you
When I was being made in secret
    intricately wrought in the depths of the earth. (Ps 139:13–15)

It used to be that husband and wife, after learning they would have a child, kept it secret for a while, often until the wife began "to show." Now, when the woman discovers she is pregnant, she wants to spread the news the next day, or maybe call someone on her cell phone from the doctor's office. The husband, too, is eager to get the news out. And yes, there are the images of ultrasound. Even so, we still have a profound realization that the beginning of human life takes place in secret.

The Bible also tells us that ultimate beginnings, if we may call them that, are known only to God. Other great beginnings on the stage of human history take place quietly, simply, and in secret. Weiss says, "Those immediately concerned are too much wrapt up, at the time, in the marvelous things they are experiencing, to give any thought to a consecutive account of them; while outside observers, who might provide such a narrative, are, as a rule, wholly absent."[3]

To this we may add that those individuals experiencing God's marvelous doings know them only partially, and in faith. Certainty, if and when it comes, is achieved later, often much later. The chosen few have no idea where the beginnings will go. The larger world, which can include family and friends, knows little or nothing about what God is doing. Only on the rarest of occasions is there a Simeon or Anna to raise a voice in thanksgiving for what God is doing and will do (Luke 2:25–38).

Jesus's Life Began and Developed in Secret

If the beginnings of the early church took place in secret, and they certainly did, what are we to say about the birth, life, and ministry of Jesus? The birth narratives in Matthew and Luke are judged by scholars today as being the last to be affixed to gospel tradition, and we may wonder if, during Jesus's ministry, or even in the years immediately following his death and resurrection, there were any who knew the details about Mary and Joseph's

3. Ibid.

journey to Bethlehem, Jesus's birth in a Bethlehem manger, and the flight to Egypt. Luke says after reporting the visit of the angels in Shepherd's Field, and the witness of the shepherds after they found the babe in a manger, that "Mary kept all these things, pondering them in her heart" (Luke 2:19), which speaks volumes!

Our Christmas carols speak of the stillness and silence surrounding Jesus's birth. Phillip Brooks's "O Little Town of Bethlehem" (1868) begins:

> O little town of Bethlehem
> How still we see thee lie
> Above thy deep and dreamless sleep
> The silent stars go by . . .

It continues:

> How silently, how silently
> The wondrous gift is given
> So God imparts to human hearts
> The blessings of his heav'n
> No ear may hear his coming
> But in this world of sin
> Where meek souls will receive him still
> The dear Christ enters in.

I used to think this and other Christmas carols were largely romantic portrayal of the nineteenth century, but now I am not so sure. Things may well have happened that way.

It is common to speak also about the "hidden years" of Jesus's youth. Yes, we read in the Bible about how he stayed behind in the temple when his parents began the journey home after Passover (Luke 2:41–51), and how when he came home he was obedient to them. Then Luke tells us again that "his mother kept all these things in her heart" (v. 51). But what else do we know about Jesus's growing-up years? Sermons are preached about him working as a carpenter beside his father in the Nazareth workshop, and artists have portrayed him as a young boy looking at nature's beauties—the lilies of the field, the birds of the air, the mustard plant, sheaves of wheat, clusters of hanging grapes—all of which turn up in his later teachings,[4] but

4. So Warner Sallman in his painting *The Boy Christ* (1944), where the boy Jesus is sitting outside Nazareth in the surrounds of his Father's world. In the upper left is Nazareth, "a city set on a hill that cannot be hid" (Matt 5:14); overhead are the "birds of the air," below which are the "lilies of the field" (Matt 6:26, 28); flowers at right include

what do we really know about Jesus's youth? Practically nothing. Did he ever have a girlfriend? Did he ever get into innocent mischief with other boys? Did he throw stones at a distant tree trying to hit it? Did he make his mother something of wood, worked on in the carpentry shop, and give it to her as a gift? He doubtless went to synagogue with his father, maybe also his mother, but what do we know about family life on the Sabbath? Nothing. In these hidden years, so called, God was working out in secret an act of salvation for the whole world.

During Jesus's years of public ministry, particularly in Galilee, when large crowds began to gather about him to hear him preach, there remained a great secret about who this man really was. William Wrede called it "the messianic secret," which appears prominently in the Gospel of Mark.[5] Jesus conceals his messianship, calling himself "Son of man," and in Wrede's view, this secret antedates the Gospels in which it appears. To Peter and the other disciples he reveals himself at Caesarea Philippi as the Messiah, but Mark follows up this confession by saying, "he charged them to tell no one about him" (Mark 8:27–30). Only at the end of his ministry does Jesus admit to the High Priest that he is the Messiah (Mark 14:61–62), but he refuses to tell Pilate he is "King of the Jews" (Mark 15:2–5). Wrede points out, too, how Jesus concealed his teaching by speaking in parables, explaining things only to his disciples in private (cf. Mark 4:11–12, 33–34; Matt 13:10–13; Luke 8:9–10).[6]

There was a secrecy in the garden before Jesus's arrest, according to John Henry Newman (1801–1890), who wrote the Anglican hymn "Praise to the Holiest in the Height." One verse goes,

> And in the garden secretly
> And on the cross on high
> Should teach his brethren and inspire
> To suffer and to die.

More nineteenth-century romanticism? Probably not.

---

blossoms of a mustard plant (Matt 13:31–32; 17:20); sheaves of wheat grow amidst thorns and thistles (Matt 13:7, 24–30); and clusters of grapes hang from an overhead vine (Matt 20:1–15; 21:28–32, 33–41; John 15:1–2). The picture is intended to illuminate the "hidden years" of Jesus's youth; see Jack R. Lundbom, *Master Painter: Warner E. Sallman* (Macon, GA: Mercer University Press, 1999), 90–91.

5. William Wrede, *The Messianic Secret*, trans. J. C. G. Greig, Library of Theological Translations (Cambridge: James Clark, 1971).

6. Ibid., 211

Our God Is a Hidden God

The reason God begins all his great works in secret is that our God remains a hidden God. In Christianity, as in Judaism, we put the emphasis on our religion being a revealed religion, and so it is. But we need to remember that the reason for this emphasis is that our God also continues to be a hidden God. Paul Ricoeur says,

> The idea of revelation is a twofold idea. The God who reveals himself is a hidden God and hidden things belong to him . . . The one who reveals himself is also the one who conceals himself. And in this regard nothing is as significant as the episode of the burning bush in Exodus 3. Tradition has quite rightly named this episode the revelation of the divine name. For this name is precisely unnameable.[7]

So while we affirm that our God has chosen to make himself known to people of the world, preeminently in the person of Jesus Christ, we must not forget that God continues nevertheless to be hidden. Revelation and hiddenness must be kept in tandem in any doctrine of God. It is a paradoxical tension, never one without the other.

I should now like to go into the Old Testament and have us look at five texts, each of which shows in its own way how God begins great works in secret: 1) the creation of the world, 2) the call of Abraham and covenant with Abraham, 3) the election of Israel, 4) the call of Jeremiah and 5) the promise to Israel after its inglorious end of nationhood. I will then close with a great work begun in secret over a century ago in central China.

The Creation of the World Began in Secret

In Genesis we have not one but two accounts of creation (Gen 1–2). They are beautiful stories, but nevertheless stories, not telling us how the creation of heaven and earth and man and woman actually took place. Modern science today is revealing bits of this great secret, but there is still much we do not know.

So far as what God was doing before creation, the Bible tells us nothing. When the biblical stories are compared with stories much older, stories upon which the biblical accounts draw, we see that all precreation ideas

7. Paul Ricoeur, "Toward a Hermeneutic of the Idea of Revelation," *HTR* 70 (1977) 17–18.

have been eliminated by the biblical writers. Gone are the commingling of fresh and sea waters, and the birth of the gods, and gone is the primordial battle with forces of chaos. In the Babylonian story of creation, Marduk has combat with Tiamat, and after defeating her, cuts her body in pieces to do "artful works" of creation.[8] Second Isaiah, it is true, does resurrect an ancient story about Yahweh doing battle with Rahab the dragon (Isa 51:9), but there is no trace of any primordial battle in Genesis. Gen 1:1 simply begins: "In the beginning God created the heaven(s) and the earth" (KJV; RSV), or as many now translate: "When God began to create the heaven and the earth . . . " (NJV; cf. NRSV). The story in Gen 2 begins similarly: "In the day that the LORD God made the earth and the heavens . . ." (Gen 2:4b, NRSV).

Martin Luther understood the Bible's silence about what took place before creation. When someone asked him the schoolboy question as to what God was doing before creation, he is reported to have said, "He went into the woods to cut rods from which to punish good-for-nothing questioners."[9]

The Call of Abraham and Covenant with Abraham Began in Secret

Abraham was born in Ur of the Chaldeans, the southernmost part of ancient Babylonia and today the southernmost portion of Iraq (Basra). At the beginning of recorded history it was called Sumer. Abraham's family emigrated north to Haran, which is in Syria, where they settled for a time (Gen 11:27–32). Then Abraham received a call from God to go to a strange land that God would show him, and God promised to bless him and make him a blessing to all families of the earth (Gen 12:1–3). So Abraham journeyed down into the land of Canaan.

The departure from Chaldea, a busy, populated area in the ancient world, the sojourn in Haran, and the journey to Canaan were doubtless events that went unnoticed in the world at the time. Even the few who did know about them could not have anticipated that a great work of God was in the making. For Abraham it was a journey of faith, as the writer of Hebrews rightly says (Heb 11:8–9). The covenant God made with Abraham (Gen 15) was another great act planned and carried out in secret, and here

8. "The Creation Epic," Tablets IV–VI, *ANET*[3], 61–68.

9. James Muilenburg, "The Biblical View of Time," *HTR* 54 (1961) 251.

the writer of Hebrews names Sarah as the great woman of faith in seeing this promise fulfilled by the birth of a son (Heb 11:11).

We may, of course, attribute this seeming obscurity to the literary genre in which the events are preserved. The patriarchal stories, after all, are legends,[10] and in legends generally the field of vision is limited to two—maybe three—persons at one time.[11] There is little or no background; everything is foreground.[12] And yet, I would aver that God's dealings with Abraham were still a great secret hidden from most all his contemporaries.

Israel's Election Was and Still Is a Secret in the Mind of God

The question has been asked many times: why did God choose the Jews as his special people? A student asked me this just recently. It is reported in Deuteronomy, chapter 7, where Moses tells the children of Israel:

> For you are a people holy to Yahweh your God; Yahweh your God has chosen you to be a people for his own possession, out of all the peoples that are on the face of the earth. It was not because you were more in number than any other people that Yahweh set his love upon you and chose you, for you were the fewest of all peoples, but it is because Yahweh loves you, and is keeping the oath which he swore to your fathers . . . (Deut 7:6–8)

The love of God, like the covenant made with the fathers, is an act of pure grace, and we learn from the Bible that God's grace never needs a reason. God's judgments yes; but not God's grace, which can come for a reason or not for a reason.[13] Most of the time, and certainly here in

10. Hermann Gunkel, *The Legends of Genesis: The Biblical Saga and History*, trans. W. H. Carruth (New York: Schocken, 1964).

11. Axel Olrik, "Episke Love i Folkedigtningen," *Danske Studier* 5 (1908) 69–89. English: "Epic Laws of Folk Narrative," in Alan Dundes, ed., *The Study in Folklore* (Englewood Cliffs, NJ: Prentice-Hall, 1965), 129–41.

12. Erich Auerbach, *Mimesis*, trans. Willard R. Trask, Princeton Paperbacks 124 (Princeton: Princeton University Press, 1974), 3–23, 70–75, 99–122; cf. Jack R. Lundbom, "Parataxis, Rhetorical Structure, and the Dialogue over Sodom in Genesis 18," in Philip R. Davies and David J. A. Clines, eds., *The World of Genesis*, JSOTSup 257 (Sheffield: Sheffield Academic, 1998), 136–38.

13. Jack R. Lundbom, "God's Use of the *Idem per Idem* to Terminate Debate," *HTR* 71 (1978) 201; Lundbom, "God in Your Grace Transform the World," *Currents in Theology and Mission* 34 (2007) 278–81.

God's choice of Israel as his holy (i.e., set-apart) people, no reason is given. G. Ernest Wright says that this election was "a secret of God which Israel did not know."[14] Paul understands this fully in Rom 11, where he can only exclaim after talking about a great mystery:

> O the depth of the riches and wisdom and knowledge of God! How unsearchable are his judgments, and how inscrutable his ways! "For who has known the mind of the Lord, or who has been his counselor?" (Rom 11:33–34, RSV)

The election of Israel remains a secret even today—to the Jewish people, to Christians, to everyone.

The Call of Jeremiah Was Made in Secret

The Lord informed Jeremiah of his call to be a prophet while he was still a young boy, walking about in an almond orchard. The call was not being made just now, however; it had been made long ago. The Lord says to Jeremiah:

> Before I formed you in the belly I knew you
> and before you came forth from the womb I declared you holy
> a prophet to the nations I made you. (Jer 1:5)

Some have suggested that Jeremiah was called from the time he was in his mother's womb, like the Servant of Second Isaiah (Isa 49:5), or like John the Baptist (Luke 1:15), but the text will not yield this interpretation. God is telling the young Jeremiah that his call took place *before* he was formed in the womb, which means it took place at a time known only to God. Hence, another divine secret, and the young Jeremiah is the first to hear about it.

A Secret for Israel after the Loss of Nationhood

Later in Jeremiah's life, when the prophet was confined to the court of the guard and his nation was spiraling toward inglorious defeat, this word came to the prophet:

14. G. Ernest Wright, "Deuteronomy," *IB* (New York: Abingdon-Cokesbury, 1953), 2:380–81.

Thus said Yahweh, who made it
    Yahweh who formed it to establish it
    Yahweh is his name!
Call to me and I will answer you
    and let me tell you great things and hidden things
    you have not known. (Jer 33:2–3)

Nationhood for Israel will end; people will die by the sword, from hunger, or from disease; and most of those who survive will have to make the long walk to Babylon, where they will be exiles. But, wonder of wonders, the Lord tells Jeremiah that he has in store for Israel great and hidden things. The Hebrew can also be translated "great and secret things." What are they? We are not sure, but they are probably the promises in the following oracle: the healing of the people, the sweet smell of peace and security, the restoration of fortunes lost to the Babylonians, the building up of the people, the cleansing of sin, and, most important of all, the forgiveness of sin (Jer 33:6–9).

A Great Work in Central China Began in Secret

Peter Matson was born in Dalarna, Sweden, on March 27, 1868. His family emigrated to America in 1879, settling on a farm in Alexandria, Minnesota. On a summer day in 1887, or 1888, Matson knelt by a haystack and promised the Lord he would give half his income to missions or become himself a missionary. After schooling in Minneapolis and at the Chicago Theological Seminary, he was called by the American Mission Covenant (Missionsförbundet i Amerika) for missionary service to China. In the fall of 1890 he sailed for China, arriving in Shanghai on October 28.

Matson sailed up the Yangtze (Chang Jiang) to Hankow, and found his way over to the China Inland Mission (CIM) headquarters on Woosung Road. He recalled: "I was all alone, nobody knew of my coming, I did not even have a letter of introduction. Fortunately I had my certificate of ordination and, of course, my passport."[15] After talking with the CIM director, it was decided that he should study Chinese at the CIM language school in Ganking. Matson was also advised to shave the front part of his head, and shed Western dress for Chinese dress, which he did. So Matson went the

15. Peter Matson, "Chinese Reminiscences," *Our Covenant* 15 (1940) 19.

three hundred miles up the Yangtze to the CIM school, and there spent four months learning Chinese.

Then Matson received a letter from Chicago suggesting that he locate in the neighborhood of newly arrived Swedish missionaries, who subsequently established a station at Wuchang in the winter of 1891. But he did not envision a cooperative union with the Mission Covenant of Sweden, deciding rather to enter new territory where the gospel had not been preached.[16] The summer of 1891 was "the summer of the Yangtze riots," a time when much antiforeign agitation was going on, but Matson spent his time traveling up and down the Yangtze in search of a suitable field for mission work. His search led him to Hupeh (Hubei) Province. In November, on a boat trip up the Han River in the company of Dr. Howard Taylor, son of J. Hudson Taylor, Matson was led to consider the need for mission work in Fancheng, a city on the Han in northern Hupeh. The province as a whole was new to Christian missions. The CIM had worked in Siangyang and Fancheng for two or three years, but now the site was vacant. Matson wrote to Hudson Taylor, founder of the CIM, and after an exchange of letters Taylor wrote to Matson on April 16, 1892, saying that the CIM had decided to retire from Fancheng, and that he would be glad if Matson took over their premises.[17] This decided the matter for Matson. He wrote home and told the Covenant Board he was opening a mission station in Fancheng.

Matson then decided to visit J. Hudson Taylor in Shanghai. They had a warm encounter, kneeling and praying together in Taylor's office just before midnight. Taylor laid his hands on Matson's head and asked for God's blessing upon him.[18]

Matson picked up his few belongings, and on May 11, 1892, sailed up the Han in a houseboat with three Norwegian Lutherans: Halvor Ronning of the Hauge Synod, Daniel Nelson of the Norwegian-American Lutheran Church, and J. B. Brandtzaeg of the Norwegian China Mission Society,[19] on

16. Matson gives his account of the choice of a field in "The Siang Fan District," in Peter Matson et al., eds., *Half a Century of Covenant Foreign Missions* (Chicago: Evangelical Covenant Church of America, 1940), 20–21; see also Matson, *Sowing in Tears, Reaping in Joy* (Chicago: Covenant Book Concern, 1923), 17.

17. Matson, *Sowing in Tears, Reaping in Joy*, 21.

18. Ibid., 24–25.

19. Kenneth Scott Latourette refers to Norwegian Lutherans, organized into the Norwegian Lutheran China Mission Association in Bergen in 1890, as being in the area; see Latourette, *A History of Christian Missions in China* (New York: Macmillan, 1929), 400.

a tour of investigation.[20] The Norwegians, too, were interested at the time in opening a mission in Hupeh.[21] All dressed in Chinese clothes to make themselves less conspicuous. James Scherer, Professor of Missions at the Lutheran School of Theology in Chicago, reports:

> Coming to the twin cities of Fancheng and Siangyang, the men climbed a small mountain for a spectacular overview and for a time of prayer. They were filled with thanks for God's guidance, and joyous in their anticipation of the work which could be done in spreading the gospel in this unevangelized area. According to one account, they heaped together some stones as a memorial to their first visit to the place of their future labors. Matson chose Siangyang for the Mission Covenant; Brandtzaeg decided on Laohokow; Nelson and Ronning selected Fancheng and its surrounding territory, taking over the work already begun in a small way by the China Inland Mission.[22]

An agreement with Hudson Taylor allowed Matson to take over the rented CIM premises at Fancheng, and in that spring he took up residence in the city.[23] A decision had been reached that the Lutherans would work north of Fancheng, and the Mission Covenant would work south. Both would carry on work in Fancheng, but the Mission Covenant would have its main station across the river in Siangyang.

For the next fifty years Matson gave leadership to Covenant missionary work in Hupeh Province. He was married in 1893 and joined in the missionary enterprise by his wife Kristina, who transferred over from the Swedish Covenant Mission. They worked together from 1893 until 1922, when Kristina died. She had been in poor health ever since the murder of close missionary friends and the death of her firstborn son. She also put a second son into the grave. Yet despite poor health and these personal tragedies, Kristiana endeared herself to the Chinese, and had a particularly profound impact among Chinese women. She was a pioneer of school work for girls in Hupeh Province.[24] Peter's second wife, Edla, was also a good partner in the work, working as an evangelistic and educational missionary

20. Matson refers to this in "China Reminiscences," 28.

21. Rolf A. Syrdal, "American Lutheran Mission Work in China" (Unpublished PhD thesis, Drew Theological Seminary, Drew University, 1942), 31–32.

22. James A Scherer, "The Lutheran Missionary Pioneers: Who Were They?" *Currents in Theology and Mission* 17 (1990) 352.

23. Matson, "The Siang Fan District," 22.

24. Leonard Larson, "Educational Work in China," *Our Covenant* 1 (1927) 49.

in Siangyang. They were married in 1924. I had the privilege of knowing Edla Matson in my growing-up years in Chicago, and remember her as a wonderfully warm and gifted woman. Peter Matson died on May 30, 1943, and was buried in Ridgewood Cemetery in Des Plaines, just north of Chicago. He was seventy-five years of age.

The work of these pioneer missionaries bore fruit. After a decade of labor, in 1903, the Covenant Missionary Society of China had eight missionaries on the field, assisted by sixteen Chinese workers.[25] A number of schools had been started, and a dispensary in Siangyang had treated 1400 patients. There were twenty-nine converts to Christianity, and by 1905 the number increased to 167. By 1908 the total adult membership was 534, in 1912 it was 1000, and in 1915 it was 1500.[26] The autumn of 1910 saw a great revival.[27] By this time the Covenant had head stations at Fancheng, Siangyang, Nanchang, Icheng, and Kingmen, and thirty outstations operated by a staff of twenty-five missionaries and eighty-five Chinese workers. Covenant Mission work reached its high-water mark in 1925, a year before the Communists were expelled from the Chinese National People's Party (KMT), and much unrest came to central China. In 1925 the Covenant China Mission had fifty-two missionaries on its staff, 175 Chinese workers, forty-six outstations, and 2,255 students in the various schools. In its churches were approximately 2500 adult members.[28]

In 1909 the Covenant of America joined hands with the Covenant of Sweden to launch a preparatory school and a seminary at Kingchow, a city at the southern end of Hupeh Province where the two fields met.[29] The theological seminary was dedicated on December 4, 1909, with many people in attendance, including Chinese authorities. One of the first teachers was Marcus Cheng, who went on to become a well-known evangelist, and even after the Revolution of 1949 he was pressed into service as an interpreter for Chou En-lai.

At Siangyang the dispensary was treating an ever increasing number of people. In 1908 it had 5,522 outpatients, and 263 inpatients.

25. Karl A. Olsson, *By One Spirit* (Chicago: Covenant Press, 1962), 447.

26. Ibid., 448.

27. Matson, "The Siang Fan District," 27.

28. Olsson, *By One Spirit*, 450.

29. Matson, "The Siang Fan District," 26; John Peterson, "Kingchow and Shasi," in Matson et al., eds., *Half a Century of Covenant Foreign Missions*, 53–54; Olsson, *By One Spirit*, 448–49.

Dispensary work was carried on there until 1914, when Bethesda Union Hospital opened. This hospital, although built by the Covenant Mission, was a joint venture with the Lutherans, who had doctors and nurses on the staff. The joint venture lasted until 1933,[30] when the Covenant took over the work entirely. Bethesda Hospital was a substantial two-storey brick building with light and airy wards, eighty-five white-enameled comfortable iron beds, and by 1927 it had electric lights and x-ray capability. It was the only institution of its kind in northwest Hupeh Province. About seven hundred patients were treated annually in the hospital, and approximately ten thousand treatments were given in the dispensary. Patients came from the twin cities of Siangyang and Fancheng, and from villages and towns within a radius of fifty to two hundred miles.[31] The Covenant Mission had also opened dispensaries in other parts of the province.

Mission work in Hupeh Province continued during the difficult years of Japanese bombing and occupation, also during the civil war that ended with the establishment of the People's Republic in 1949. By this time all but a very few missionaries had left China, and for the next thirty-plus years the Chinese Church struggled and lived incognito under Communist rule, especially during the Cultural Revolution (1966–76). But God's work that began simply, and in secret, has borne much fruit.

I visited Hubei Province in the summer of 2008 and was gladdened at what I saw in the five cities where the Covenant Mission had head stations: Xiangyang (Siangyang), Yicheng (Icheng), Nanzhang (Nanchang), Jingmen (Kingmen), and Jingzhou (Kingchow). I was accompanied by my student Dr. Cao Jing and her husband. In all these cities we found vibrant churches. In Yicheng a smaller congregation was meeting in rented facilities, hoping to get land to build a new church; but in all the other cities were new, large church buildings, in which, I was told, between five hundred and one thousand people gather for worship each Sunday. The churches had Sunday schools and activities during the week, and when we were there, money was being raised for victims of the Chengdu earthquake in Sichuan Province.

30. Rolf A. Syrdal, "American Lutheran Mission Work in China," 215.

31. K. M. Nelson, "Glimpses from Our Medical Work in Siangyang," *Our Covenant* 1 (1927) 26.

What Great Works of God Are Beginning Today in Secret?

I often wonder, as I teach my classes here at LTS, and sit with students around the table at lunch and dinner, what great works of God are perhaps beginning now in secret. Do you wonder about that? You should, because extraordinary beginnings are doubtless taking place in our midst, hidden largely from our eyes and the eyes of people around us. I think, too, that we should pray for such things to happen, for the Bible teaches that "the prayer of a righteous person has great power in its effects" (Jas 5:16, RSV). Abraham was called a prophet because he was a man of prayer (Gen 20:7). Jeremiah was a great man of prayer. Peter Matson knelt in prayer at a Minnesota haystack, later with Hudson Taylor in Shanghai, and still later with his Lutheran missionary comrades on a mountain in Hupeh, asking for God's direction in the work they were beginning. He prayed many other times, as did all the missionaries. People in churches back home prayed. Chinese Christians prayed. May we be doing the same today, remembering that all great works of God begin in secret, and the God who begins them will bring them to glorious flower in a way no one can imagine.

13

Theology in Language, Rhetoric, and Beyond[1]

Theology as Assertion and Philosophically Driven Doctrine

CHRISTIAN THEOLOGY, WHICH IS discourse about God and things related to God, and divine revelation, which is discourse about God's self-disclosures from individuals and communities that have come to believe them, possess two distinguishing characteristics: 1) both discourses, almost without exception, are proclamatory and certain, made in the assertive mode;[2] and 2) both discourses tend to become systematic in nature, due to a joining of faith assertions with philosophic inquiry.

That Christian theology be assertive—strongly and aggressively assertive—should occasion no surprise, since Christian preaching from earliest times has 1) centered on gospel proclamation (*kerygma* in Acts 2:14–36 and elsewhere); 2) embodied confessions, creedal formulas, and hymns used in the early church (Rom 1:3–4; 1 Cor 11:23–26; Phil 2:5–11); and 3) over time evolved into the creeds recited today in public worship: for example, the Apostles' Creed and Nicene Creed.

In ancient Israel prophetic preaching was carried on largely—though not exclusively—in the assertive mode, the Hebrew prophets possessing an

1. Parry Lecture, Plymouth Congregational Church, Fort Wayne, IN, October 20, 2006; Public Lecture at the Lutheran Theological Seminary, Hong Kong, October 8, 2010; published in *Theology & Life* 34 (2011) 253–76.

2. Paul Holmer, "Can We Educate Ministers Scientifically?," in Keith R. Bridston and Dwight W. Culver, eds., *The Making of Ministers* (Minneapolis: Augsburg, 1964), 20–21.

authority commensurate with their office as divine messengers in the service of Yahweh God. George Kennedy says the essential rhetorical quality of the Old Testament is its "assertion of authority."[3]

Today an equivalence of assertive discourse and the language of faith is assumed when dogmatic teachings of the Roman Church are "once and for all delivered to the saints" (Jude 3),[4] and when Fundamentalist preachers in the Protestant tradition, with Bible in hand, preface assertion after assertion with "The Bible says, . . ." For the latter dialogue becomes impossible with modern intellectual thought, or with liberal Protestant groups, most notably the World Council of Churches. Even in Protestant evangelicalism, "witness" and "dialogue" have become almost mutually exclusive concepts, the latter said to be a concession to religious relativism that destroys Christian integrity, and the former preserving Christian integrity by conveying the "truths revealed in Scripture."[5] In each of these religious communities, and many others in between, it is assumed that revelation, witness, or truth requires the assertive mode of discourse; any other mode yields something less.

From early times there has also been a joining of biblical texts and Christian testimony with philosophy inherited from the Greeks. One can see beginnings in the Apostle Paul,[6] then a flowering in the church fathers, who had to defend Christian faith against the Jews, on the one hand, and internal gnostics, on the other. Church councils met the same threats from within and without by promulgating doctrines aimed at regulating the faith: for example, Nicaea (AD 325) and Chalcedon (AD 451) debated and then issued definitive statements on the Trinity and the two natures of Christ. In the High Middle Ages it was Scholasticism developing a system of philosophy, theology, and teaching based on writings of the church fathers and Aristotle. Anselm (1033–1109) and Aquinas (ca. 1225–1274) crafted arguments for the existence of God, assessed the role of reason and revelation in attaining salvation, and declared themselves on a range of other matters

3. George A. Kennedy, *Classical Rhetoric and Its Christian and Secular Tradition from Ancient to Modern Times* (Chapel Hill: University of North Carolina Press, 1980), 121.

4. See Paul Ricoeur, "Toward a Hermeneutic of the Idea of Revelation," *HTR* 70 (1977) 1–2.

5. Arthur F. Glasser in Arthur F. Glasser and Donald A. McGavern, *Contemporary Theologies of Mission* (Grand Rapids: Baker, 1983), 205–19.

6. See e.g., 1 Cor 13:11 ("when I became a man I gave up childish ways"); and Rom 2:14–15 ("while their conscience also bears witness . . .").

where philosophy had to be pressed into service. Theology in the Middle Ages was "queen of the sciences," where *science* did not have the restricted meaning it has today, but denoted every academic discipline studied at the university (German: *Wissenschaft*).

The Reformers used their intellectual powers to define the nature and authority of God's word, determinism and freedom of the will (Luther, Erasmus, Calvin), the meaning of the Eucharist (Luther, Zwingli), and a host of other theological topics requiring a mastery of philosophic thought. Today theologians are working to develop a doctrine of the Holy Spirit, which, not surprisingly, is proving to be an elusive undertaking. Small wonder! My guess is that the Holy Spirit will not submit to tidy analysis, but we shall have to wait and see how this quest plays out.

The modern period has witnessed on the Continent, particularly in Germany, theologies driven largely by ideology. Walther Eichrodt, for example, in his *Old Testament Theology* sought to discuss everything under the single idea of "covenant,"[7] admittedly a dominant theme, and possibly even the preeminent theme in the Old Testament, but not a rubric under which all Old Testament theology can be subsumed. In Germany, Gerhard von Rad in his *Old Testament Theology* identified defining theologies in the various strands of the Pentateuch,[8] employing also an evolutionary scheme postulating an early "Exodus theology" in ancient Israel (Deut 26:5–10), then a later "Creation theology" (Second Isaiah).[9] Here too we have come to recognize, particularly with regard to creation theology, substantial oversimplification.[10]

Anglo-American theology has tended to begin not so much with ideas as with language, specifically language of the biblical text.[11] Here the

7. Walther Eichrodt, *Theology of the Old Testament*, vol. 1, trans. J. A. Baker, OTL (Philadelphia: Westminster, 1961).

8. Gerhard von Rad, *Old Testament Theology*, vol. 1, *The Theology of Israel's Historical Traditions*, trans. D. M. G. Stalker (Edinburgh: Oliver & Boyd, 1962), 105–305.

9. Von Rad, "The Theological Problem of the Old Testament Doctrine of Creation," in *The Problem of the Hexateuch and Other Essays*, trans. E. W. Trueman Dicken (New York: McGraw-Hill, 1966), 131–43; Von Rad, *Old Testament Theology*, vol. 1, *The Theology of Israel's Historical Traditions*, 121–28, 136–39.

10. Jack R. Lundbom, *Jeremiah Closer Up*, HBM 31 (Sheffield: Sheffield Phoenix, 2010), 53.

11. See, for example, S. R. Driver, *An Introduction to the Literature of the Old Testament* (Gloucester, MA: Smith, 1972), 49–50, 99–103, 130–35; Driver, *A Critical and Exegetical Commentary on Deuteronomy*, 3rd ed., ICC (Edinburgh: T. & T. Clark, 1902), lxxvii–xcv.

feeling runs deep that battles, when they occur, will be won or lost not in the air, but on the ground. History has also been given a greater role in theological formulation. The American Old Testament scholar G. Ernest Wright developed a theology of the "mighty acts of God,"[12] putting theology squarely in the realm of history.

Other trends in both Europe and America have sought to bring theology out of the realm of philosophy and ideology and into the realm of language, once again the biblical language. I give just two examples. The *Theological Dictionary of the New Testament*,[13] and now-complete *Theological Dictionary of the Old Testament*,[14] examine all significant biblical words for their theological content: for example, *grace*, *love*, *fear*, *chosen*, *righteousness*, *justice*, and so on. Of course, many biblical words (for example, *walk*, *burn*, *cease*, *house*, *become fat*) contain little or no theology, which means theology must be created from the contexts in which these words appear. A more serious problem with the otherwise excellent *Theological Dictionary of the Old Testament*, to which I have contributed a number of entries, is knowing how to evaluate the language in biblical Wisdom literature, which is not theological per se, and which is paralleled in wisdom literature throughout the ancient Near East.

An important article by Paul Ricoeur appeared some years ago,[15] in which he argued that our current concept of revelation is too authoritarian and totalitarian, being derived ultimately from speculative philosophy where propositions such as, God exists, God is immutable, and God is omnipotent, dominate. What we need, said Ricoeur, is a concept more pluralistic, one that gives priority to modes of discourse original to the community of faith. To find these he went to the Old Testament, where the major modes were said to number five: 1) prophetic, 2) narrative, 3) prescriptive (e.g., laws), 4) wisdom, and 5) hymnic (e.g., psalms). In the prophetic mode of discourse, which I call the assertive mode, Ricoeur found the original nucleus of the traditional idea of revelation.

I believe Ricoeur was on the right track in returning to the discourse of the Old Testament for a more pluralistic concept of revelation, to which

12. G. E. Wright, *God Who Acts: Biblical Theology as Recital*, Studies in Biblical Theology 1/8 (London: SCM, 1952).

13. Gerhard Kittel and Gerhard Friedrich, eds., *Theological Dictionary of the New Testament*, 10 vols. (Grand Rapids: Eerdmans, 1964–1976).

14. G. Johannes Botterweck et al., eds. *Theological Dictionary of the Old Testament*, 17 vols. (Grand Rapids: Eerdmans, 1974–).

15. Ricoeur, "Toward a Hermeneutic of the Idea of Revelation," 1–37.

I would simply add a fuller and more precise understanding of theology. But instead of form-critical categories, I prefer linguistic ones. The linguist speaks of four modes of discourse: 1) the assertive, 2) the injunctive (or imperative), 3) the interrogative, and 4) the optative (basically the wish). Particular attention needs to be given to the interrogative mode, for that mode more than any other stimulates audience involvement and makes dialogue a possibility. True dialectic may have begun with the Greeks—but not dialogue, and surely not question and answer. Question and answer is well documented among the ancient Hebrews, which means we must read the Bible not only for the answers it provides but for the questions it asks. Modern Jewish discourse can be instructive at this point. The story is told of a person who, in a fit of consternation, said to a rabbi, "Why is it you always answer me with a question?" The rabbi responded, "So what is wrong with a question?"

I intend in this lecture to examine five biblical texts containing idioms, rhetorical language and structures, and juxtapositions emanating from individuals we seldom credit with having any theological sense: biblical scribes. I hope these will show how theology, also revelation, resides in places other than in propositional affirmation and philosophically driven doctrine. I have no desire to discount either. Christian faith requires well-thought-out doctrines articulated by theologians and church councils, and benefits enormously from affirmations in the Bible and from lay folk—learned and unlearned—who down through the centuries have lived and died for the faith. The need, as I see it, is simply to expand the parameters of theology, looking for theology in biblical discourse not otherwise assessed, or else assessed improperly. Why do we need expanded parameters?

1. We need to recognize that the Bible has something to say about the hiddenness of God, that revelation and hiddenness exist in tandem at crucial self-disclosures of the divine Person.

2. We need to honor genuine attempts to seek God, not simply be asserting at every turn that God has found us, or taking as definitive the witness of others who have found God.

3. We need to find God in the questions, not just in the answers. This includes questions we ask of God, and questions God asks of us, some of which turn out to be open-ended because God expects us to answer them for ourselves.

4. We need to find theology not only in assertions but in dialogue, for the God we worship wants nothing more than to be in dialogue with the men and women of his creation.
5. We need to discover in the Bible a theology that is implicit, which merits as much attention as theology that is explicit. Any theology that is intentional by the biblical writers is important for our understanding of the Christian faith.
6. We need also to keep together issues that the Bible keeps together, not develop little systems that separate matters belonging to a larger whole.

Doing all of these will a) deepen the faith of those who are already Christian; b) give hope to those having faith but who struggle—in some cases mightily—with doubt, uncertainty, and questions that seemingly go unanswered; and c) give entré into the Christian faith to people who live deeply in the world but who have not yet embraced the Christian faith.

Our world today is filled with people who have questions rather than answers, who are seeking God rather than claiming to have found God, and who know more about the hiddenness of God than the revelations we celebrate every Sunday in public worship. Nothing less than the Christian witness is at stake, for people today are looking for honesty and humility in the testimonies we give, not for boasting, triumphalism, or a never-ending litany of authority-based assertions on this point or that. My subject then: "Theology in language, rhetoric, and beyond."

Exodus 3:12–14

Chapter 3 of Exodus contains the *locus classicus* of divine revelation. Here God reveals himself to Moses in the burning bush, and tells him he intends to deliver his people out of Egypt, after which he will bring them into a land of their own (3:8). Moreover, he wants Moses to go along as the people's leader. Moses's first assignment will be to go to Pharaoh and secure the people's release. Moses resists. God says, "But I will be with you," and Moses is given a sign (3:12). But Moses says that when he goes to the people, they will want to know God's name, so he asks, "What shall I say to them?" God replies, "I will be what I will be . . . Say this to the people of Israel, 'I will be has sent me to you'" (3:14). "I will be" later becomes "He will be" (= Yahweh).[16]

This tautological idiom, called an *idem per idem*, has traditionally been rendered "I am who I am," which appears to betray influence from the LXX of Exod 3:14 (ἐγώ εἰμι ὁ ὤν) and Jesus's "I am" sayings in the Gospel of John (John 5:35, 48–51; 8:12, 58; 10:7–14; 11:25; 15:1). Scholars and theologians have therefore gone on to talk about God's "being" (e.g., Paul Tillich's "Ground of all Being"), which is a notion entirely foreign to the ancient Hebrew mind. The verb in question can also be translated as a future: "I will be what I will be," which is how I have just rendered it, and which the RSV and NRSV place in a footnote. This has to be the correct translation, since the idiom repeats what God has just said in v. 12: "*But I will be* with you," where everyone translates the Hebrew verb as a future.

God is using this idiom to terminate a debate he is having with Moses. A look at other *idem per idems*, both in the Bible and in modern discourse, show that they consistently function as closure devices, and in argumentative discourse terminate debate. From the Bible:

- Jacob, reluctant to let Benjamin go with his brothers to Egypt, fears he may lose him, as he did Joseph. Finally he relents and lets Benjamin go, saying, "But if I am bereaved I am bereaved" (Gen 43:14).
- Esther, knowing that to appear uninvited before the Persian king is to court death, agrees finally to approach the king and petition him on behalf of the Jews. Her concluding words: "And if I perish I perish" (Esth 4:16).
- Pilate, responding to Jews who object to the title he has written on Jesus's cross, says, "What I have written I have written" (John 19:22). The debate is over, and nothing more is said.

In modern discourse the idiom functions similarly:

- The husband who says of his marriage: "What's spoiled is spoiled," wants to terminate any discussion about reconciliation with his wife.
- The judge who says, "The law is the law," wants to terminate debate with the defendant in court.
- And the dean in college who says to the student, "But rules are rules," terminates all discussion about a requirement being waived.

16. Lundbom, "God's Use of the *Idem per Idem* to Terminate Debate," *HTR* 71 (1978) 193–201.

Some years ago two American songwriters took the Spanish proverb *Qué será, será*, and gave it a closure function in a popular song. In this song a little girl asks her mother questions about the future, such as, "Will I be pretty?" and, "Will I be rich?," to which the mother replies, "Qué será, será; whatever will be, will be." The idiom here gently puts an end to questions the mother cannot answer. One could cite many other *idem per idems* in everyday use that serve as closure devices or that terminate debate. Parents, for example, say to their children in tones not always gentle: "And that's that." My mother terminated debate with this one.

Regarding the debate between God and Moses in Exod 3, scholars have often argued over whether God gives or does not give a name. Some say that he does; others think he does not. The uncertainty should not surprise us, for anyone who has been on the receiving end of an *idem per idem* used to cut off debate will attest to the fact that such an answer will be perceived at the same time as a nonanswer. Here in Exodus I do not think the tension needs to be resolved, but can and should be allowed to remain. Why? Because, as Paul Ricoeur says in commenting on this episode, "The God who reveals himself is a hidden God and hidden things belong to him."[17] Put another way, the God who says, "I will be with you," which is the preeminent promise in all of Scripture, refuses further self-disclosure by saying, "I will be what I will be."

The Bible is a remarkable book in that it contains God's revelation of himself to humankind. Yet we need to keep in tandem another truth just as important, namely, that God continues to be hidden. Abraham Heschel says, "There is an alternative to God's presence, namely His absence. God may withdraw and detach Himself from history. While exposed to the overwhelming presence, the prophets predict the absence."[18] The prophets, who knew better than anyone the overpowering presence of God, knew also of his absence, experienced painfully when evil was rife. Hosea says:

> With their flocks and herds they shall go
>   to seek the LORD
> but they will not find him
>   he has withdrawn from them. (Hos 5:6, NRSV)

Similarly, from the prophet Micah:

17. Ricoeur, "Toward a Hermeneutic of the Idea of Revelation," 17–18.

18. Abraham J. Heschel, *The Prophets*, vol. 2 (New York: Harper & Row, 1962), 211–12.

> Then they will cry to the LORD,
> but he will not answer them;
> he will hide his face from them at that time,
> because they have acted wickedly. (Mic 3:4, NRSV)

Sermons and personal witness should not, then, speak only about a God who has found us, important a truth as this is, but confess at times a hidden God who must be sought and found by the contrite and humble. The great prophet of the exile says:

> Seek the LORD while he may be found,
> call upon him while he is near;
> let the wicked forsake their way,
> and the unrighteous their thoughts;
> let them return to the LORD, that he may have mercy upon them,
> and to our God, for he will abundantly pardon
> (Isa 55:6–7, NRSV)

Christians in the throes of doubt, living through personal crises, or in full-blown rebellion against God, need to hear this message. The same goes for people who do not know God at all. To all of these a confident—or overconfident—Christian witness can be as much a stumbling block as no witness at all. The Bible is clear: the God who reveals himself remains a hidden God.

Exodus 33:17–23

Farther on in the book of Exodus is another divine self-disclosure where the same idiom is used (Exod 33:17–23).[19] Here and in what precedes, God is testing the man whom he has chosen. Once again the two are embroiled in a debate, only now their positions are reversed: Moses is committed to the journey, but God, after the Golden Calf episode, objects to going along. Instead he offers to send his angel (32:34; 33:2). But Moses insists that God himself must come. Finally God relents and says his "presence" (lit. "face") will go (33:14). But the argument continues. Moses presses this time to see God's "glory," which here means God's bright, beneficent face. God says:

> I will make all my goodness pass before you, and I will proclaim before you my name, "Yahweh"; but I will be gracious to whom I will be gracious, and I will show mercy on whom I will show

19. Lundbom, "God's Use of the *Idem per Idem* to Terminate Debate," 198–99.

> mercy. Thus he said, "You cannot see my face; for no one shall see me and live." (Exod 33:19–20)

God will let Moses see only his back after he has passed by (vv. 21–22). A second time Moses has been silenced. A double *idem per idem* this time terminates their debate.

As in the earlier text, here we are introduced to a God who both reveals and remains hidden. God has given his grace or favor to Moses, yet now his grace or favor is withheld. In both Exodus texts is also another matter, which from a theological point of view is potentially problematic. The *idem per idem* cuts off debate, and from the point of view of the one being silenced, the termination will seem abrupt and premature. We must therefore come to terms with the fact that anyone using the idiom in this manner lies open to the charge of behaving irrationally. If that person is someone in authority (as is usually the case, and is certainly the case here, where God is speaking), that person will be perceived as acting in a high-handed sort of way. How unlike the irenic Socrates is this God of the Old Testament! Why does God act in such a manner, or are we to conclude that because God is God, he can act any way he wants?

Happily, the problem is not a serious one, because in both Exod 3 and 33 God is acting in a gracious capacity. In Exod 3 he is promising to lead his people out of slavery and be with them on their journey. In Exod 33 the discussion itself revolves around grace and mercy. This, I believe, makes perfectly acceptable God's use of the *idem per idem* to terminate debate. For we can accept and indeed trust a God who withholds in the present only good from us. And although it may baffle and frustrate us, we can accept a God who at times is irrational in the way he dispenses his goodness. Just so long as God does not behave this way when he metes out judgment. We would feel differently, I am sure, if we heard God say, "I will judge whomever I will judge." That sounds capricious, and would tend to undermine any faith and trust we might have in him.

One can find supporting evidence from the Bible that the Judeo-Christian God does indeed act irrationally—if we may use that term—in the dispensation of his grace. His judgments, meanwhile, are accompanied by reasons, and they are valid reasons. How unlike other deities of the ancient Near East, who rain havoc on the people of earth for no reason at all, or else for reasons that are ludicrous. In the Babylonian Flood Story, for example, Enlil sends the flood because the earth is becoming overpopulated, and the noise people are making keeps him from getting a good night's sleep![20] In the biblical story, the flood comes because of human wickedness.

Claus Westermann has also pointed out that judgment speeches of the prophets are almost always accompanied by a reason, whereas in salvation speeches reasons are conspicuously absent.[21] One can read Second Isaiah in vain to find a reason why God is delivering his people out of exile. In gracious acts God is motivated only by his love and faithfulness (Isa 43:4; cf. Deut 7:6–8), and since these qualities originate with him, they need no rationale. In the New Testament we see the irrational God of grace vividly portrayed in Jesus's parable of the Labors in the Vineyard (Matt 20:1–15). This is the parable in which laborers work a different number of hours in the field, but at the end of the day all receive the same wage. A transparent teaching about God's infinite and irrational grace.

Thus I would conclude that the Lord God uses the *idem per idem* only to hide from our eyes his infinite grace and unlimited goodness. It is this kind of God who withholds from Moses a full revelation of his name and a complete unveiling of his face.

Isaiah 5:18—6:5

Occasionally one finds in the Old Testament scribes deliberately juxtaposing materials in order to set up a contrast, much in the way modern journal, magazine, and newspaper editors run contrasting articles in succession or place them side by side on a page.[22] They do not tell you they are doing this; nevertheless, the editing is intentional, and an effect on the readership is expected. When such subtle and implicit statements are made in the Bible, we must be alerted to them and look for any theology they might contain. This phenomenon of juxtaposition has not gone unnoticed in Jewish tradition. Rabbi Akiba (d. AD 134) is reported to have said, "Every section in Scripture is explained by the one that stands next to it" (*Sifre Num.* 131).

20. "Atrahasis" A (Tablet II), i, in *ANET*[3], 104.

21. Claus Westermann, *Basic Forms of Prophetic Speech*, trans. Hugh Clayton White (Philadelphia: Westminster, 1967), 97–98.

22. Lundbom, "Scribal Contributions to Old Testament Theology," in Bradley J. Bergfalk and Paul E. Koptak, eds., *To Hear and Obey: Essays in Honor of Fredrick Carlson Holmgren* (Chicago: Covenant Publications, 1997), 42–49.

Some years ago the well-known Jewish scholar Robert Gordis pointed out in the book of Proverbs, amid a collection dealing with "fools" (26:1–12), these proverbs in succession:[23]

> *Answer not* a fool according to his folly
> lest you be like him yourself
>
> *Answer* a fool according to his folly
> lest he be wise in his own eyes (Prov 26:4–5)

One proverb says not to answer a fool with foolishness; the other says to give fools a foolish answer. Each has its reason. The scribe responsible for this juxtaposition knew precisely what he was doing, and maybe wanted to teach us something about the limits of wisdom. One can be right doing either. One can be wrong. It all depends. Proverbs have broad application, but are not universal truths.

An important juxtaposition occurs in the book of Isaiah, where a theologically minded scribe had a statement he wanted to make. In this book, the prophet's call comes not in chapter 1, where one would expect it, but in chapter 6. Older scholars, assuming chronological order in the book, concluded either that the call took place after Isaiah had been preaching for some time, or that chapter 6 was a "call of renewal" following an inaugural call not recorded. Tannaitic interpreters (rabbis from 50 BC to AD 200) wanted the call to be at the beginning of the book, which is where the calls of Jeremiah and Ezekiel are placed. The consensus now is that chapter 6 is the prophet's inaugural call, and that the preaching in chapters 1–5 came later. Chronology was not followed. But why?

The answer, it seems to me, is that the compiler of the book of Isaiah placed the prophet's call where he did in order to juxtapose it with Isaiah's woe oracles of 5:8–22. In 5:8–22 Isaiah cries *woe* on the rich, the drunks, the liars, the conceited, and Jerusalem's unjust elite. These people are greedy for more real-estate holdings, acquit the guilty for a bribe, and deprive innocent folk of their rights. Then in 6:5 he is seen turning the spotlight on himself, saying, "*Woe is me!* For I am lost; for I am a man of unclean lips, and I dwell in the midst of a people of unclean lips" (RSV). A divine messenger then touches his lips with a burning coal from the Lord's altar, and the prophet is told that his guilt is taken away and his sin is forgiven

23. Robert Gordis, "Quotations in Wisdom Literature," *JQR* 30 (1939–40), 137.

(6:6–7). In all we have seven woes, which is probably significant in that the number 7 in Hebrew thinking signifies completeness.

The combined message of the two passages, although not made explicit, should nevertheless be obvious. The good prophet called by God to judge others is seen to have rendered an earlier judgment on himself, which goes some distance, surely, in humanizing the prophet. More important, this candid bit of self-examination is what gives Isaiah his warrant to preach. Someone recognizing his or her own woeful state can venture forth to point out the woeful state of others, a theme reiterated in Jesus's Sermon on the Mount (Matt 7:1–5). And it is a scribe who has articulated this theology by juxtaposing Isaiah's call with his oracles against Jerusalem's unholy and unjust.

We would do well to appropriate such a theology today, living as we do in a world where people are speaking judgments on this social ill or that, but saying nary a word, or else are being dismissive, about their own uncleanness. Personal morality must go hand in hand with the censure of social ills. Without the former the latter rings hollow.

Jeremiah 20:14–18; 1:5

The outburst emanating from Jeremiah in Jer 20:14–18 is one of the most shocking in all of Scripture, rivaled only by a similar outburst from Job in the book bearing his name (Job 3:1–26; 10:18–22). Jeremiah speaks a double curse: the first on the day of his birth, the second on the man who brought his father the news.[24] Most commentators include this passage among Jeremiah's so-called confessions, which are individual laments, basically, of the type that occur in the Psalms. But some are not so sure that Jeremiah's complaint is directed to God, so they simply call it a self-curse. John Calvin says the utterance is blasphemy; others agree it borders on blasphemy. I believe the concluding question in v. 18 is directed to God—Job's words in Job 10:18 are directed to God—therefore, I take this to be one of the Jeremianic confessions. The poem goes as follows:

> 14 Cursed be the day
> on which I was born
> the day my mother bore me
> Let it not be blessed

24. Jack R. Lundbom, "The Double Curse in Jeremiah 20:14–18," *JBL* 104 (1985) 589–600; Lundbom, *Jeremiah 1–20*, AB 21A (New York: Doubleday, 1999; New Haven: Yale University Press, 2009), 864–74.

[15]Cursed be the man
  who brought my father the news:
"A male child is born to you"
  making him very glad

[16]Let that man be like the cities
  which Yahweh overthrew and did not pity
Let him hear a cry in the morning
  and an alarm at noon time

[17][Let that day be like . . .]
  because he did not kill me in the womb
So my mother would have been my grave
  and her womb eternally pregnant

[18]Why from the womb did I come forth
  to see hard times and sorrow
  and end my days in shame?

This confession, concluding as it does the First Edition of the book of Jeremiah (chaps 1–20), does not receive a divine response. Other confessions in the book do. Von Rad says, "the God whom the prophet addresses no longer answers him."[25] It is true; there is no answer here in chapter 20. But a rhetorical structure in this earliest of the Jeremiah scrolls provides the wrenching question with an answer, and it is a divine answer. Tying together chapters 1–20 is a rhetorical device known as the *inclusio*, which is a closure device returning the hearer of a literary work to the beginning.[26]

The inclusio is employed throughout the Old Testament, in writings of Greek and Roman authors, and in speeches, poems, and literary works of our own day. The American poet Carl Sandburg was especially fond of the inclusio. For example, in Sandburg's poem "Chicago," the following phrases appear both at the start and at the end: "Hog Butcher," "Tool Maker," "Stacker of Wheat," "Player with Railroads," and "Freight Handlers." Other Sandburg poems employ this same device.[27]

The book of Jeremiah opens with God informing the prophet of his call into divine service:

25. Gerhard von Rad, *Old Testament Theology*, vol. 2, *The Theology of Israel's Prophetic Traditions*, trans. D. M. G. Stalker (Edinburgh: Oliver & Boyd, 1965), 204.

26. Jack R. Lundbom, *Jeremiah: A Study in Ancient Hebrew Rhetoric*, 2nd ed (Winona Lake, IN: Eisenbrauns, 1997), 42–44; Lundbom, *Jeremiah 1–20*, 229, 869.

27. See Lundbom, *Jeremiah 1–20*, 76.

> Before I formed you in the belly I knew you
> and before *you came forth from the womb* I declared you holy
> a prophet to the nations I made you (Jer 1:5)

In the larger composition of 1–20, this word becomes the answer to Jeremiah's wrenching question:

> Why *from the womb came I forth*
> to see hard times and sorrow
> and end my days in shame? (Jer 20:18)

The compiler of an early Jeremiah book, who may well be Jeremiah's colleague and friend, Baruch the scribe, has given Jeremiah's question an answer: The prophet came forth from the womb because God called him before he came forth from the womb, indeed, long before. What has happened, you see, is that someone other than Jeremiah has helped to answer the prophet's existential question. That person has taken an earlier word from God, one known to Jeremiah and doubtless reported by him, and used it to answer a later question that seemingly went unanswered. Jeremiah may even have been party to this editorial handiwork, for we know the prophet had a hand in compiling the first scroll of his utterances (Jer 36:1–8). In any case, when the First Edition of the book of Jeremiah was read to a gathered assembly, which took place a year after it was written up (Jer 36:9–10), the final question of the suffering prophet may already have had a divine answer. The dialogue, of course, was not explicit. It was embodied in the book's structure, and only the careful listener alert to such structures would get the message. But some would. Ancient listeners were little different from listeners today. Some make connections immediately. Other dreamy folk miss them entirely. Still others need someone to make the connections for them.

What does this have to teach us? First of all, I believe people must be permitted to express their deepest hurts, even doubts about the worth of life and the Author of Life. Theology in some cases resides in the questions people ask—honest and humble questions, such as we have here in Jer 20:18. Allowing people to express their deepest hurts, anxieties, and doubts runs an admitted risk, particularly if like Jeremiah people may be harboring suicidal thoughts, for psychologists tell us that most people who actually commit suicide have spoken about it to someone beforehand. Nevertheless, I believe people must be allowed—as Jeremiah was allowed—to give vent to their deepest feelings. And they should also not think that God is scandalized by unreasoned outbursts. God has heard it all before. Yes, they can speak even the unspeakable.

Then, after some time has passed—preferably not too much time—questions candidly asked can hopefully get an answer: either by the individual himself or herself, because a subsequent word of assurance was forthcoming (as so often happens in the Psalms), or because someone else—a family member, a friend, even someone loosely connected to the individual—comes with an answer: "Yes! Your life is worth living." You or I may be that individual. Christian faith is a dialogue, between God and individuals, and between individuals with one another.

Jeremiah 5:1–8

In Jer 5:1–8 we have a dialogue poem weighing in the balance divine pardon for Jerusalem.[28] It has unmistakable echoes of the dialogue between Abraham and God over Sodom (Gen 18:23–32). The poem is divided into five stanzas, demarcated by repeating key words and an alternation of speaker and audience. The whole makes a large *chiasmus*, a rhetorical structure in which defining elements build to a center point and then repeat in reverse order to the end:

Yahweh to Jeremiah and others:

Yahweh to	[1]Run back and forth in the streets of Jerusalem
Jeremiah	look please, and take note
and others:	Search in her squares (to see)
	if you can find a *man*
a	If there is one who does justice
	and searches for truth
	that *I may pardon her*
	[2]For if they say, "As Yahweh lives"
	surely in vain *they swear*
Jeremiah to	[3]O Yahweh, your eyes
Yahweh:	do they not look for truth?
	You struck them down, but they writhed not
b	you annihilated them, but they refused correction
	They have made their faces harder than rock
	they have refused to repent
Jeremiah to	[4]Then I said, but these are the *poor*
Self:	they have no sense

28. Lundbom, *Jeremiah 1–20*, 371–85.

For they know not Yahweh's way
the justice of their God

c
[5]I will go to the *great*
and I will speak with them
For they know Yahweh's way
the justice of their God

Jeremiah to Yahweh:
But both alike had broken the yoke
they had snapped the bonds
[6]Therefore a lion from the forest *will strike them*
and a wolf from the desert will devour them

b'
A leopard will prowl around their cities
anyone going out from them will be torn apart
For their rebellions are many
their regressions are great

Yahweh to Jerusalem:
[7]Why should *I pardon you*?
your children have forsaken me
and have *sworn* by "no-gods"

a'
When I fed them to the full they committed adultery
and to whore-houses they trooped
[8]they were well-fed lusty stallions
Each *man* neighing for his neighbor's wife.

God begins the dialogue by instructing Jeremiah and a larger search party to find *one* righteous man in Jerusalem. If they succeed, he will pardon Jerusalem.

Jeremiah then asks God about his passion for truth, a move simply to get audience attention, for Jeremiah knows that God cares deeply about truth. Jeremiah continues by expressing outrage at precisely what outrages God: the ineffectiveness of punishment in bringing about repentance. He may have learned this from the prophet Amos (Amos 4:6–11), although everyone knows that sometimes punishment does no good.

In the center the audience becomes privy to a dialogue Jeremiah had with himself while out on the mission. It occurred to him that perhaps poor folk clung to wrongdoing because they did not know God's law (*torah*); perhaps if he went to the city's elite, he would find such knowledge, and also would find a people who practiced justice and were seekers after the truth. If God has a hope, so does Jeremiah.

In the next stanza Jeremiah shifts into the assertive mode, but since God is the addressee, the discourse does not translate into authority preaching. Jeremiah gives God a sad report of the mission: All turned out to be covenant breakers. Then in vivid metaphors he anticipates the dire consequences upon Jerusalem. Again, this is not judgment preaching, which is how it is often interpreted. Jeremiah may even be trying to forestall judgment, which is what Abraham did in his dialogue with God over the fate of Sodom. By expressing fears to God about what will happen to Jerusalem, Jeremiah's impact on the audience will be totally different from what it would be if he preached uncompromising judgment. Now instead of people being angry and defensive, they will be fearful along with him. Jeremiah has made himself one with the people. Indeed, it is this oneness with both God and people that makes Jeremiah a true divine mediator, one with the likes of Moses and Samuel (Jer 15:1).

In the final stanza God resumes the discourse. He now speaks directly to the inhabitants of Jerusalem, asking them the question on which the whole dialogue turns: "How can I pardon you?" It is a question they will have to answer. The poem concludes with more indictment, but no judgment, and with no answer to the pardon question. At the end is a heavy silence.

Theology once again is seen to be embodied in a question, this one posed by God, which the audience is left to answer for itself. In the New Testament something similar occurs in Jesus's parable of the Lost (Prodigal) Son (Luke 15:11–32), although there the open-ended conclusion is not embodied in a question. But the strategy is the same. In this parable, the ending, as New Testament scholar Kenneth Bailey has shown, has been intentionally left off.[29] The older son must decide for himself whether he will go in to the party, even as the Pharisees and scribes must decide for themselves whether they will enter the kingdom opened up to them by Jesus.

Preaching from our pulpits and teaching done in other venues must not always be dispensing ready-made answers, although fifteen years of experience as a parish pastor has taught me that this is what many people want. And today this is what many are getting, as preaching becomes more and more a "dumbing down" to young children, and to children, I might add, who are not terribly bright. Have another look at the preaching of the prophets, and read again the Gospels with an eye to discerning the character of Jesus's preaching. Both Jesus and the prophets addressed common folk, but they did so with intelligence, subtlety, and great imagination. People walked away in astonishment and wonder. Occasionally they were

29. Kenneth E. Bailey, *Poet and Peasant; and, Through Peasant Eyes: A Literary-Cultural Approach to the Parables in Luke* (Grand Rapids: Eerdmans, 1983), 191, 201–3.

left with a question they had to answer for themselves. It was expected that they had the resources to answer these questions. What we need today is a life-giving dialogue with the God of heaven and earth, who wants nothing more for us than our salvation and ultimate good.

Author Index

Ackroyd, Peter R., 140
Akiba, Rabbi, 174
Alonso-Schökel, Luis, 138
Alt, Albrecht, 60
Anderson, Bernhard W., 84, 86, 93
Anderson, Herbert, xi, xii
Anderson, Richard, xi, 49
Anselm, Saint, 165
Aquinas, Saint Thomas, 165
Antiochus Epiphanes, 138
Ap-Thomas, D. R., 1
Aristotle, 165
Auerbach, Erich, 156
Augustine, Saint, 99

Bailey, Kenneth, 181
Baker, J. A., 166
Barton, John, 86
Baumgartner, Walter, 100, 106, 107, 108, 109, 110, 111, 112, 113, 114, 116, 118, 120, 121, 122, 124, 125, 126, 127, 130
Begrich, Joachim, 101, 139
Berg, Signe, 78
Bergfalk, Bradley J., 174
Bergquist, Helen, 78
Best, Thomas, 106
Biddle, Mark E., 101
Blackman, A. M., 141
Blau, Joshua, 22
Boadt, Lawrence, 125
Bonhoeffer, Dietrich, 48, 56
Bowden, John, 143
Botterweck, G. Johannes, 167
Brandtzaeg, J. B., 159, 160
Bridston, Keith R., 164
Bright, John, 103, 123
Brook, Philip, 152
Buber, Martin, 103
Budde, Karl, 100
Bullock, Michael, 103

Caffee, Gabrielle L., 135
Calvin, John, 166
Cameron, George G., 139
Cao Jing, 162
Capps, Donald, 134
Carruth, W. H., 156
Cervin, Russell A., 49, 57
Cheng, Marcus, 161
Chou En-lai, 161
Chow, Simon, 150
Christensen, Duane L., 62
Clifford, Richard J., 73
Clines, David J. A., 156
Conzelmann, Hans, 1, 14
Cooke, G. A., 3
Cross, Frank Moore, 73
Cullman, Oscar, 49
Culver, Dwight W., 164

Dahood, Mitchell J., 1, 4, 5, 33, 104
Dallas, A. K., 101
Daube, David, 45, 59, 67, 69, 70
Davies, G. Henton, 103, 140
Davies, Philip R., 156
Diamond, A. R., 100, 123
Dicken, E. W. Trueman, 84, 166
Dittes, James E., 144
Driver, S. R., 13, 29, 65, 166
Duhm, Bernhard, 29
Dundes, Alan, 138, 156

Dunn, James D. G., 75
Durham, John I., 103, 140
Dwight, Martha, 78
Dyer, Donita, 132, 133

Ebeling, Erich, 33
Eichrodt, Walther, 84, 166
Eissfeldt, Otto, 140, 143
Erasmus, Desiderius, 166
Erikson, Erik, 134, 137

Faley, R. J., 35
Fischer, Max, 101
Fitzmyer, Joseph A., 33, 67
Fohrer, Georg, 22, 24
Freedman, David Noel, 1, 13, 21, 65, 73, 95, 137, 139, 140, 141, 142
Friedrich, Gerhard, 167
Fretheim, Terrence E., 93
Freud, Sigmund, 134

Gennep, Arnold van, 135, 136
Gilmour, John S., 134
Ginsberg, H. Louis, 66
Glasser, Arthur F., 165
Gordis, Robert, 175
Graf, Karl Heinrich, 29
Grant, Frederick C., 97, 150
Greig, J. C. G., 153
Gunkel, Hermann, 82, 100, 101, 102, 103, 104, 105, 106, 107, 108, 110, 111, 112, 113, 114, 116, 118, 120, 121, 122, 124, 125, 126, 127, 128, 129, 130, 139, 156
Hanson, K. C., 101
Hanson, Paul D., 36
Harrelson, Walter, 84
Harris, Zellig S., 3
Hartwell, Herbert, 139
Herder, Johann, 103
Hermission, Hans-Jürgen, 86
Heschel, Abraham, 171
Herodotus, 31
Hertzberg, Hans Wilhelm, 143
Hinneberg, Paul, 101
Holladay, William L., 12, 36
Holmer, Paul, 164
Holmgren, Fredrick C., 174

Homer, 136
House, Paul R., 106
Huddlestun, John R., 65, 95

Jastrow, Marcus, 23, 28
Jerome, Saint, 88
Johnson, Aubrey R., 140
Jung, Carl, 134

Kashishian, George, 132, 133
Kashishian, Pearl, 132, 133, 144
Kaufmann, Y., 93
Kennedy, George, 165
Kittel, Gerhard, 167
Köhler, Ludwig, 102
Koptak, Paul E., 174

Lambert, W. G., 33, 35
Landes, George M., 93
Larson, Leonard, 160
Larson, Viola, 78
Latourette, Kenneth Scott, 159
Levinson, Daniel, 134
Lofthouse, W. F., 1
Lundbom, Jack R., 13, 16, 26, 30, 32, 36, 47, 73, 74, 93, 97, 106, 108, 109, 111, 112, 117, 124, 125, 126, 128, 130, 137, 153, 156, 166, 170, 172, 174, 176, 177, 179
Luther, Martin, 41, 155, 166

Marsh, James, 103
Matson, Edla, 78, 160
Matson, Kristina, 160
Matson, Peter, 158, 159, 160, 161, 163
Mayer, W., 2
McCarthy, Dennis J., 64, 84
McGavern, Donald A., 165
Meissner, Bruno, 32
Mendenhall, George E., 64
Meyers, Carol L., 137
Moran, William L. , 62
Mowinckel, Sigmund, 139
Muilenburg, James, 84, 101, 102, 105, 106, 142, 155

Nelson, Daniel, 159, 160
Nelson, K. M., 162

Nelson, Mildred, 78
Neubauer, Karl Wilhelm, 1
Newman, John Henry, 153
Nicholson, E. W., 65
Nogalski, James D., 101, 139
Norden, Eduard, 102
Nordlund, Mildred, 78

O'Connor, Kathleen M., 100
O'Connor, M., 137
Oesterley, W. O. E., 34
Ohlson, Hulda, 76, 77
Ohlson, Otto, 77
Ohlson, Virginia, 77
Olrik, Axel, 156
Olsson, Karl A., 161
Orlin, Louis L., 139
Orton, David E., 100

Palache, J. L., 1
Peake, A. S., 29
Peterson, John, 161
Pfeiffer, Robert, 65
Porter, J. R., 103, 140

Rabin, Chaim, 21
Rad, Gerhard von, 61, 83, 84, 91, 92, 129, 130, 166, 177
Rashi, 96, 108
Reed, William L., 1
Reventlow, Henning, 103
Ricoeur, Paul, 154, 165, 167, 171
Robinson, H. Wheeler, 65
Ronning, Halvor, 159, 160
Rudolph, Wilhelm, 29

Sallman, Warner, 152
Sandburg, Carl, 177
Sanders, James A., 22, 91
Sauer, G., 21
Scherer, James, 160
Schiele, Friedrich Michael, 101
Schmid, H. H., 84, 93
Sheehy, Gail, 134
Simpson, D. C., 141
Simpson, W. H., 21
Smend, Rudolph, 103
Smith, George Adam, 139
Smith, Mark S., 100
Smith, Ronald Gregor, 103
Smith, William Robertson, 136
Soden, W. von, 2
Stalker, David M. G., 61, 84, 130, 166, 177
Stegemann, Hartmut, 22
Stoebe, Hans-Joachim, 1
Strange, James F., 146
Streck, Maximilian, 33
Syrdal, Rolf A., 160, 162

Tamez, Elsa, 39
Taylor, Howard, 159
Taylor, J. Hudson, 159, 160, 163
Terrien, Samuel, 139
Thorsell, Vanette, 78
Thureau-Dangin, F., 33
Tillich, Paul, 170
Tournier, Paul, 134
Trask, Willard R., 156
Trumbull, H. Clay, 135, 136

Vaux, Roland de, 34
Vermès, Géza, 32
Vespasian, 147
Vizedom, Monika B., 135
Volz, Paul, 109

Warner, Martin, 86
Weidner, E. F., 33
Weinfeld, Moshe, 65, 67
Weis, E. A., 75
Weiser, Artur, 108, 139
Weiss, Johannes, 97, 150
Wellhausen, Julius, 65
Westermann, Claus, 174
Whitney, K. William Jr., 82, 101
Wickstrom, Fern, 78
Wilhelm, G., 2
Willi-Plein, Ina, 1
Wilson, R. A., 60
Wiseman, D. J., 64
Wrede, William, 153
Wright, G. Ernest, 157, 167

Zimmerli, Walther, 1, 14
Zwingli, Ulrich, 166

Scripture Index

Genesis

1–2 154
1 80, 81, 89, 92, 97
1:1 97, 155
1:26–27 89
1:27 97
1:28 83, 94
2–3 92, 97
2 89, 155
2:4b 97, 155
2:7–8 93, 97
2:18–24 83
2:18–23 89
2:19 93, 97
3:1 97
3:23–24 147
4:5–6 28
6–9 92
6:8–9 40
6:8 11, 14
6:9 14
8:17 83
8:21 36
8:22 96
9:1 83
9:7 83
9:8–17 95
11:27–32 155
12:1–4 48, 55
12:1–3 47, 54, 155
12:4 48, 56
15 47, 54, 155
15:5 95
15:6 48, 56
17 47, 54
17:7 95
17:13–14 95
17:14 47
18:1 16
18:3 16
18:23–32 179
18:30 24
18:32 24
19:19 5, 16
20:7 163
22 48, 56
22:17 83
25:25 73
26:3 141
26:24 141
30:2 23
30:27 8
31:32 23
31:35 24
31:36 22, 23
32–33 11
32:6 [5] 11
32:8 [7] 11
32:31 [30] 12
33:1–11 44, 51
33:3ff 8
33:4–11 12
33:5–11 38
33:5 7, 14
33:8 11
33:10 11, 12, 44
33:11 7, 14
33:15 11, 12
34:7 27
34:11 9
38 27

Genesis (continued)

39:4 9, 11, 44, 50
39:14 23
39:17–19 23
39:21 3, 4, 13, 14
42:21 3, 9
43:14 170
43:29 20
44:18 24
45:5 24
47:25 7, 43, 50
47:29 8, 9, 43, 50
49:1–27 72
49:11 86
50:4 9, 43, 50

Exodus

1–15 47, 54
3 154, 169, 171, 173
3:1 73
3:8 169
3:12–14 169
3:12 141, 169, 170
3:14 13, 170
3:21 17
4 25
4:14 25
4:22–23 45, 52
11:3 17
12:36 17
15 46, 53, 136
15:18 74
20–23 47, 54, 58
20:1–7 73
20:1–17 59
20:2–3 45, 52, 59
20:2 47, 54
20:8–11 60
20:17 60
21:18–27 64
21:28–22:15 64
22:22–27 39
22:23 [24] 25
22:24–26 [25–27] 14
22:26 [27] 6, 12
22:27 39
24:3–8 47, 54
29:38–42 34
32:10–11 25, 26
32:19 25, 27
32:22 24
32:34 12, 172
33 173
33:2 172
33:12–13 14
33:14 172
33:16–17 14
33:17–23 172
33:17 44, 50
33:19–20 173
33:19 13, 20, 44, 50, 51
33:21–22 173
34 47, 54
34:1–9 40
34:6–7 13, 39
34:6 6, 12, 17, 39, 44, 45, 50, 52
34:7 17
34:9 14, 40
34:29–35 5

Leviticus

6:2–6 [9–13] 34
6:2 [9] 34, 36
6:5 [12] 36
6:6 [13] 36
17–26 58, 61
19:2 61
22:27 4

Numbers

6:25–26 20
10:33 73
11:1 25
11:10 25
11:11 14
11:15 14
11:33 25
12:9 25
14 25
14:3–4 137
16:15 28
22:20 25

22:22 25
22:27 23
23:21 74
24:10 22, 23
25:3 25
25:9 25
25:11–13 95
28:2–8 34
32:5 9
32:10 25
32:13 25

Deuteronomy

1–28 58
1–4 47, 54, 65
1 47, 54
1:1–5 59, 65
1:15–17 68
1:19–46 62
2:34–35 62
3:6–7 62
3:23 15
4:1 67
4:5 67
4:6 67
4:9–10 67
4:14 67
4:26 47, 54
5–26 47, 54
5 59, 65
5:1–21 59
5:1–5 60
5:2–3 73
5:6–21 73
5:6–7 45, 52, 59
5:6 47, 54
5:7 60
5:12–15 60
5:21 60
5:22 60
5:30–31 60
5:31 67
6–11 61
6:4–9 47, 54, 61
6:4 61
6:6 67
6:7 67
6:13–14 61
6:14–15 25
6:20–25 67
7:1–5 63
7:1–2 62
7:2 18, 20
7:4 25
7:6–8 61, 156, 174
7:6 61
7:7–8 74
7:12–16 68
7:14 83
7:16 63
8:1 68
8:6–10 68
8:6 61
8:7–10 84
9:4–6 61
9:6 61
9:7–29 61
10:12–13 61
10:17–18 69
10:18–19 39
10:20 61
11:1 61
11:11–12 88
11:13–15 88
11:13 61
11:16–17 25, 89
11:17 25
11:18–21 61
11:18–20 47, 54
11:18 67
11:22 61
11:26–29 47, 54
12–26 59, 63, 65
12 68, 86
12:5–14 63
13–18 63
13:1–18 63
13:1–5 68
13:4 61
13:12–18 63
14:1–21 63
14:2 61
14:21 61
14:22–15:23 63
14:28–29 69

Deuteronomy *(continued)*

14:29 39
15:1–11 68
15:12–18 68
16:1–17 63
16:10–11 69
16:11 39
16:13–14 69
16:14 39
16:18–18:22 63
16:19 68
18:12 63
18:15–18 66
18:21–22 68
19–25 63
19:1–21 63
19:14 64
20:1–20 64
20:8 70
20:16–18 63
20:16 62
21:1–9 64
21:10–14 62, 64, 68
21:15–17 64, 68
21:18–21 64
21:22–23 64
22:1–8 64
22:1–4 70
22:6–7 69
22:8 68
22:9–12 64
22:13–30 64
22:13–21 70
23:1–18 64
23:1 71
23:15–16 68
23:18 70
23:19–25 64
23:19–20 68
24:1–5 64
24:1–4 70
24:1 10, 38
24:6–13 64
24:6 68
24:8–9 70
24:10–11 68, 70
24:12–13 68
24:14–22 64
24:14–15 68
24:17 39, 69
24:19–21 39, 69
25:1–3 64, 71
25:4 64, 69
25:5–10 64, 71
25:11–12 64, 71
25:12 71
25:13–16 64
25:17–19 64
26 63
26:5–10 166
26:12–13 39
27–28 65
27 47, 54, 63
27:19 69
28 47, 54, 59, 63, 65
28:9 61
28:12 88
28:23 89
28:24 89
28:50 18, 40
29:1 59
29:25–26 [26–27] 25
29:26 [27] 24
30:11–14 45, 48, 52, 55, 59
30:15–29 68
30:19 47, 54
30:28 47, 54
31–34 72
31–32 47, 54
31:9–13 65
31:10–13 47, 54
31:16–17 25
31:19–22 67
31:24 65
31:26 65
32 36, 137
32:1–43 58, 72
32:1–18 92
32:1 47, 54, 65
32:4–6 85
32:6 85
32:7–9 62
32:10–18 84
32:15–22 30, 31
32:13–18 90

32:22 34, 35, 36, 82
32:22a 30
32:26–27 35
32:32–33 85
32:46–47 68
32:46 65, 67
32:47 137
33 58, 72
33:1–5 72
33:2–5 61, 72, 73
33:3 74
33:5 74
33:24 4
33:26–29 72, 74
33:26 74
34 58, 72
34:10–12 66
34:10 58

Joshua

4:19–24 137
6:21 62
7 26
7:1 26
7:11 26
8:8 29
8:19 29
10:28–40 62
10:40 62
11:10–20 62
11:20 6, 18, 20
20:10–15 62
23:16 26
24 47, 54

Judges

2:13–14 26
2:14 26
2:20–23 26
2:20 26
3:7–8 26
3:8 26
6:12 141
6:17 16
6:39 24
8:23 74
9 30
9:15–20 30
9:30 24
9:49 29
9:56–57 30
10:6–7 26
10:7 26
14:19 27
21:22 7, 38

Ruth

2:2 9
2:10 8, 9
2:13 9

1 Samuel

1:18 5, 16, 43, 50
8 74
11:6 27
12:12 74
15 49, 56
15:11 28
16:22 9, 44, 40
17:28 24
18:8 23
20:3 9
20:7 23
20:29 9
20:30 23
25:8 8, 9
27:5 9

2 Samuel

3:8 23
6:7–8 28
6:7 26
6:8 26
7 47, 54, 137
7:12–16 95
9–20 137
12:5 24
12:22 15
13:21 27
14:22 8, 9
14:30–31 29

2 Samuel (continued)

15–19 140, 143
15:25 15
16:2 140
16:4 8, 9
16:5–13 141
16:14 141
17:27–29 141
18–19 143
18:6–8 143
18:33 [19:1] 143
19:43 [42] 23
20:11 4
22 26
24:1 26

1 Kings

1–2 137
8 17, 19
8:22–23 93
8:28–53 40
8:28 6, 17
8:30 17
8:33 17
8:37–38 17
8:38 17
8:44–45 17
8:45 17
8:46–49 17
8:47 17
8:49 17
8:52 17
8:54 17
8:59 17
9:3 17, 18
9:7–9 18
11:19 9
18:29 35
18:38 35
19:10 99
19:14 99

2 Kings

1:13 16
13:3 26
13:23 5, 18, 40
15:8–30 30
16:15 35
18:4 63
18:22 63
19:15 93
22:13 29, 30
22:15 76
22:17 29, 32, 36
22:17b 30
23:21–23 47, 54
23:26 26
24:2 31

1 Chronicles

13:10–11 28
13:10 26
13:11 26
21:1 26

2 Chronicles

6 17
6:19 17
6:21 17
6:24 17
6:28–29 17
6:29 17
6:34–35 17
6:35 17
6:36–39 17
6:37 17
6:39 17
25:10 23
25:15 26
29–31 63
30:9 6, 12, 19, 41
33:13 15
35:25 100

Ezra

9:8 6, 18

Nehemiah

1:3 28, 29, 32
2:17 28, 29, 32
3:20 22
3:33 [4:1] 23
4:1 [7] 23
5:6 24
9:6–15 92
9:17 6, 12, 19
9:31 6, 12, 19

Esther

2:15 4, 9
2:17 4, 5, 9
4:8 9
4:16 170
5:2 4, 9
5:8 4, 9
7:3 4, 9
8:3 9
8:5 4, 9

Job

3:1–26 176
5:10 88
8:5 15
9:15 15
10:18–22 176
10:18 176
19:5 11
19:11 22, 26
19:16 8
19:21 11, 15
26:12 86
32:2–3 24
33:24 17
38:8–11 86
40:27 [41:3] 13
41:2b-3 [10b-11] 13
42:7 26

Psalms

1 101, 105
1:1 104, 105
1:6 104
2 105
2:12 21, 105
3 104, 142, 143
4 15, 143
4:1 44, 51
4:2 [1] 15
5 104
6 104, 128
6:2 40, 44, 51
6:3 [2] 15, 16
6:10 [9] 15, 16
7 104
8 101, 105
8:1 105
8:9 105
9:13 40
9:14 [13] 15
13 104, 128
13:1 38
13:2 [1] 5, 44, 51, 124
16:1 105
16:12 105
17 104, 125
17:1 104
17:15 104
18 26
18:8 [7] 26
19:1–6 101
20 105, 142
20:4 105, 142
21 105, 142
21:2 105, 142
22 104, 128, 143
22:1 124
23 xi, 132, 133, 138, 139, 142, 143, 144
23:4 139
23:5 139, 141
24 101
24:7–10 74
25 104
25:6–7 124
25:16 5, 15, 40, 44, 51
25:18 15
26 16, 41, 104
26:11 15
27:7 15

Psalms *(continued)*

27:9 5, 38
28 128
28:2 15, 16
28:6 15, 16
30 15, 16, 128
30:2 105
30:7 38
30:8 [7] 5
30:9 [8] 16
30:11 [10] 15, 16
30:12 105
31 128
31:3 [4] 141
31:9 40
31:10 [9] 8, 15, 16, 128
31:13 128
31:23 [22] 5, 15, 16
35 126, 128
35:7 127
37:1 22, 27
37:7–8 22, 27
37:8 27
37:21 11
37:26 11
38:5–8 125
39:2 124
41:5 [4] 15
41:11 [10] 15
42 101
42:9 124
42:10 125
43 101
43:2 124
44 104
44:23 124
45:2 38
45:3 [2] 7
45:7 [8] 141
46 101
50:2 74
51 104
51:1–2 40
51:3ff [1ff] 15
51:3 [1] 15
55:2 [1] 5, 15
56:2 [1] 15
57:2 [1] 15
59:6 [5] 16
67:2 [1] 20
68:25 [24] 74
69:1 105
69:35 105
70:1 105
70:5 105
74 104
74:1 124
74:2 124
74:3 124
74:10 124
74:18 124
74:19 124
74:22 124
77:8 124
77:9 39
77:10 [9] 16
78:19 140
79 104
79:5 124
79:6–7 113
80 104
83 104
84:1 105
84:11 40
84:12 [11] 5, 14, 105
86 40
86:3 15
86:6 15
86:15 6, 12, 39
86:16–17 6
86:16 5, 15, 40
88:14 124
89:12 [11] 91
89:19–37 96
89:38–51 104
89:47 124
89:50 124
93:1 74
94:1–7 104
94:9 93
95:3 74
96:1–2 129
96:10 74
97:1 74
98:1 129

98:6 74
99:1 74
99:4 74
102:4 [3] 34, 36
102:11 36
102:13 [12] 36, 41
102:14–15 [13–14] 2
102:14 19
102:15 [14] 10
102:26 [25] 91
103 101, 105
103:8 6, 12
104 80, 105
104:2–9 91
104:4 [3] 21
104:9 86
104:10–16 88
104:26 93
105 105, 129
106 105, 129
106:40 26
109:12 10
111 129
111:3 6
111:4 6, 12, 39
111:10 67
112 6, 129
112:1–9 6
112:3 6
112:4–5 11
112:4 5, 6
112:9 6
112:10 6
113 129
116 15, 40
116:1 15
116:5 12
117 129
119 15
119:29 15
119:58 4, 15
119:132 5, 15, 40
119:170 15
123 104
123:2 13
123:3 19, 41
124 27
124:2–3 27
128 83
129:1 103
130 15, 104
130:2ff 15
130:2 15
135 105, 129
135:7 90
137 22, 101
139:13–16 97
139:13–15 150, 151
140 16, 41
140:7 [6] 15
143:1 15
143:11 141
145:4–9 39
145:8–9 6
145:8 6, 12
146–150 105, 129
147:8 88
148:5–6 91
148:6 86
149:1 129

Proverbs

1:9 7
3:1–4 40
3:4 14
3:12 4, 38, 44, 50
3:22 7
3:34 14, 40
4:9 7
5:18–19 38
5:19 7, 43, 50
8:29 86
11:16 7, 38, 43, 50
13:15 9
14:21 11
14:31 11, 39
17:8 7, 43, 50
18:23 8
19:17 11
21:10 3, 11
22:1 8
22:11 4, 7, 38, 43, 50
24:19–20 27
24:19 22, 27
26:1–12 175

Proverbs *(continued)*

26:4–5 143, 175
26:25 2, 3, 7, 43, 50
28:8 11
28:23 4, 10, 38
31:30 4, 7, 43, 50

Ecclesiastes

9:7–8 141
9:11 10
10:12 7, 38

Song of Solomon

1:6 22, 23
3:1–4 145, 146, 147, 148

Isaiah

1–5 175
1:4 61
5:1–7 30, 86
5:2 86
5:8–22 175
5:18–6:5 174
5:24–25 26
6 175
6:1–5 74
6:3 61
6:5 175
6:6–7 176
9:17 [18] 29, 30
9:18 [19] 30
10:16 34, 35
11:6–9 83
13:10 81
21:10 103
24:4–7 88
26:10 3, 14
27:2–6 30
27:4 30
27:11 18
30:14 34
30:18 19, 41
30:19 19, 41
33:2 19
33:10–12 30
33:12 29, 30
33:14 34, 35
33:15ff 35
33:17 35
33:20 35
33:22 74
37:36–38 35
40:3–5 138
40:21–31 80
41:11 22, 27
42:5–9 80
43:1–7 80
43:4 174
44:1–5 80
44:21–28 80
45:12–18 80
45:12–13 92
45:24 22, 27
49:5 157
49:20–21 95
51:1–10 97
51:1 141
51:5 141
51:9 155
51:10 138
51:12–16 80
54:1–3 95
55:6–7 172
56:4–5 71
65:5 34, 36
65:17 80

Jeremiah

1–20 90, 129, 130, 177
1:5 93, 129, 130, 131, 157, 176,178
1:8 141
1:10 94
2–3 107
2:2–9 84
2:2–3 25
2:7 84
2:15 29, 31
2:17 31
2:20–22 85
2:20 86

2:21 86
2:23–25a 89
2:23–24 89
2:27ab 85
3:2–3 88
3:3 88
3:4 85
3:16 95
3:19–20 85
3:21–25 107
3:21–22a 107
3:21 18
3:22a 108
3:22b-25 104, 107
3:22b 107
3:23 107
3:24–25 107
3:25 107
4:7 29
4:19–22 108, 112
4:19–21 108, 113
4:19c 109
4:22 87, 108, 112
4:23–26 80, 81, 93
4:28 88
5:1–8 179, 180
5:7–8 89
5:10 86
5:20–25 86
5:22–23 86, 87
5:24–25 88
5:24 87, 88, 96
5:25 87
6:1–7 117
6:4–5 63
6:7 87
6:8–12 117
6:14 49, 56
7:13 48, 55
7:20 63, 82
7:22–23 49, 56
8:4–9 90
8:4–7 87
8:6 90
8:7 87
8:15 120
8:18–21 106, 109, 110, 111, 125
8:18 109, 110
8:19 110, 111
8:19a 110
8:20 110
8:21 110
8:22–9:11 110
8:22–9:2 110, 111, 121
9:1 109, 111, 112
9:3 109
9:9 [10] 29, 31
9:10–11 81, 110, 111, 112
9:10 111
9:11–13 [12–14] 31
9:11 [12] 29, 111
9:17–22 100
10:1–16 90
10:1–10 90
10:11 90
10:12–16 90, 91
10:12–13 90
10:13 90
10:16 93
10:19–22 112
10:19–21 112, 113
10:19 112, 122
10:20 112
10:21 112
10:23–25 113, 114
10:23–24 113
10:24 114
10:25 113
11:16–17 31
11:16 28
11:18–23 114, 115
11:18–20 114, 117
11:18–19a 115
11:18 114, 117
11:19 117
11:19bc 115
11:20 114, 115, 117, 124, 128
11:21–23 114
11:21 114
11:22–23 117
12:1–6 116, 117
12:1–3 116, 117
12:1 114, 117, 124
12:2 117
12:3 117
12:4 88, 116

Jeremiah *(continued)*

12:5–6 116
12:5 22, 116
12:6 116, 117
12:11 88
12:14–17 94, 95
14 104
14:1–10 88
14:1–6 88
14:1 118
14:2–10 118, 119
14:2–6 104, 118
14:2–3 148
14:7–9 104, 106, 118
14:7 114, 141
14:10 118
14:11–16 118, 120
14:17–15:4 119, 120, 121
14:17–19ab 119
14:17–18 120
14:17 120
14:19–15:2 120
14:19–22 104, 106, 120
14:19c 120
14:20–22 120
14:20 114
14:22 88, 120
15:1–2a 120
15:1 181
15:2b-3 120
15:4 120
15:5 120
15:10–12 121, 122, 123
15:10 113, 121
15:11–12 121
15:12 122
15:14 36
15:15–21 122, 123, 124
15:15–18 122
15:15 114, 123
15:16 123
15:17 123
15:18 123, 124
15:19–21 122
15:19 123
15:20 123
15:21 122, 123
16:2 83
16:13 5, 18
16:19 124
17:1–4 36
17:4 36
17:11 90
17:12–18 125
17:13–18 125, 126
17:13–16a 106, 125
17:13 114
17:14 124
17:16b-18 125
17:18 125
17:19–27 31
17:27 29, 31
18:1–10 93
18:6–10 94
18:13–17 88
18:14–15 88
18:18–23 126
18:18 126
18:19–23 126, 127
18:19 114, 124
18:20 127
18:21 127
18:22 31, 127
20 177
20:7–13 106, 127, 128, 129
20:7–12 128
20:7–10 127, 128
20:7–9 127
20:7 114, 124
20:10–13 127
20:11–13 127, 128
20:11–12 100
20:12 114, 124, 128, 129
20:13 100, 128, 129
20:14–18 129, 130, 176, 177
20:16 130
20:17 130, 131
20:18 130, 131, 176, 178
21:6 63, 82
21:14 32
22 32
22:7 63
22:10 100
22:15 22
22:18–19 100

22:23 3, 18
22:28–30 100
23:3 95
23:10 88
23:18 48, 55
23:21–22 48, 55
24:6 94
27:4–7 92
27:5–7 94
27:5 93
29 94
29:1–23 94
29:5–6 94
29:24–28 94
29:28 94
30–33 96
30–31 97
30:19 95
31:2 18
31:9 19, 41, 85
31:22b 97
31:27–28 95
31:28 94
31:31–34 47, 65, 80
31:35–36 96
32:17 92, 93
32:20–23 92
32:29 31
32:40 65
32:41 94
32:43 63, 82
33:2–3 97, 157, 158
33:2 93
33:6–9 158
33:10 63, 82
33:12 63, 82
33:20–21 96
33:20 96
33:25–26 96
33:25 96
36:1–8 178
36:7 18
36:9–10 178
36:29 63, 82
37:20 6, 9
38:26 6, 9
42:2 16
42:9–10 17
42:10 94
43:12 31
45:4 94
46:19 29, 31
49:2 29, 31
49:27 31
50:32 31
51:15–19 90
51:19 93
51:30 29, 31
51:34–45 83
51:42–44a 83
51:58 29, 31

Lamentations

1:9 103
4:11 32
4:16 4, 18, 40
11:16 103
11:18–19 103

Ezekiel

3:16–21 48, 55
15:4–5 21
20:6 85
20:9 141
20:15 85
20:41 4
21:3 [20:47] 31
36:8–11 95
44:13 36
44:15 36
44:19 36
46:13–15 35

Daniel

3:6 34
3:11 34
3:15 34
3:17 34
3:20–21 34
3:23 34
3:26 34
4:24 [27] 3, 10
6:12 [11] 3, 15

Daniel *(continued)*

7:11 34
9:2ff 19
9:3 19
9:13 5
9:17 19
9:18 19, 20
9:20–27 20
9:20 19

Hosea

1:10 95
2:5 66
2:8 66, 90
2:11 66
2:12 66
2:13 66
2:16–17 [14–15] 25
2:23 94
3:1 66
4:1–3 88
4:1 87
4:2 66
4:3 82
4:6 66, 67, 87
4:13 66
4:15 66
5:1 67
5:4 87
5:6 171
5:10 66
6:1–3 106
6:3 88
6:6 66, 87
6:9 66, 67
7:7 30
8:1 66
8:5 25, 26
8:11 66
8:13 66
8:14 66
9:4 66
9:5 66
9:15 66
10:1–2 66, 67, 86
10:5 67
10:8 66, 67
12:3–6 12
12:5 [4] 12
12:7 66
12:11 66, 67
13:4 66
13:6 90
14:2–3 106

Joel

1 82
2:2 81
2:3 82
2:13 6, 12, 19, 39, 41
2:28–29 79

Amos

1:2–3:8 29
1:2 82
1:3–2:3 66
1:4 30, 31
1:7 30
1:10 30
1:12 30
1:14 29, 30
2:2 30
2:4 66
2:5 30
2:6–8 66
2:9 66
3:2 66
4:6–11 180
4:7–8 88
4:13 91, 93
5:8–9 91
5:15 18
5:18–20 81
6:6 141
8:9 81
9:5–6 91

Jonah

4:1 28
4:2 6, 12, 20, 39
4:4 28

4:9 28

Micah

3:4 172
6:6–8 49
7:7–10 103

Nahum

1:4–6 82
3:4 7, 43, 50

Habakkuk

3:3 74
3:8 26

Zephaniah

1:2–3 82

Zechariah

4:7 20
7:2 4
10:3 26
12:10 1, 20

Malachi

1:9 4, 20

1 Esdras

8:75 6

Judith

4:7 138

Sirach

40:17 2
40:22 2
51:19 22

Psalms of Solomon

1 103

Matthew

1:18–25 75
5–7 45, 47, 52, 55
5:14 152
5:38–48 44, 51
6:10 75
6:26 89, 152
6:28 152
7:1–5 176
7:24–27 48, 55
8:18–23 48, 55
11:15 48, 55
11:28 45, 52
11:29–30 59
11:29 45, 52
11:30 45, 52
13:7 153
13:10–13 153
13:24–30 153
13:31–32 153
16:18 47, 55
17:20 153
19:12 71
20:1–15 44, 51, 153
21:28–32 48, 55, 153
21:33–41 153
23 47, 55

Mark

4:11–12 153
4:33–34 153
5:24–34 49, 57
8:27–30 153
14:61–62 153
15:2–5 153
16:9 146

Luke

1:15 157
2:19 152
2:25–38 151

Luke *(continued)*

2:36–38 78
2:41–51 152
2:51 152
7:46 141
8:2 146
8:9–10 153
11:2 75
15:11–32 12, 44, 51, 181
23:29 83

John

1:1 75
1:14 37, 75
3:16 75
5:35 170
5:48–51 170
8:12 170
8:58 170
10:7–14 170
11:25 170
14–15 47, 55
14:26–27 49, 57
15:1–2 153
15:1 176
19:22 170
19:25 147
20 148
20:1 145
20:8 148
20:11–18 145

Acts

2 49, 57
2:14–36 164
8:26–39 71

Romans

1:3–4 164
1:12 49, 57
1:18–32 41
2:1–11 41
2:4 45, 51
2:6–8 41
2:14–15 165
3:23–24 37
3:24 38, 41, 44, 45, 51
5:20 44, 51
8:18–25 49, 57
11 157
11:1–36 49, 57
11:1–24 47, 55
11:25–36 47, 55
11:33–34 157

1 Corinthians

1:10–13 49, 57
7:26–31 83
11:23–26 164
12 49, 57
13:9–12 49, 57
13:11 165

Galatians

3:28 79

Ephesians

1:6 44, 51
3:7 38
4:13 49, 57

Philippians

2:5–11 75, 164

Colossians

1:15–20 75

Hebrews

10:26–31 47, 55
11:8–9 155
11:8 48, 55
11:11 156

James

Revelation

www.ingramcontent.com/pod-product-compliance
Lightning Source LLC
Chambersburg PA
CBHW031359230426
43670CB00006B/597
9781625644800